F-BOMB

Dispatches from the

WAR ON FEMINISM

BOMB

Lauren McKeon

BenBella Books, Inc.
Dallas, TX

BenBella

BenBella Books, Inc.
10440 N. Central Expressway, Suite 800
Dallas, TX 75231
www.benbellabooks.com
Send feedback to feedback@benbellabooks.com

Printed in the United States of America
10 9 8 7 6 5 4 3 2 1

Names: McKeon, Lauren, author.
Title: F-bomb : dispatches from the war on feminism / Lauren McKeon.
Description: Dallas, TX : BenBella Books, Inc., [2018] | Includes
   bibliographical references and index.
Identifiers: LCCN 2017047831 (print) | LCCN 2017052368 (ebook) | ISBN
   9781946885180 (electronic) | ISBN 9781946885012 (trade paper : alk.
paper)
Subjects: LCSH: Feminism. | Anti-feminism.
Classification: LCC HQ1155 (ebook) | LCC HQ1155 .M375 2018 (print) |
DDC
   305.42—dc23
LC record available at https://lccn.loc.gov/2017047831

Edited by Jill Ainsley
Proofread by Lisa Marietta
Front cover design by Oceana Garceau
Full cover design by Sarah Avinger
Spray paint: mr pliskin, iStock.com
Page design by Julie Scriver, Goose Lane Editions
Printed by Lake Book Manufacturing

Distributed to the trade by Two Rivers Distribution, an Ingram brand
www.tworiversdistribution.com

Special discounts for bulk sales (minimum of 25 copies) are available.
Please contact Aida Herrera at aida@benbellabooks.com.

Contents

ONE
How feminism became
today's dirtiest word

TWO
On the front lines of the new
women-on-women gender wars

THREE
The future is feminist

ONE

How feminism became
today's dirtiest word

1 We've got a long way to go, baby: Confronting the dangerous myth that we've made it

One of the greatest lies of the twenty-first century is that women have made it—"it" being some magical place, a Gloria Steinem-esque take on Walt Disney's Tomorrowland where aspiring and talented girls and women flock to rides like Equal Pay Mountain and Mission to CEO Country. I imagine them munching on Get Out of the Kitchen Funnel Cakes, riding the Reproduction Rights Monorail, or having a blast on the Safe Campus Voyage. Don't forget the Violence-Free Zone, the Carousel of Greatly Lucrative Science, Tech, Engineering, and Math Jobs, and Adventures Thru Respecting You as a Person. Feminist Tomorrowland gift shops sell Wear Whatever the Hell You Want T-shirts and Anti-Slut-Shaming hats. It's the best place on earth. But it's all as ridiculous as it sounds.

I was twenty-four and nearly a year into my first big-name magazine gig when I realized Feminist Tomorrowland was very far away indeed. By then, I'd already decided I was a feminist. I discovered feminism in my high school gender studies class, slipping into the label as easily as I did my favorite pair of jeans. I'd read the word before in books, of course, and on some cellular level the concept called to me. I mean, I signed up for the elective even though I knew most of the school considered it an easy pass. I joined idealistic young teens like me as well as a hulking dude who had a seemingly endless wardrobe of camouflage, at least three stoners who so rarely showed up that I was always surprised when I saw them, and our school's lone Jehovah's Witness, who grimaced through the entire unit on gender and religion. Our teacher was a stalwart, gnomish man whom, at the time, I pegged as eighty, but who was very likely closer to a grizzled sixty. He had a doctorate—he was not Mr. Porter but *Dr.* Porter—and even at sixteen I wondered why he chose to put up with high school kids.

For an old white man, Porter's introduction to feminism was admirable. I learned about the history of feminism and sampled the smorgasbord of core feminist theory: impossible beauty standards and the male gaze, the wage gap, the prevalence and cultural normalization of rape and violence against women, and the importance of reproductive rights. My introduction was wicked old skool—as I'm only slightly ashamed to admit I would have called it back then—and, I now realize, absent of today's hallmark intersectionality, a term coined by American law professor Kimberlé Crenshaw in the late 1980s. Today's feminists use intersectionality to examine and acknowledge the interplay between systems of discrimination and oppression—and as a powerful antidote to "white girl feminism." Growing up in a sleepy and not particularly progressive Ontario suburb, I had never even heard the word "transgender." For all the course's flaws, though, it set me on the right path, and by university I was already starting to find my own way through the movement, its theories, and its causes. Today, I can't point to just one moment that defines my choice to self-identify as a feminist, but many.

Even in 2008, when I was twenty-four, being a feminist wasn't a popular pick. I knew firsthand that (according to my demographic, at least) cool feminists were a rarity. I'd been to many booze-fueled parties where intellectual men and women expounded on the troubles in Afghanistan and the silliness of George W. Bush but received my thoughts on feminism like a fart in the room. A couple of years earlier, I'd even published an article about these observations in *Chatelaine*, a Canadian women's magazine. I argued the single most unattractive thing for a young woman to be was a feminist, akin to gaining twenty pounds overnight. This wishy-washy belief in women's rights, I wrote, was setting us up for a dangerous backslide. Not everybody agreed with me. One woman wrote a letter to the editor that said, in part, "I have a traditional role in my home, but I don't see things as unequal—I see them as how it is. How will you reach your utopian 'equality' if you are born a woman and someone else is born a man? It's your estrogen against his testosterone. It's biology, baby. McKeon needs to grow up, experience life, and get the chip off her shoulder. I'm proud to say I'm not a feminist."

And yet it wasn't until this job at a big-name national business magazine—my first one in my chosen field—that I discovered how much being a woman mattered. The magazine's senior editor didn't seem to like me very much. He was uniformly unimpressed with my writing and never assigned me anything, and whenever I entered his messy office to discuss a story, he demanded I bend over and fetch a stapled report off a stack of teetering paper. He made comments about my shirt, my hair, my shoes, calling my sartorial choices "interesting" and "nice" in a tone that heavily implied the contrary. I convinced myself I just needed to work harder to win him over. I was a newbie, after all, and that's how initiation worked. I was a feminist but also a desperate overachiever. I wanted to believe in equality of opportunity. I wanted to believe that girl power meant showing the old curmudgeon he was wrong about me. And so I ignored the lunchtime comments about cunnilingus. I silently recycled the photocopied articles about weight loss, laser eye surgery, and birth control left on my desk each morning.

Then one night at the pub, during a celebration of our recent round of awards nominations (including one for an investigative feature of mine *not*, unsurprisingly, written for the magazine in question), I finally saw that no amount of trying would get me ahead.

The table was crowded and sticky with spilled beer. During a lull in the conversation, the editor turned toward me, the broad slabs of his ruddy cheeks hitched up in a smile. "I bet you spend your days crying in a corner, writing poetry nobody will ever read," he said. "You should quit now because you'll never make it in journalism." As far as insults go it was a weird one, but the message was clear: *get out*. He laughed and my colleagues laughed while my mouth did its best impression of a Cheerio. He never spoke to me again; it was like I'd become a ghost. I quit a few months after that.

Attraction name: the Young Woman Who Hit a Very Low Glass Ceiling.

As far as encounters with the old boys' club go, my experience was depressingly normal. In the several years since, I've had at least a dozen similar ones and, in interviews with other women, heard about hundreds more. Yet what truly scared me as I grew up (as the *Chatelaine* letter writer so helpfully suggested) wasn't the entrenched patriarchy but just how many women were convinced feminism had won, and a long time ago, too. Everywhere I turned, it seemed more and more women were proudly proclaiming, "I'm not a feminist." They treated the women's movement as a quaint 1960s relic. And why not? The surface gains women have made in my lifetime have allowed us to spin a dangerously sweet bedtime story of success and equal opportunity. It tells us we've already reached our happily ever after, and it's easy and seductive enough to believe.

After all, in recent years, gender-equality awareness has surged across North America. We are saturated with tampon, soap, and food commercials that proclaim girl power. Brazen feel-good feminists like Malala Yousafzai, FEMEN, and Pussy Riot are household names. In every industry is one famous woman who has made it, allowing everybody to believe we all have—as if women are dolls on a paper chain. But painting feminism as triumphant poses an insidious risk.

At best, this post-feminist lie means buying into the rebranding of the status quo as sexy, fun, and free. At worst, it means accepting the status quo as the best we can do. Such victory blindness can freeze us in second place and threaten to send us rocketing backward. What would happen then? The more women I met who snubbed feminism, the more I craved answers and the more I kept writing about them. Soon, I couldn't help but see these stories as connecting pieces of a bigger picture.

In 2013 I published a profile of a young and prominent anti-abortion activist in Canada's biggest city magazine, *Toronto Life*. My mother and grandmother couldn't finish reading the article. My granny, a former union head who'd fought for equal rights in the workplace, had put her husband through school and kept working even after he earned enough to support the family, just because she liked her job. As for my mom, she'd always told me that being a mother was a woman's choice, not her duty. She ensured that both my sister and I were on birth control as soon as we were old enough to have sex, which was something she believed we should do with pleasure. That any woman could fight to end reproductive rights was unfathomable to either of them. "Why write about *this* girl, Lauren? She could ruin everything!" They had a point: why her indeed?

As I delved deeper into the anti-feminist movement and continued interviewing women who appeared to advocate against their own rights, I often encountered the argument that I'd be a better feminist if I left them alone. By paying attention, my critics (and loved ones) argued, I legitimized them. I understand the concern. We hope that if we don't pay attention to people whose ideas we find repugnant, they will disappear, silently slinking away until — *poof!* — they have no public platform and thus no power. This unfortunately ignores the fact that online communities and social media enable the viral dissemination of ideas without any help at all from mainstream media. We should ignore scary movements that are so far on the fringe they might as well be dusty 1970s macramé, but the anti-feminists aren't hiding in a dark cave, quietly talking to their three trollish BFFs. Why would they, when they can connect with and broadcast to thousands? As a journalist, I've always believed the real danger comes in ignoring and dismissing, particularly when we don't like what we uncover. If we ignore these ideas we don't like, they don't go away; they fester unchecked. We can't engage with something, critically or otherwise, if we pretend it doesn't exist.

Perhaps if I interviewed enough anti-feminist women, I thought, I could understand them. If I only knew why they'd abandoned feminism, I could convince them they were wrong. I also hoped the interviews would prove *me* wrong: they'd show I'd overreacted, that things weren't so bad. If only. Every time I interviewed one—from a young anti-abortion activist to a self-styled trophy girlfriend to a woman re-embracing housewifery—I asked the question, "What about feminism?" More often than not, I received a variation of the same shrug: *What* about *feminism?*

I knew we were really in trouble when the Women Against Feminism campaign went viral in August 2014. It featured selfies of women holding up signs on which they'd written reasons why they were against feminism. Full pages, Post-it Notes, giant poster boards, even paper plates detailed their beefs. The same themes emerged: feminism is a hateful and violent force, one that exponentially exaggerates women's oppression, dwells too much on small personal slights, devalues traditional roles, turns all women into victims, and dresses men up in villains' costumes while simultaneously ignoring their issues. It is petty, constrictive, probably racist, totally useless, and 100 percent irrelevant in the modern Western world. Here is just a small sampling of what you would have found on the movement's Tumblr and Facebook sites:

"I don't need feminism because equality of opportunity *already* exists."

"I don't need feminism because I don't see women as weak and pathetic victims of a non-existent patriarchy."

"I reject feminism because being a wife and mother is the greatest joy in my life."

"This isn't 1920. We're not fighting for anything anymore. Women have freedom!"

"I don't need feminism because I love men. All my friends are men. They're way nicer and less dramatic than women—especially feminists."

"I don't need feminism because your vaginas can't silence my voice."

When the movement's memes went viral, many feminists rushed to poke holes in the anti-feminist argument. The campaign had feminism so wrong, they said. It was as if those other women had taken the definition of feminism from a dictionary published on another planet: Mars, maybe. Headline after headline blared smug sentiments such as "Actually, women, you *do* need feminism."

Others cheered the anti-feminists. Some felt we'd already won: feminism was beating a dead horse. Perhaps capital-F feminism, the movement as monolith, deserved questioning? It had become tone-deaf, too turned in on—and against—itself. "These arguments need to be engaged, not dismissed and ridiculed," wrote Cathy Young, a *Boston Globe* journalist who frequently and critically tackles gender issues, often sympathizing with the rhetoric of men's rights. "The anti-feminist egalitarians," she wrote, "believe that, whatever feminism's positive past gains, its dominant modern version is hostile to men and demeaning to women. They are right."

Maybe.

Even a self-proclaimed diehard feminist like me could see feminism was constricting on itself like a snake, squeezing out criticism. The result was a broken sisterhood, its fault lines both varied and numerous: race, class, age, sexual orientation—it went on and on. White women especially were guilty of pancaking all women's experiences together, flattening out differences and erroneously adopting a skewed Musketeers all-for-one mentality.

Patricia Arquette unwittingly revealed the privilege problem during her 2015 acceptance speech for the Oscar for best supporting actress. "It's time for all the women in America," she said, "and all the men who love women, and all the gay people, and all the people of color that we've fought for, to fight for us now." She stuck to her statement, even as other feminists, particularly Roxane Gay, wondered at the implications: Did Arquette think racism was a thing of the past or that all those groups were mutually exclusive?

This myopic view isn't limited to the rich and famous. Women of color repeatedly report being relegated to the sidelines of the movement. Many give up and are pushed out entirely. A handful of them have even become vocal anti-feminists. They're not the only women the movement is hemorrhaging. From the start, feminism has been notoriously unkind to transgender women. Even today, one of feminism's grandmothers, Germaine Greer, has repeatedly, publicly, said transgender women are "not women" but men.

She's not alone. In response to the increasing advocacy around transgender rights, a whole branch of anti-trans feminism has sprung up, calling itself "trans-exclusionary radical feminism." The TERFs, as they've dubbed themselves, have derided any attempt to include transgender women in the movement, barring them from their own feminist events and bullying them at others. When I organized a "We Need More Feminism" speaker series in March 2015, one transgender speaker almost bowed out because she was so afraid of the TERFs; they were already targeting the event, calling it a celebration of fake feminism and fake women. While she ultimately went on stage, she admitted she wasn't sure if feminism still had a place for her. I heard the same painful uncertainty from the women of color who spoke at the event. Women with disabilities, women in the sex trade, those on the LGBTQ spectrum—anybody, really, who doesn't neatly fit into the binary of what we like to deem normal—echoed it.

It occurred to me that night, and not for the first time, that for all its dedication to equality, feminism suffered from institutionalized exclusion, and it wasn't doing much for its bad image, not to mention the women who felt abandoned. This wasn't a case of respectfully arguing over what direction battleship *Feminism* should steer, or what issues it should focus its missiles on. A war was brewing within the movement, between women who believed feminism already included everyone it needed and those who knew it did not. No wonder the anti-feminists were gaining traction: we were handing out ammunition like free candy and helpfully showing them where to point the gun.

In October 2014, with the shaky state of feminism heavy on my mind, I went to the Women's Forum des Femmes, held in Canada's capital city of Ottawa. More than one hundred women of all ages filled an auditorium with laughter and hisses, cheers and boos. My thoughts were on the recent criticism of the movement, its discord, and the high stakes of it all: our lives. As feminism publicly crumbled, and the undercurrents of anti-feminism spilled over, we were already losing ground at home, at school, at work, on the streets, and in our bedrooms, courtrooms, and boardrooms.

Then in its third year, the forum had set itself a bold goal: it would define the feminist agenda, for today and for the coming years. "We can, and we must, do this," boomed Niki Ashton, a New Democratic Party member of parliament in her early thirties. "Canada is waiting." A feminist agenda for *whom*, I wondered. Should there be only one? Can there be only one? I remember this as the time when I stopped avoiding the question: If we wanted to bring women back to feminism, did we need to overhaul the movement? I wasn't alone. In the opening panel discussion, one of the speakers, Sonia Lawrence, director of the Toronto-based Institute for Feminist Legal Studies at Osgoode Hall Law School, described herself as a "critical race feminist." She urged us to be "generous across our differences." To a background of tentative cheers, she went on, "We need to keep the movement open and inclusive so that our disagreements do not overwhelm the many things we do agree on." As the audience's clapping became more confident, she added, "I am not the feminist police, and I don't want to be." Later, she remarked that the demonization and polarization sweeping the movement surprised and disappointed her. "We have to find a way to talk about the things we disagree on and pursue those," she said. "It's not clear what we have to gain from this divisiveness; it is clear what we have to lose." She suggested the movement adopt flexible coalitions within itself: hundreds of groups with different key goals that could still work together to lobby for the big goals.

After her speech, I wanted to hoot and holler like I was at a riot grrrl concert, not the National Library of Canada. My enthusiasm was short-lived. During the question-and-answer period, a woman in the audience asked how we could stop all the feminist-on-feminist hate she was seeing on social media, especially Twitter. "It's vicious. It's extremely discouraging and confusing," she said. "How do we build a space where we don't slip into attacks publicly?" The problem with such attacks, she argued, is that in addition to creating disunity, they perpetuated all the worst stereotypes about feminism. Women are turned off from the movement, and anti-feminist groups, sensing a wounded lion, take advantage of its weakness.

One of the other panelists, Erica Violet Lee, a twenty-three-year-old Indigenous protestor who, minutes earlier, had received a standing ovation after reading her rallying cry, "We are the Revolution," told the women gathered that she'd had to quit Twitter for just that reason. She couldn't take the hate. Sonia Lawrence quickly jumped in. "By no means did I want to suggest we should be quiet in the name of unity," she said. "Feminists should not," she noted, "fear to discipline each other, particularly if a mainstream feminist is out of line." In a way, I agreed: for far too long, women have been taught to play nice and be polite. Historically, the feminist movement has hushed many women's voices under a misguided pledge for unity. It needs to stop. Still, as I glanced at my social media feeds, my smile sagged. Peer discipline and call-out culture on Twitter often manifests as neither respectful yet firm nor as even correctively caring. What we largely get instead are vicious and unforgiving attacks. No wonder people like Lee were bowing out of the conversation. Though dissent isn't inherently terrible, it's hard to understate how much it is fracturing us. There are no easy answers: feminism's vibrant acrimony is turning women away, and so is its demand that all women kowtow to one capital-F unified version. It's lose-lose at a time when women's rights need it to be win-win.

I was thinking about all this as I walked back to the hotel, after the conference. The parliament buildings were old and gigantic and beautiful, a testament to nation building and legacy. But construction was everywhere. One building, larger than a city block, was almost entirely covered with an outer shell of scaffolding wrapped in white plastic. The entire thing looked like it was plopped inside a bag, except where wind had ripped makeshift windows. Roughly half of all the storefronts located in the city's pedestrian-only area were in the midst of remodeling, flimsy plywood shelters doing a poor job of disguising the chaos. This being Canada, plenty of signs asked passersby to "Please excuse our mess." Construction was in progress, but soon, said the signs, everything will be good again. It occurred to me that the feminist movement was a lot like these buildings: an old, mammoth institution, proud and important, but falling apart—and still trying to convince us there was nothing to see. All the while, its scaffolding was showing.

❦

The backlash against the women's rights movement, in and of itself, is nothing especially new. Those with a vested interest in seeing the movement fail have always existed: yes, sometimes it was men, but it was also the religious right and conservative traditionalists. In 1991, when I was seven years old, journalist Susan Faludi published the

Pulitzer Prize–winning book *Backlash: The Undeclared War Against American Women.* Faludi charted the rising 1980s anti-feminist movement and emergence of what she called the "New Right" woman. I imagine Faludi must look at much of what's going on today with a serious case of déjà vu. In *Backlash,* she argued that male antifeminists enlisted women to do the heavy lifting in the campaign against their own rights. Conservative activist Phyllis Schlafly, whom I like to think of as the first president of the female anti-feminist fan club, headed the Stop ERA campaign against the (still unratified) Equal Rights Amendment because she believed it would "take away the marvelous legal rights of a woman to be a full-time wife and mother in the house supported by her husband." Economist Sylvia Ann Hewlett, who claimed to be a reformed feminist (thanks to Schlafly) and whose book *A Lesser Life: The Myth of Women's Liberation in America* sparked a six-publisher bidding war, argued that feminism reviles motherhood. Faludi also introduced us to Camille Paglia, who was then rising to fame for dismissing date rape as feminist nonsense.

On my bookshelf, I have the fifteenth-anniversary edition of *Backlash,* which includes a preface that wryly notes the latest wave of anti-feminists were right-wingers who said *they* were the true feminists. Faludi calls women like Christina Hoff Sommers, author of *Who Stole Feminism? How Women Have Betrayed Women* and *The War Against Boys: How Misguided Feminism Is Harming Our Young Men,* a "sleeper cell of pod feminists" who have hijacked the feminist movement. Other potential pod members are Lucianne Goldberg and Jeannie Sakol, who co-founded the Pussycat League in 1970 to oppose the women's lib movement and bring back "charm, chic and clinging gowns," and Danielle Crittenden, author of *What Our Mothers Didn't Tell Us: Why Happiness Eludes the Modern Woman* and founder of the magazine *Women's Quarterly,* which ushered in "new"—ahem, anti-—feminism.

This latest iteration of the anti-feminist backlash reminded me of a *Glee* mash-up song, only depressing (well, depending on how you feel about musicals). Maybe Britney Spears's "Oops! . . . I Did It Again" meets Guns N' Roses's "Welcome to the Jungle." The same rhetoric was re-emerging, only now it was wilder and, also, everywhere. Social media allows the ideas underpinning both anti-feminism and post-feminism (the idea that we're *past* the need for feminism) to spread and to connect, and the anti-feminist movement—and its many octopus arms—have grown beyond the usual suspects. This popularity makes a certain kind of sense. My fellow millennials and I are, quite literally, the daughters of the powerful anti-feminist wave Faludi wrote about in *Backlash*. But it's not just my generation. This new pukey-face-emoji reaction to feminism may have historical roots, but it also has its contemporary reasons. I've never before seen such a blanket rejection of feminism from those who actually have a vested interest in seeing it achieve its goals. To me, these women are harder to explain away. I can't credibly claim they are all misogynists, and too many of them are not traditional, right wing, or even remotely devout. I also can't quite convince myself they are all under the big, fat, hairy thumb of men or are misguided, approval-seeking drips.

Lest we think it is only Women of the Internet, let's not forget the spate of celebrities who once rushed to distance themselves from the f-word: Sarah Jessica Parker, Demi Moore, Carrie Underwood, Susan Sarandon, Kelly Clarkson, Lady Gaga, Björk, and (until recently) Taylor Swift, Katy Perry, and Madonna. (Both Donald Trump and Beyoncé can likely take some credit for pushing female celebs to join Team Feminism—albeit for different reasons.) In June 2014, pop star Lana Del Rey infamously declared: "Feminism is just not an interesting concept." Shailene Woodley, star of the blockbusters *Divergent* and *The Fault in Our Stars* (both based on wildly popular teen fiction) has said she's not a feminist because, as she put it, "I love men, and I think the idea of 'raise women to power, take the men away from the power' is never going to work out because you need balance."

Most of these women are also outspoken advocates for empowerment, independence, and strength. And yet—and yet—they repeat
the same strange rhetoric of many anti-feminists: they love men, believe in equal rights, but feel feminism limits and confines them. It
reminded me of a game I used to play with my friends when I was a
kid: Opposite Land. Everything we said, we meant the opposite. Yes
became no, and green became red. Our shirts would go inside out or
backward, and sometimes we'd do a Superman with our underwear.
Often, we'd wait for a parent to enter the room before we started
playing it, just so we could annoy them. Looking at pop culture, I
was that annoyed parent all the time.

The uproar became so great that in May 2013 the *Washington
Times* gleefully announced: "Feminism may be dead." It wasn't just
hot air. At the time, in a countrywide survey, more than half the
US female population had declared itself "not feminist." About
5 percent said they were actually "anti-feminist." And, in a series of
subsequent polls, women consistently said they felt there was nothing
positive about the term "feminist." A year later, one 2014 *Economist/
YouGov* joint poll showed that more than 30 percent of women still
said "no" to the f-word *after* being read the dictionary definition of
feminism ("someone who believes in the social, political and economic equality of the sexes").

A May 2014 Ipsos Reid survey of fifteen countries—including
Canada and the US, but also places such as Sweden, Japan, and
Argentina—put feminists on the majority side again, but just barely.
Drastically less than half of the respondents said they "strongly" identified as feminists, leaving the pollster to conclude only one in six
were "core" feminists: the type who'd be likely to engage in activism
or talk rights at dinner parties.

In Canada, for instance, only 17 percent of women said they
strongly identified as feminist; in the US, the number sat at 20 percent. In all cases, those polled were then read a dictionary definition
of feminism that stressed social, political, and economic equality. It

made a negligible difference. The numbers only bumped up once the poll asked respondents if they believed in equal opportunities for men and women and that women should be treated equally to men in all areas based on their competence, not their gender. In Canada, 67 percent strongly agreed; in the US, only 63 percent. The average for all fifteen countries surveyed was just 60 percent. To find out the story behind the words, I contacted John Wright, a Canada-based executive with Ipsos whose job it was to turn the company's raw data into meaningful narratives.

"Words in and of themselves are absolutely critical and can become pejorative," said Wright, his voice heavy with a Nicolas Cage drawl. Survey results can vary wildly based on the precision of the language used when crafting the questions, even when considering the small differences between terms such as "in favor," "support," and "acceptable." Each suggests a different level of commitment—what we're willing to accept as true to us. And some words, simply put, are loaded. This can result in survey respondents answering negatively to something with which they actually agree. Based on the polling, that's what Wright, a man in his late fifties, thought had happened to the word "feminist." It was like a tea bag steeped in water too long, gone sour from all the negative social connotations. Many women may want to avoid calling themselves feminists, Wright said, even if they agree with equal rights.

The word "feminist" has a long history of debate, and some of those debates were so negative, he argued, that it could be time, at least for pollsters, to redefine the word, or use an entirely different term. He had a point, though I was torn between whether it made me relieved or angrier. Wright, however, may have thought I was confused, because he suddenly told me about his old phone, a Motorola Flip the size of two hands and something many of the younger, smartphone-tethered staff in his office have never seen. Wright keeps it at the back of his desk and whenever anyone in his office is so fixated on something they believe is right, he will whip out the old cell and point to the gawky antenna. He does it to re-mind his younger staff that things have not always been the way they are now, that sometimes something that seems forever ago, wasn't.

I wondered whether Wright meant that feminism as a unified movement was about as outdated as an old phone, or that thinking feminism was a good label was naive in the same way that believing all phones had always been smartphones was naive. Either way, it was bad. I am sure what he really wanted was for me to be optimistic that, at least for some women, ditching the f-word didn't preclude them from believing in equal rights. But I don't think avoiding the word helps women; it hushes our voices and makes it harder to act. When I asked Wright if he was arguing for future polls to not include the word "feminist," he paused. He was silent for longer than I expected. "I think this is just new ground," he finally said. "And we just have to think about it." Some countries, he surmised, still had a great need for the word and all that it represents. He was mostly talking about countries in Asia that, in his mind, still needed the Germaine Greer–type definition of the movement. "This is their time for feminism," he said.

But, I wondered: Had our time really passed?

Once I started seeing women (and men) embrace this hardline re-jection of feminism, I couldn't stop seeing it or its effects. I pictured it as a giant f-bomb that had exploded, leaving a nuclear-sized mush-room cloud filled with hypersexualization, scary new conservatism, mid-century values, and a new generation of women who were eager to ditch the feminist fight. Famous women who ardently rebuffed the label and the thousands of Women Against Feminism weren't the cause of this change, though, or even the final outcome; they were a single symptom of a much wider cultural shift. Just one generation ago, asserting the existence of such a regression would have seemed silly, conservative, wishful thinking. Not today. Today, evidence all around us shows that women see feminism as a tool for their mothers' and grandmothers' apron pockets, *but it is not for them.*

I would love for the women who believe we are in a post-feminist world to be right. I want nothing more than for all the women who have dedicated their lives to feminism to retire and sip piña coladas on a beach while women and girls everywhere enjoy the fruits of their labor: equal pay, lives free of violence, equal representation in positions of political power, absolute reproductive rights, harassment-free working environments, and about a bazillion other things. But I just don't see that paradise yet.

That's not to say women haven't made huge gains; they have, and thanks largely to feminism. In 1967, for example, only 11.7 percent of mothers were the family breadwinners, and just over 15 percent were co-breadwinners. This is according to the 2014 *Shriver Report*, a 415-page study on the state of women in North America completed by the Center for American Progress under the guiding fear women were on the brink of societal backslide. As of 2009, those numbers had jumped to 41 percent and 22.5 percent, respectively. In recent years, twice as many single women as single men were new home buyers. Globally, women control more than $20 trillion in spending. Also gone were the days when only men pursued post-secondary education; we now outnumber them in most programs. We keep making impressive gains in employment, too: back in the 1970s, scantly more than 15 percent of us were managers in the private sector. That number is now closer to 50. In the US, women-led businesses account for a staggering $3 trillion of the country's GDP.

We are also leading companies that, years ago, nobody would have ever thought we'd run. Sheryl Sandberg was at Facebook and Marissa Mayer at Yahoo. The CEO of General Motors was Mary Barra. Before her, in Canada, Maureen Kempston Darkes became the company's first woman president. In grade four we had to write to a CEO for a school assignment. I wrote to Darkes, confessing I idolized her. I was the only one in the class who received a handwritten response, which I still have. My dad worked at GM and, to his credit, explained that the fact a woman was his big boss was special; it meant I could do something like that one day.

But it's dangerous to let these victories fool us into thinking we've won. At the time of the *Shriver Report*'s release, one in three adult women in North America lived in poverty or on the brink of it. We made up roughly 47 percent of the labor force but more than 60 percent of minimum-wage jobs. As a result, we were likely to have poorer health and more stress than men. We continued to earn somewhere around seventy-five cents for every dollar a man earned, and some studies of the past decade showed that gap was growing, not shrinking. The average Black woman earned only sixty-four cents to a white man's dollar, and Latinas earned fifty-five cents. Paid family leave was still a dream for close to 90 percent of women workers. And while there were close to three million more of us enrolled in post-secondary education than men, they still hugely outnumbered us in program majors that tended to pay more after graduation, including science, technology, engineering, and math, disciplines jointly known as STEM. The field, in fact, is overwhelmingly male. Despite a few high-profile women at the top, we comprised less than 20 percent of the industry's employees. Considering STEM is widely acknowledged as the driver of our future economy, this portends bad things for working women.

Beyond these hard numbers were hundreds of anecdotes that charted the ways women were still losing. Take, for instance, just a few of the things that happened during the week I wrote the sentence you're reading right now: a woman was shot and killed in Detroit after refusing to give a man her phone number; three men in Atlanta gang raped and then set fire to a woman because she beat them in a freestyle rap battle at a house party; Microsoft's CEO told a predominately female audience at a tech conference to never ask for a raise but instead "know and have faith that the system will give you the right raise"; American talk show host Wendy Williams told

Hunger Games star Jennifer Lawrence that the hacked, leaked nude photos of her were not a "sex crime," as Lawrence had told *Vanity Fair*, because, according to Williams, the hacking "has actually made your career even hotter"; and numerous rape scandals rocked the New York alt-lit scene, supposedly a bastion of progressive values. And that was just an average news week. I could have picked any week at random and found similar results, or worse.

Also consider the moment in 2016 when most of us realized we were in trouble — the Trump in the room, if you will. First came the Hillary Clinton effigies hung in front of houses. Then Donald Trump called Clinton a "nasty woman" during a live televised presidential debate. Perhaps it shouldn't have come as a shock. That same month, October 2016, a 2005 recording was leaked of Trump bragging about his treatment of women to *Access Hollywood* host Billy Bush. "I'm automatically attracted to beautiful [women]. I just start kissing them. It's like a magnet. Just kiss. I don't even wait. And when you're a star they let you do it. You can do anything," Trump boasted. "Grab them by the pussy. You can do anything."

Trump's resurrected words, and his response to the leak, launched many "This pussy grabs back" T-shirts, memes, and rallying cries — and prompted many women to come forward with sexual assault allegations against Trump. By the end of the month at least seventeen women had shared their experiences, alleging unwanted sexual advances that included touching, groping, and kissing. Among the women who spoke out against Trump's behavior were former Miss Teen USA contestants who accused Trump of entering their changing room when they were undressing or, in some cases, already nude. The teens were as young as fifteen. Trump had previously gloated about this, too, on Howard Stern's show, also in 2005, saying that because he was the owner of the pageant, he could "sort of get away with things like this." When not calling his accusers liars, Trump and his supporters dismissed his talk as harmless locker room banter.

People either believed the Trump team spin or didn't care about his behavior, because he won the election. I was less surprised than most to learn that 53 percent of white women voted for Trump. Their ballot marks disproved conventional wisdom that his gross actions and comments toward women would make him about as appealing as a dirty gym sock. Many women resented the presumption that they'd vote for Clinton based on her gender. Even supposedly diehard Democrats had piled on the misogyny, claiming they simply preferred Bernie Sanders for the job while also calling Clinton supporters "Hillary bots" and Clinton herself other, worse things. They earned their own nickname, "Bernie Bros," which, in turn, spawned several think pieces and much online chatter about whether feminists were making up the misogyny. Never mind the death threats.

Scott Goodson's 2012 book, *Uprising: How to Build a Brand—and Change the World—by Sparking Cultural Movements*, offers surprising insight into anti-feminism's growing popularity. To help explain the rise of social movements, Goodson turned to Bob Johansen, a director at the forward-looking think tank Institute for the Future. "In times of turbulence, anything that gives people a sense of meaning tends to grow," Johansen explained. In a modern era of super-connectivity—and yet concurrent in-person disconnectivity—movements are the new gathering points, today's Rotary Club or Tupperware party, if you will. While technology facilitates today's lightning growth, Goodson argues, it's really passion of belief that inspires people to move on an idea together.

Goodson cites Barack Obama's 2008 campaign as the start of today's movement mania. While Obama offered hope, his campaign also sparked the Tea Party, one of the most successful recent countercultural movements. The Tea Party swiftly sprang up in opposition to Obama's policies and positions, zeroing in on people's anger. Like anti-feminism and men's rights activism (MRA), it started out, as Goodson wrote, "unclear and chaotic and messy," but as Obama's popularity grew, so did the Tea Party's ability to oppose his message. Their own message soon crystallized. (Fast-forward and we get Trump.) So it goes with feminism and anti-feminism. As feminism grows and stalls and fails and grows some more, like all major movements, anti-feminism responds, plucking at the restlessness and dissatisfaction that feminism misses, paving the way for a new vision of womanhood.

According to Goodson, hundreds and thousands of movements are happening all around us—some commercial, some social, some big, some small—and together they've put us in a cultural moment of movements. We're on a hunt for meaning, and technology has accelerated our ability to connect with others on that same hunt. In 2009, shortly after Barack Obama's second election win, and way before @RealDonaldTrump broke the internet, Clay Shirky, the author of *Here Comes Everybody: The Power of Organizing Without Organizations*, gave a TED talk on the power of social media. He called our current age "the largest increase in expressive capability in human history." The internet, he explained, was the first-ever medium that allowed for a many-to-many communication pattern: it can facilitate the building of groups and mass conversation among those groups.

Some researchers are beginning to argue that the relationships we form online can be as strong and as real as the ones we form offline. That's how we get a Women Against Feminism Facebook group that, by early 2017, had grown to amass more than 42,000 likes, or a "Feminism is Evil" Facebook page that claims "Feminism is about female supremacy, not gender equality" with more than 52,000 likes. (For a chilling comparison, the pro-feminism campaign "Who Needs Feminism?" had earned just under 39,500 likes by 2017, despite massive media attention upon its 2012 founding.) These aren't just idle conversations; people are building bonds and social groups, no matter how trollish they might seem to outsiders. *Fizz. Bang. Explode.* There is no recorking that champagne bottle. "The question we all face now," Shirky told his audience, "is 'How can we make best use of this media?'"

If this were a different type of book, I might focus on the uplifting actions and the optimistic work of those who are forging new feminisms for the future, documenting how they are making best use of our moment of movements. We will meet more of those people soon—they *do* exist—but what I wanted to know first was: Why are women so hell-bent on throwing feminism in the historical trashcan? And if feminism is not what they want, what *do* they want? What can we learn from those who oppose us?

I knew that, in many ways, whatever I discovered would be inadequate. There is so much that feminism must pay attention to right now, so many life-or-death issues from which we can't afford to turn away: the hugely disproportionate rates of discrimination and violence against Indigenous women, women of color, women with disabilities, transgender women, and so many more who do not fit the white, middle-class status quo. These are undeniably feminist issues, and they're also ones wrapped up in painful, long histories of colonialism, racism, white supremacy, ableism, homophobia, and transphobia.

The statistics on violence against women are both depressing and alarming. In 2016, for instance, twenty-seven transgender people were murdered in the US, nearly all of them transgender women of color; in the first five months of 2017, that tragic number had already hit eleven, and all of the victims were transgender women of color. Sixty percent of women with disabilities experience some form of violence. Indigenous women, including First Nations women, Inuit women, and Métis women, are six times more likely to be killed than non-Indigenous women and more than 2.5 times more likely to be survivors of violence. In Canada, the number of murdered and missing Indigenous women is staggering—a national crisis that our federal government took an unforgivably long time to acknowledge, let alone act upon. The two-year, $53.86-million independent national inquiry launched in September 2016 has been soundly and rightly criticized by activists, leaders, and family members for its inadequate communication with families. Those same critics demanded an extended timeline to allow proper hearings for those families, and to demand more care and awareness so that families are not re-traumatized by the process. What's more, the commission put the onus on families to reach out to participate; as of May 2017, less than three hundred had done so. Numerous studies show that when women of color report violence, they're taken less seriously and their perpetrators receive more lenient sentences. No woman should ever have to experience violence; that society seems to judge some women more worthy of our sorrow than others is inexcusable.

We need to write a hundred, a thousand, books about this. We must shine a ceaseless spotlight on these issues, and so many others. Investigating the rise of anti-feminism and post-feminism and its allure among today's girls and women is only one small part of all the feminist work that needs to be done. In choosing to focus on the areas in which the anti-feminist movement has gained the most ground, particularly among women, I know I'm missing so many other feminist issues, including those that are dear to me. The onslaught against women is broad, and the scope of my book is narrow. It is impossible for one book to cover it all. I set out on this project with the hope that if I could understand women's anti-feminist discourse, it would help me—and others—to understand more, and in that understanding we would wake up: we would investigate more, make more connections, become thunderous in our feminist fights.

Many women seem convinced that the gains we've made are enough. The US presidential election felt like proof that we were willing to settle for *almost* there, not realizing, or unwilling to admit, it would mean *never* there. And somehow, in the process, both what we'd achieved, and our unattained goals, were being turned into tinder for the anti-feminist fire.

How did this happen? If I refused to dismiss women who didn't believe in feminism or rejected the label, then it followed they must have been responding to *something*. What was it about feminism that women weren't connecting with? To find out, I knew I had to go deep inside the anti-feminist movement; I needed to keep meeting the people who had decided women's rights were achieved, or had at least been realized enough for us to stop fighting for them. I needed to not look away. But before I could go forward into the fire to see what the wholesale rejection was costing us now and what it might cost us in the future, I knew I needed to take a step back and focus that same critical eye on today's feminist movement and our fractured sisterhood. Because if I was scared of what all the female anti-feminist sentiment was doing to us, I was even more worried these women may have a point.

2 Feminists eat their young: The fourth wave, a fractured sisterhood, and the cataclysmic divide between feminist generations

Feminism is a movement that is at once feared and loved, sometimes by the same people. I stepped into this project to find out why women were abandoning the f-word and the consequences of that. I'd guessed the reasons were complex, but I wasn't quite prepared for just how muddled our thinking had become.

The *Washington Post* and the Kaiser Family Foundation Survey Project have been asking Americans what they think about feminism and women's issues since 1995. The results are both broad and enlightening. As I expected, the 2016 poll showed that women were feeling lukewarm about feminism. Only 60 percent saw the movement favorably and just more than half thought the movement had, à la Joan Jett, a "bad reputation," and that it should definitely give a damn. A smidge less than 40 percent of women thought the movement was angry, and another 30 percent thought it was outdated. Just about half the women felt the movement focused on changes they wanted (younger women were, on the whole, slightly more inclined to believe feminism cared about the same issues they did, while older women were more likely to give it the thumbs down). Only half, again, felt it reflected the views of all women, a number that hasn't seemed to budge since 1989. And 40 percent of women felt it unfairly blamed men for their challenges, suggesting the man-hating stereotype has more pop-culture staying power than even Oprah.

At the same time, the vast majority of women felt equal pay for equal work, affordable child care, and the reduction of sexual harassment should be "top priorities" when it comes to improving women's lives—all things feminism has worked diligently toward for decades. Other feminist priorities women agreed with were reducing domestic violence and discrimination against women of color and increasing the number of women in STEM. More than two-thirds of women felt a strong need for a women's movement (note that pollsters didn't use that dirty word *feminism*), a number that had *increased* since 1989, when only 59 percent of women surveyed felt there was a strong need. This is what psychologists call cognitive dissonance: the discomfort of holding two competing beliefs, ideals, or values at once. Many women, it seems, believe that feminism is for angry old man haters, as outdated and unhelpful as shoulder pads. *And* they see a strong need for better social policy and political movement to help women, which suggests that women believe we may not have achieved equality yet. This, I think, more than anything else explains how we really arrived at that now infamous saying, "I'm not a feminist, but . . ." We're afraid and maybe a little apathetic, and some days we think we made it, but deep down inside *we also know better.*

And we've known better for a while. A 1996 research paper called "I Am Not a Feminist, But" published in the journal *Political Psychology* set out to explore the then new (but still totally baffling) trend of post-feminism in college-age women. The authors studied those who labelled themselves feminists, post-feminists, and anti-feminists, and their reasons for identifying as such. After they'd completed their research, they were forced to add a fourth label: precarious feminists. They slotted more than 40 percent of women into this category, more than any other (though the next highest, at 35 percent, was post-feminist). As a result, they concluded that precarious feminists are similar to post-feminists in that they see advancement resulting from individual abilities. Unlike the post-feminists, however, they are dissatisfied with women's current status, but they are still lukewarm on the label "feminist."

In another study, "Feminists or 'Postfeminists'?" published nearly ten years later in the journal *Gender & Society*, scholar Pamela Aronson noted that the majority of young women she interviewed about their views on feminism and gender relations "were, in the words of one woman, 'fence-sitters.' They embraced a number of feminist principles yet rejected others and failed to classify themselves as either feminists or non-feminists . . . Despite this ambiguity, nearly all of the interviewees were supportive of feminist issues." Fast-forward to today and it seems that equally musty adage "The more things change..." holds true.

Part of this might be explained by the perception women have about how *others* view feminism. A 2013 YouGov poll showed that, regardless of their own views on feminism, only 27 percent of women respondents thought that the majority of other women considered themselves feminists. Only 5 percent of women thought that men considered themselves feminists. In a poll the following year, 24 percent of women said they considered calling someone a feminist an "insult." Women may, in their hearts, believe in the movement, but that doesn't mean they're going to don a "feminist" T-shirt or sip from an ironic "male tears" mug (as in "I drink male tears," an idea expertly explored in Amanda Hess's 2014 *Slate* essay "The Rise of the Ironic Man-Hater," in which she noted that "on its most basic level, ironic misandry functions like a stuck-out tongue pointed at a playground bully"). Or if they do, they might not broadcast it, particularly offline.

Consider how this tension plays out for teen girls in the peer pressure cookers—i.e., the classrooms and hallways of high schools. "I have friends who believe in feminism but choose not to wear the feminist label because it comes with a lot of stigma, especially in school," a young feminist named Majella Votta told me. "One day in school I heard a girl classmate say, 'Ugh, feminism really annoys me,' to try and impress these two guys in our class. Never in my life have I felt such pity for someone."

When I recounted a similar story to a group of thirty-and-over women academics at a dinner party, many of them expressed shock. "But Justin Trudeau says he's a feminist!" one exclaimed. And it's true: the Canadian prime minister won over women in Canada and elsewhere with an endearing combination of snuggly panda photo ops, shirtless selfies, and this retort to critics, after choosing a gender-balanced cabinet: "Because it's 2015." It all depends on who's claiming the label and in what context, with race, class, and life experiences all coming into play. What does Trudeau risk by declaring himself feminist? Feminism is experiencing an odd moment right now, where it is at once completely marketable (if you believe in a feminism that is soft on critical analysis but big on empowerment, looking hot, and buying dope shit) and distinctly uncool, like granny panties (if you believe in the kind that requires political action, tough reflection, and constant work).

The *Washington Post* observed this same tension in its article accompanying data graphs from the Kaiser survey. *Post* reporters recounted what one college sophomore (and feminist) told her professor when asked for her personal thesis: "Feminism is not a political movement." For younger generations, wrote the journalists, feminism "stresses personal freedom as much as it does equality." Call it an extension of choice feminism, a term that rose to worried prominence at the turn of this millennium's first decade. In a 2010 paper, Michaele L. Ferguson of the University of Colorado at Boulder argues that *choice feminism* is a response to three common criticisms of feminism: that it is too radical, too exclusionary, and too judgmental. "Ultimately," she concluded, "the problem with choice feminism is not that it celebrates women's choices without having a political consciousness. The problem is that, even complemented by a political consciousness, the turn to choice feminism is motivated by a fear of politics." What good was political consciousness, she asked, if women were afraid to use it?

In addition to seeing feminism as a bad thing, nearly 70 percent of women also saw it as "empowering." Because what does empowerment mean? Whatever you want it to. It's a term I've heard both feminists and anti-feminists use, each to describe their own movement. "I have a bad case of empowerment fatigue," *Bitch* magazine editor, and one of its three founders, Andi Zeisler wrote in "Empowering Down," a chapter in her 2016 book *We Were Feminists Once: From Riot Grrrl to CoverGirl, the Buying and Selling of a Political Movement.* "As a catchall phrase that can be understood to mean anything from 'self-esteem-building' to 'sexy and feminine,' to 'awesome,' empowerment has become a way to signify a particularly female way of being that's both gender essentialist—when was the last time you heard, say, a strip aerobics class for men described as 'empowering'?—and commercially motivated." She argues that the word has been used to sell and embrace hundreds of contradictory messages, including everything from high heels and cosmetic surgery to having children, being an asshole, buying a gun, and more. "By the time the satirical newspaper *The Onion* announced 'Women Now Empowered By Everything a Woman Does,'" she added, "it really did seem that 'today's woman lives in a near-constant state of empowerment.'"

As feminism does the necessary work of practicing intersectionality, these pluralities of meanings are both vital and confounding. When I asked a seventeen-year-old named Mia Salvato who lives in northeastern Ohio why she thought her peers could be reluctant to politically rally around feminism, she told me the movement needs its Rosa Parks. "I feel like feminism is so disembodied," she told me. "There's not somebody we can look at and say, 'This is who we're fighting for. This is *what* we're fighting for.' And, personally, I would like to see that happen, even if it's a straight, white woman." So long as it's someone, she said, that anyone could look to and say, "See, *this* is the problem."

It's a call for focus—a sort of reverse Beyoncé, somebody who doesn't just make feminism cool because she's killing it but urgent because she's *losing*. We don't need a champion, necessarily, but somebody to champion, a subtle but distinct difference. And so, depressingly, this is where we return: trying to hurdle over the idea that women have nothing left to win.

❧

Well-intentioned mainstream, white feminism—the kind the second wave and even the third wave have embraced—reminds me of my high school self. I grew up in a now large suburb one quick train ride away from Toronto. My school was big and multicultural, a hodge-podge of different-colored bodies teeming through the hallways, sitting in classrooms, eating at the cafeteria, and running through our sports fields. For two years in a row, our valedictorian was a Black woman. We had a step team. The entire school attended our two-hour Black History Month production every year. My friends' faces reflected the school's make-up: a mix of religious, cultural, and racial backgrounds. As I listened to them dish about their families and their lives, I leaned toward our similarities. All our moms annoyed us. We all faced pressure to maintain brainiac status and bring home top marks. We liked the same TV shows. We made the same jokes. In modern parlance, these girls were my ride-or-dies. I saw us as the best girl gang ever.

And we were. Those friendships were real. Some of those girls remain my closest, dearest friends today. But I cringe now at how little I understood then. The diversity of the school wasn't reflected in Dr. Porter's gender studies course; only one of my friends took the class with me. Of course, I knew that my friends' families and communities were unlike mine, yet in so many ways I benevolently and naively shrugged it off. I deliberately chose not to see the biggest differences, and I thought that was a good thing. *We are all humans! We are all the same! Look at our colorful mosaic of people! I'm a good white person!* You've met my high school self; maybe you're her right now. Hell, I can still be her sometimes. I sincerely, sweetly, and 100 percent wrongly believed I was doing the right thing: championing equality. I was actually discounting their own realities and experiences, and the worlds they lived in when they were not at school. I had taken a person-sized eraser to their selves and, with the best intentions in the world, scrubbed them out.

Mainstream feminism slides down the same slope with its all-for-one, one-size-fits-all approach. The we're-all-the-same narrative is threaded through our discourse, stitched through our academic papers, public events, and online conversation, hemmed tight into both our history and the statistics we use to battle for better rights. This universality assumes that the unfair system affects all women in the same manner, or that all of our issues, from gay rights to racial discrimination, are divided from each other.

Consider the historical milestones feminism celebrates. We're fond of saying Canadian women earned the right to vote in federal elections in 1921. We make less of the fact that it was only white women who earned that right. Many women of color weren't allowed to vote until the late 1940s, and Inuit women only won the right in 1960. We celebrate Canada's Famous Five for winning equality for privileged white women while making less of the fact that they spewed racism and xenophobia elsewhere. Three of them campaigned for forcible sterilization in Alberta, an act that passed into law in 1928 and was used to mutilate more than four thousand people, mostly women, before it was struck down in 1972.

We bandy about statistics on lower earnings, scant economic representation, violence, rape, and more — some with such frequency that they've reached near celebrity status, like the Kim Kardashian of numbers. But we often fail to mention those numbers correspond to straight white women, many of them middle class and able bodied.

For women of color, gay women, transgender women, women with disabilities, and so on, those storied and outrageous numbers are often far worse. And yet, time and again, we iron out the nuances, turning feminism into a pressed shirt. No wonder so many women feel left out.

In some ways, the Great Lump-In makes a lot sense: feminists had to eke out basic rights before they could focus on the details, or at least that's always been the argument. It's a convenient one. It allows us to forget that many of the women who have led feminism are those able to do so largely because they weren't the ones on the fringes struggling to survive. But that's only part of what makes our homogenizing of feminism so inexcusable. Let's think about it: The more feminism surges toward exclusion, building those moats and drawbridges and whole fortresses around itself, the more it becomes part of the same establishment it's fought so hard to tear down (or at least gain access to). From where many women sit, the white, established, straight, upper-class, male-dominated society doesn't look a whole lot different from white, established, straight, upper-class feminism. And why would it? Both are only speaking to, and about, themselves.

At everything from cocktail parties to panel events, I've found myself in the company of older feminists who expect me to speak on behalf of my generation and corner me as if I'm a magical unicorn — or a sacrificial lamb. I'm praised for being there and for caring about women's rights, but few women listen to what I have to say. Conversations tend to oscillate between outright dismissiveness, historical lecturing, and demands for answers. One night, I sat in an upscale pizzeria in Toronto (the type of restaurant that pairs your pinot grigio with your pepperoni) with three women, all in their fifties and sixties, who had worked together in the finance industry for decades. Successful, cultured, and firmly rooted in the middle- to upper-middle class, they were well coiffed and well off: hair cut into precision bobs, clothes tailored and neutral, makeup tastefully applied. I adored and admired them. Every winter they bought a "culture package" comprising tickets to the city's plays, musicals, ballets, operas, and speaker series. Sometimes, when one of the women had a ticket to give up, it was benevolently bestowed upon me, the starving writer. I'd been with them before, but this was the first time we'd ever talked about feminism.

They were delighted to find out that I am a feminist, too. "Good for you," they said. They told me that, in the 1970s and '80s, early into their careers, they realized the importance of feminism when they battled to gain equal footing with the men in their offices. They fought hard to have their job titles and salaries reflect the actual work they did. One was almost fired, more than once, for refusing to be the coffee girl at meetings. We laughed uproariously as she recounted how she'd told a boardroom full of men where they could put their cream and sugar. (Guess!) It wasn't lost on any of us that I was too young to have been alive back then, or that I owed a lot to women like them.

Then the mood shifted. Suddenly, they wanted me to explain how young women could possibly complain when men harassed them in the office, given how they dressed like "sluts." Well, actually, they wanted me to condemn these supposedly slutty women, as they had. Were they not *trying* to sleep their way to the top? Did they not realize it was inappropriate to wear a skirt that tight or short? How could these young women expect men to take them seriously when they paraded their cleavage? Did they really expect men not to look? Had the older generation fought so hard to gain a toehold, only for these boob-baring young women to ruin it all? One bomb after another, and I was expected to field them. I felt like I'd been designated Young Feminist, Vice President of Explaining Everything. It was an impossible job. I fumbled a subject change, but they sat patiently undeterred, knives at sharp angles, suspended over their pizza. I imagined the serrated blades as long-nose saw sharks out for blood. It was ridiculous, I know: me conjuring these women as menacing, threatening. But in that moment, it didn't feel like we were all part of the same sisterhood; it felt like civil war.

I couldn't translate my generation's sartorial choices in a way that made sense to my dining companions, not in a way that squared my generation's aversion to victim blaming and rape culture with their struggle to have men see them as equals in the workplace — hell, to even let them into the workplace. I tried every tactic, every argument. Didn't every woman deserve a safe, harassment-free work zone, no matter what she wore? Wasn't it a slippery slope down to "asking for it" territory if we scrutinized work clothes? Did they truly believe all these young women were trying to sleep their way up the corporate ladder? But whatever case I made came back to the question of *why*. Why were young women dressing like that? Why were they ruining everything? Eventually, frustrated, I gave up. "I have no idea," I answered tensely, honestly, throwing my fellow young women under the bus. I felt like a fraud.

Later that night, on my way home and pondering the earlier exchange, my mind darted back to an interview I'd done months earlier. I'd asked a feminist about ten years older than me why the sisterhood seemed so fractured. She'd answered immediately and ominously: "Feminists eat their young."

In the midst of other older women who grilled me, like the women at dinner had, but rarely inquired about what mattered to women my age and younger, I often forgot I had a right to be there, too. I forgot I could call myself a feminist without having to pass a test. Which is to say that I would often run to the washroom and pep-talk myself in the mirror, reminding my red-faced reflection that I was the editor of one of the country's oldest progressive magazines for eff's sake. It was my *job* to have opinions about this shit. This sideline feeling continued to happen into my early thirties, well past the age anyone could realistically mistake me for a spring chicken. And I knew it wasn't just me.

"Age is the single most divisive issue in the women's rights movement right now," Ottawa-based Julie Lalonde told me.

When I interviewed her, Lalonde was twenty-nine, with a Governor General's Award already under her belt for her feminist work. She was also part of several feminist organizations, had spearheaded even more projects, and worked part-time as an anti–violence against women educator. Aside from her GG award, Lalonde was most well known for her role in securing a student-run women's sexual assault center at Carleton University. Lalonde had returned to the school for her master's degree after completing a bachelor's in women's studies. During her first year back, in 2007, a horrific sexual assault occurred on campus. It took seven years for her to get the student-run support center to open, but she refused to back down. Basically, she was a badass.

She was also keenly, painfully aware of the fractures in the feminist movement and had become disillusioned with academic feminism during her fight for the support center. While she acknowledged women's studies is what brought her to feminism, she added that she was embarrassed to admit it now. She contended that many tenured professors in the women's studies department had refused to support the push for the center. They avoided the picket lines and instead urged silence. Lalonde said they told her they feared showing support would harm funding for their department. To her, that idea was outrageous. Even the woman who taught Lalonde's feminist activism class refused to get involved.

That people with such privilege refused to use it to help those with less or none appalled Lalonde. "I just couldn't accept it then," she said, "and I can't accept it now." Her entire outlook on the movement changed. She could see the fracture lines. When Lalonde said age is the most divisive thing, she didn't mean older feminists are duking it out with younger ones, rock 'em, sock 'em style, but that the movement has split along different points of view, old and new. The feminist waves are all crashing into one another, and we're in turmoil. As much as older feminists can seem surprised and baffled by younger feminists, the lines aren't strictly generational; they're ideological. One woman's feminism can seem as different from another's in the same way Cheerios barely resemble Lucky Charms—both cereal in name only.

Bitch co-founder Lisa Jervis also argued against the generational divide in a 2004 op-ed. She confessed to loathing the question "Are you in the third wave?" To her, the distinction of which wave she was born into was irrelevant. "We've reached the end of the wave terminology's usefulness," she wrote. "What was at first a handy-dandy way to refer to feminism's history and its present and future potential with a single metaphor has become shorthand that invites intellectual laziness, an escape hatch from the hard work of distinguishing between core beliefs and a cultural moment." By definition, first-wave feminism encompassed the suffrage movement. The second wave was, by comparison, a spark. The women's liberation movement, as it was known at the time, rose quickly in the 1960s and '70s, urging equality beyond the right to vote. While the third wave's start date is murky, it's generally characterized as pro-sex, pop-culture hungry, man friendly, and, well, young. If you're under 40, you're part of it.

The problem, Jervis argued, is that it's all chronological. Categorizing feminism into waves flattens the differences in feminist ideologies within the same generation and discounts the similarities between different ones, all in one fell swoop. Second-wave feminists become the worst stereotypes: lipstick averse, hairy-legged, celibate man haters. Third-wave feminists become fluffy, crop-top-wearing sex fiends who have historical amnesia. Categorizing makes it easy for the mainstream media to write alarmist stories and can create an almost cartoonish divide between generations, amplifying discord. One generation forgets the mothers of the movement; the other dismisses the activism of its daughters. When we buy into the wave theory, we forget common goals, like the fight for abortion rights, equal pay, and ending violence against women.

Jervis and many other feminists who dislike the wave terminology have begged women to recognize the generational divide as "an
illusion." I agree that age doesn't dictate a woman's feminist ideology. To assume a woman's personal politics derive solely from her
age—and that the same principle could be blanketed across an entire generation—is absurd and, in itself, sexist. And yet, here we are
again. Technology and social media are changing the movement.
Younger feminists today are acutely aware of feminism's intersections
with other battles: anti-racism, Islamophobia, anti-poverty, disability
rights, transgender rights, sex worker rights. The connection points
are many. Perhaps dividing the feminist movement according to age
was acutely unfair, but it didn't stop us and, as a fourth wave now
emerges, the movement is having trouble bearing the weight of our
differences.

The shift, so far, only seems to exacerbate the movement's age-
ism. "The two issues that are bound to divide a room of feminists
are sex work and transgender inclusion," Lalonde told me. "And
I think the controversy around those two issues is born from the
generational divide within the feminist movement." Some women, in
other words, believe sex worker and transgender inclusion belong in
the movement and are central issues going forward; others do not.
As I see it, Lalonde could have added any number of uncomfortable
issues around privilege to the list of room separators. For all our
careful tiptoeing around generational stereotyping, it seems clear
that one subset of women close their eyes and see white, straight,
middle-aged, middle-class, able-bodied women as the feminist movement, and others close their eyes and see a complex rainbow.

Yes, the feminist movement can thrive on difference—a whole
mass of women working apart but also together toward the ultimate
goal of, as writer bell hooks put it, gender justice. But for many
young women I've interviewed, it doesn't feel like we are united
at all. Instead, it's more like we are building our own generational
islands, erecting fortresses, and then catapulting stones. Those who
happen to wander onto our islands are often treated with hostility,

like they are bumbling tourists, if not outright enemies. We've become distracted with fighting each other. We hurl questions, insults, and harassment at dinner parties, on Twitter, and at women's conferences and committee meetings.

"It isn't doing us any good," Lalonde told me. "It's only perpetuating the idea that we can't get along."

And the anti-feminists love us for it.

I once attended a panel on feminism during which one of the speakers, a white, sixtyish feminist, with a luminous moon-white bob and graceful hands, expressed her bewilderment over the movement's current divisiveness. She was clearly brilliant and dedicated, a grandmother of the movement who had spent much of her life researching the law as it pertained to gender, race, and the uneven application of justice. And yet she felt that the movement was much better at diversity in the 1960s and '70s. Women of all colors were at those early modern rallies, she said, all working together. They were *there*, she emphasized, as if that were enough.

Though she sat poised and not at all gawky, she reminded me of my high school self—the one that buffed over differences, sanding them down to a dull uniformity. I couldn't help but wonder if, all those years ago, she'd ever asked those women how they felt; if those "others," those women of color, were ever given the opportunity to speak, to lead; if even then she wondered who wasn't *there* at all. Mostly, I wondered why she thought that simply being at a place meant meaningful involvement, and for all women, not just for those who were, in fact, present.

Any woman who has existed in the world should know better than that. Just think of the times you were in a room of men, maybe at work or at school, or even in your own home, and they all talked over you. Think about the times men explained your own experiences to you, the times they confidently stole the spotlight, the times you felt the smallest even when you had the biggest things to say. That's what feminists like Lalonde mean when they criticize feminism for its exclusivity. It doesn't matter that girls and women are there; it matters that we let all women speak and then make the room to listen to them. And right now, we're unequivocally failing.

None of this is easy. For many women — even white ones, even rich ones, even ones in happy homes — grappling with the idea of privilege is difficult. It can seem exceedingly difficult to define, let alone acknowledge. Few would argue against the statement that the women of Hollywood's elite have more money/opportunities/ private islands/jets/beauty/everything than the average Jane. And yet even female film actors face overt sexism and are paid less than their male counterparts, proving, perhaps, that creeps and the wage gap both find all of us in the end.

I can hear the chorus now: So, then, aren't we all in it together? Don't we all have it bad? That's not the point. It's as if admitting privilege simultaneously erases both a woman's pain and the inherent unfairness she faces daily. Certainly, it's a very scary prospect for any woman still bearing the weight of her gender, as we all do, in one way or another. But this rabbiting fear has driven us to reinforce the same power structures feminism is meant to abolish. Instead of moving forward all together, as capital-F feminism claims to be doing, we've swiped sideways, an undulating wave of fallen dominoes.

It's *so* hard to know where to begin. As a white woman, even though I recognize and speak out about the root causes of feminism's divisiveness, I am part of the problem. Even as I call for all of us with privilege to shut up and listen to those who don't have as much, or any, I'm elevating my voice. As much as I do the hard work, I can also rationalize with the best of 'em. Sometimes I feel like saying, "You know what? I've done enough, I need a rest." Sometimes it can feel like I've fought so hard for my voice to ring loudly, I don't want to hush it. Sometimes it can feel like I have so much work to do in my own life — juggle several gigs to pay my bills, wash the leaning tower of plates in my sink, go to therapy — that no time is left for thinking about women's rights, let alone my privilege. In those small, selfish moments it's hard to remember that's not what a better feminism demands.

Confronting privilege means we need to open doors and cede platforms in thoughtful and consistent ways. We need to keep doing it, keep listening, keep stumbling, and keep trying to do better. That's exhausting, trying, humiliating work that turns inward to ourselves and to the movement, instead of outward to the world, a far easier task. It's uncomfortable. Trying to figure out what your privilege is and what you can do about it can feel like knotting yourself up into a roadside World's Biggest Pretzel attraction — over and over and over again. But we have to do it anyway. Well, I mean, that's one argument.

The second decade of the millennium has ushered in a new wave of feminists who are ready to live in this discomfort. They believe wholeheartedly in "half Hispanic, half Eastern European" feminist blogger and writer Flavia Dzodan's seminal and declarative 2011 essay: "My feminism will be intersectional or it will be bullshit!" In typical salty language, Dzodan describes the importance of intersectionality by likening it to a "shit puff pastry." "The shit puff pastry," she wrote, "is every layer of fuck that goes on above me, below me, by my sides, all around me." Other feminists have called it a shit sandwich. Still more have described it as moving through the world tethered to a set of weights. Add one if you're a woman, another if you're a woman of color, another if you have a disability, another if you land on the LGBTQ spectrum, another if you live in poverty. Intersectionality is, essentially, the belief that we cannot untie our oppressions from each other. It calls for a plurality of feminisms, and a movement that acknowledges that while we're all fighting for equality, we're not all standing on even ground while we do it.

Some call this growing movement the fourth wave of feminism, sometimes rather derisively. Canadian conservative *Globe and Mail* columnist Margaret Wente penned an exploration of fourth-wave feminism after learning the "new" term intersectionality in March 2016. After giving a snarky but accurate definition of it in her column, she lamented that "these folks" had influence outside university halls and prayed for it all to go away. "When I grew up, kids were urged to be blind to differences. Now they're urged to see nothing but," she wrote. "Perhaps one day we'll stop trying to identify ourselves by labels and just call ourselves human beings." Even Antonia Zerbisias, former *Toronto Star* columnist and co-creator of the hashtag #beenrapedneverreported, has railed on fourth wavers. In the wake of Canada's Jian Ghomeshi sexual assault trial, which cost the radio star his job at the Canadian Broadcasting Corporation and put him at the center of a national conversation about consent and privilege, she wrote in support of the system that acquitted him: "Memo to my sob-sister, fourth-wave feminists: get over it."

That's not to say only younger women believe in intersectional feminism. While this rising sect of the movement was born in the current generation and certainly skews younger, it's not solely age that divides us, but belief. There are those of all generations and so-called waves who think intersectional feminism is essential and vital in the push for women's rights, and then there are firm feminists, like Wente, who've never heard of the word, or those, like Zerbisias, who have, and yet see it as a trivial, even petty, term. They are the feminists who want the club to look like how I saw my high school: a happy, Kumbaya-singing circle of diversity. To them, intersectionality breeds the in-fighting that's become feminism's Achilles' heel. With a small shift, they're right: the tension of those feminists who demand intersectionality and the others who don't get it is like vinegar to baking soda. *Fizz-bang-explode.*

I'm not advocating feminism totalitarianism, rows of identical, marching Feminazis (as we're so terribly called) with Sharpied moustaches and shiny boots. Nor am I rooting for anarchy. What we need is a movement that recognizes, allows, and even celebrates its differences. In my feminist Shangri-La, we embrace the plurality of feminisms and can still work together and respect each other. We're allies. We disagree without slinging mud; we don't stage self-destructive shows for the anti-feminists' entertainment. In other words, if feminism wants to survive and grow, not shrink, it's vital that it learn how to communicate within itself.

✦

In April 2016 I attended the Saturday night headline event of Canada's national Spur Festival, a celebration of politics, arts, and ideas. The one-hour event boasted a one-word title, "Feminism," bestowing the movement with the singular power of God, or perhaps Madonna. The program booklet provided scant context: "Spur celebrates the accomplishments and contradictions of the feminist movement and explores feminism in practice." *In an hour?* How ambitious. Sitting in the audience, my bottom already going Novocaine numb on the barely cushioned seat, I wondered whether the organizers simply couldn't think of anything else to say, as if the idea of wading through the movement and drilling down past the omnipresent feminism was too daunting.

As the minutes ticked closer to showtime, I watched as the downtown Toronto theater filled to three-quarters capacity. The number of men surprised me. Fifteen minutes late, the stage lights blinked on, tiny suns that revealed the speakers' racial diversity: two white women (Constance Backhouse, a law professor, and Stacey May Fowles, a novelist and essayist); one Indigenous woman (Kim Anderson, a Cree/Métis writer and university professor); and two Black women (moderator Vicky Mochama and Lena Peters, a young activist and founding member of Toronto's Black Lives Matter). The next hour unfolded with a humming energy as the women discussed everything from racism to colonialism and from the possibility of a feminist Magna Carta to Instagram.

Mochama directed the conversation between women whose approach to their feminist practices often bore little resemblance—not necessarily a bad thing. The differences came to the forefront when Mochama asked the panelists to finish the sentence "We the feminist people, to form a more equal society . . ." As Fowles jokingly groaned "Oh, God" at the enormity of the question, the audience laughed and clapped. Anderson, who responded first, stated simply "respect all life" (though, when asked, she explained that the three-word concept must underscore all approaches to equality). Backhouse said any declaration must focus on changing the culture to dismantle discrimination. Peters emphasized that we shouldn't even try for the unity an answer would suggest: "That's the scariest version of feminism, right? The club. That's why so many people shy away from the label." She added that she doesn't want her grandchildren's feminism to resemble hers. If it did, "it would be yucky, and *old*," she laughed. Fowles agreed, adding that if such a proclamation existed, "I certainly wouldn't want to write it." Feminism should not be set in stone. The tension made for a lively discussion, and an even livelier question period.

But once given their own chance at the mic, audience members kept circling back to feminism's apparent divisiveness. One asked how to better include men, another how to better include mothers, and a third how to quell the social media infighting. Midway through, a woman's voice broke on the first word of her question. She was a young woman, close to my age, her winged glasses hitting the curls of her hair. "I'm biracial," she told the audience. Her mom's hand popped a self-conscious hello from the crowd. The young woman apologized for crying as her voice warbled. She was heartbroken, she told the panelists and everyone else in the room. "The saddest thing for me," she said, "is the divisiveness between women." Wasn't there a way we could all work together? In response, Peters chided her. She doubted, she said, that white women ever sat around a table and wondered how to get other women involved. She doubted they asked themselves how they could give up a little of their power and work together instead. For Peters, and many others, the suggestion that feminists all play nice presents a certain danger: a forced Stepford-like homogeny.

I later caught up with the young woman and her mother. It bothered her that nobody wanted to talk about the divisiveness. There had to be a way to work apart, but together. In doing so, we could acknowledge feminists' many differences, she said, but also the common goal. She worried what would become of feminism if we couldn't. It was like women were fighting over bread, she told me. That person had two slices. Maybe she had three. I could have had four. "But we all fucking don't have enough bread."

Jarrah Hodge's voice strained with diplomacy, vibrating with the plucked tension of an elastic band about to snap. Underneath her careful words, Hodge was pissed. I'd called her because I admired her Canadian feminist blog *Gender Focus*, which she'd founded in 2009. Shortly before I spoke to her, she'd won the Best Politics Blog and the Best Activism and Social Justice Blog in the juried Canadian Weblog Awards. She was only twenty-eight and had already spent most of her life, online and IRL, in the feminist sphere, organizing events and rallies, sitting on boards, and advocating for her view of a more equal world. I'd just asked her about the sexism she experienced as a young woman online, but that wasn't what she wanted to talk about. She thrummed with fake laughter: "Oh, I thought you were going to ask me about my experiences as a young woman in feminist spaces."

It had been on her mind throughout the interview, she confessed. "I'll answer that first," she told me, "and then the second question, if that's cool," the second question being the one I'd actually asked her. Of course it was cool. By now, I'd realized the frustration young women felt was always boiling in the background throughout even the most general of conversations about young feminism; it needed somewhere to erupt. Hodge was careful to say she knew other feminists meant well. But she was tired of arriving at events she'd organized, or whose committees she'd steered, and hearing older women sweetly remark that it was nice she'd made it to her first feminist event. Other times, women will tell her it's nice to see a young person, then demand to know why she didn't bring more youth with her. More than once other women have assumed her mother brought her to an event. It always makes her feel like she's not valued as an equal participant within the movement.

It's not just a matter of hurt feelings. That kind of alienation can be devastating to a teenager or early twentysomething who's just discovering women's rights, stressed Anastasia Gaisenok, who, when I spoke to her, was just wrapping up her two-year tenure as the project coordinator for the Young Women Civic Leaders initiative in Vancouver (she went on to become executive director of the Youth Global Education Network). Gaisenok, who was born in Belarus and moved to British Columbia in 2003 to attend Simon Fraser University, also landed in the "pissed" category and she was not careful, or polite, in her criticism. As she spoke about the damaging effects of "pushing out" potential feminists, her Russian accent muddied her vowels in direct relation to how irked she felt, which was very. "This is a way to turn people off the whole thing, really," she told me.

Many of the young women that she worked with, women who were interested in politics and wanted to change the world, were afraid of feminist spaces, Gaisenok noted. Once, when she suggested meeting at a local university's women's center, a place she thought was a natural fit, especially since five of the women in the group were students at the school—she was shocked to discover none of them had been to the center and balked at going. They felt they weren't feminist enough and that they'd be chastised, she told me, proving the age gap doesn't have to be wide to be felt. Gaisenok found it especially heartbreaking, she said, because she remembered being that girl: the one who knew hardly anything about formal feminist theory but who desperately wanted to be part of the movement advocating for change. Feminism needs to figure out how to bring women in who are currently on the periphery lest it turn away even more.

"It's a minefield," Gaisenok fumed, the crescents of her cheekbones tightening in anger. "You are afraid to open your mouth in one of those discussions. If you say something that is perceived as not feminist enough, or not fully thought out, or a position that this particular person doesn't agree with, then you're immediately ostracized and made to feel so horrible." She emphasized women need to be gentler and more understanding when it comes to young women discovering the movement. Instead, we've thrown up all sorts of barriers. The language of feminism can be inaccessible, said Gaisenok. At a recent panel on rape culture she wondered whether someone completely new to feminism would get lost in the maze of jargon; it took until the closing minutes of the panel to even define rape culture. If she was at entry-point level, she imagined, she'd feel so stupid listening without a clue about what was happening. She might, she surmised, even decide feminism wasn't for her, or that it didn't want her.

Considering the many roadblocks that prevent young women from adopting or aligning with feminism, from lack of education to its negative representation in pop culture, Gaisenok saw the counting-out attitude as an especially critical error. She likened feminism to a cliff: women could fall off it after being treated badly at a meeting, after threats on social media, after university, after they entered the workforce, after children, life, and so many other things got in the way. Feminism was a hard, tiring slog, she reasoned, and it was easy to topple off. No wonder so many young women weren't even bothering to find out about the f-word, she said. Feminists were too busy either building barriers or helping to throw them off proverbial cliffs.

"It's a very weird jam we've gotten ourselves into," said Julie Lalonde. Like many of the younger feminists I interviewed, including

Hodge and Gaisenok, Lalonde criticized the wider feminist movement for failing to encourage younger women to join. Technology amplified the movement's reach and allowed it to talk outside the monolith, but it didn't usually win women seats at media panels, committee tables, or at organizations that had politicians' ears. It created pressure sometimes, sure, but it was still largely older, established, and often white feminists who were given the platform to discuss issues and guide change. The movement's core feminist issues were predominately discussed in the context of younger women — reproductive rights, anti-violence in all its forms — but very seldom were young women allowed to speak for themselves.

The divide was both cataclysmic and catastrophic. "There's not just a gap between men and women," Hodge told me, echoing the gospel of modern-era feminism. "There's a gap between people of color, people of different immigrant statuses, people of different ages. We want equality that isn't just equality for middle-class, middle-aged, straight white women." I don't doubt that feminists of every generation feel the same way, but the mainstream movement has so far failed to put this new vision forward, front and center. And the longer it refuses to wholly, enthusiastically adopt the new generation's commitment to intersectionality, the more it creates all sorts of schisms. Whether they are pushed out or left out, the casualties of the breaks are becoming clearer to me: the young girls and women feminism so desperately wants and needs.

With the exception of women whose mothers were feminists, the sweeping majority of young women I spoke to across Canada only discovered feminism in university. Some claimed to never have heard the term at all until then. "I didn't know that word at all," one twenty-five-year-old feminist named Emily Yakashiro told me. "It's not because anybody prevented me from knowing it," she added. The term just wasn't used in her tiny, rural hometown. Once she started to volunteer at her university's sexual assault support center, her activist life took off. After working in the anti-violence field for a few years, she entered the animation field, deciding she wanted to be at the forefront of crafting women's portrayal in popular media. She also runs a website dedicated to dismantling sexism and racism in the fashion industry. None of it would have ever happened if she hadn't wandered into the center one day on a break.

Suggesting the route to all feminism must be through institutionalized academia is dangerous, however. While we should never fear to introduce feminism into our hallowed halls, we must also recognize that relying on our universities to teach women feminism falls into the very classist, elitist structures that intersectionality and fourth-wave feminism want to topple. Not all young women have the financial means or inclination to attend post-secondary school. Other women might only conquer their fear of the f-word after they have their first real-world encounter with sexism and misogyny (what a fun rite of passage!). It's a case of meeting people where they're at. For some newbie feminists, Twitter and Tumblr, or even Beyoncé and Emma Watson, can be as effective teachers as, well, professional teachers. If feminism truly wants to grow, it has to reach not only a younger but also a wider audience. How to do it is a harder question to answer.

Consider one of the most successful youth recruiters of our time. Its followers and leaders tweet out more than ninety thousand snippets a day, extolling their lives and togetherness. It even has its own app. Pictures stream daily across Twitter, Facebook, and Tumblr showing teen and twenty-something members scarfing down pizza, peacefully browsing through farmers markets, enjoying movie nights, riding Ferris wheels, and playing video games. The images are meant to reflect the strong bonds at work. Wannabe members not only know they're welcomed, wanted, and needed but they know it will be fun to be there. The name of that movement? ISIS. Sure, it's an extreme example of single-minded recruitment, but it's also a stark reminder that feminism doesn't want new members that blindly follow. It wants thinking ones.

We don't need feminism as monolith, but we could all use a multipronged approach: more social media, more pop culture, more books, more Dr. Porters, and less fear, less stigma, less apathy. I worry that without all those things, those faced with an institution that isn't doing very much to welcome them, speak to them, listen to them, or take them seriously at all will either leave the movement, stop caring, or never join to begin with. They'll be the women and young girls who never had a chance to knock on feminism's door. They won't even know the door is there. Of course these women will believe feminism isn't for them: that's the message the movement itself is broadcasting.

3 F-bomb generation: Empowerment, millennial women, and the "I'm not a feminist, but..." choir

Janice Fiamengo, an anti-feminist University of Ottawa English professor, stepped onto the stage at Queen's University in Kingston, Ontario. She wore a smart wraparound dress with a delicate geometric pattern, and her voluminous hair covered her face every time she looked down to check her notes, which was frequently. It was the evening of Thursday, March 27, 2014, and the room was packed. "My goal for the evening is to encourage students to join the Men's Issues Awareness Society, or to give men's issues some serious consideration," she opened. "My feeling right now is that I really hope more women will decide to join with men in pursuing equality. I hope that women will consider rejecting the feminist idea that the only suffering that really matters is the suffering of women and the best men can hope for is the right to apologize for their so-called privilege."

Fiamengo would go on to hit, in under three minutes, all the major pillars of the men's rights and anti-feminist movements: that men have lost their status and their jobs, that nobody cares about the rape of men in prisons, that there are no shelters for battered men, that men have to accept discrimination in government and public sector hiring competitions, that they're denied the right to father their children, that they're treated unfairly in divorce. Fiamengo assured the crowd that men suffered many more other injustices she did not have time to name. It went by so quickly that audience members didn't have time to unpack the contradictions and implications of her statements. If feminism is presumably built on outrage, as critics claim, the men's rights movement has perfected its use. Fiamengo stressed to the crowd that she used to be a wrongheaded feminist, too — laughing "Cry me a river, white boy" with her smug feminist friends — but that she was now reformed. They could be, too.

Queen's University is widely considered one of the best universities in the country, one of our very own Ivy League, and it boasts one of Canada's richest student populations. At less than 30 percent, the proportion of Queen's students receiving financial aid is the lowest of any of the province's twenty-two universities. The 175-year-old campus looks like a more austere, capitalist version of Hogwarts: buildings are turreted, roads are made of cobblestones, and old-growth trees hang romantically over scurrying young intellectuals. Just replace J. K. Rowling's whimsy with Gordon Gekko's greed.

Queen's students themselves have mocked the exclusive prestige of the university in the viral YouTube video "I go to Queen's!" which jokes about the school's whiteness, its frat-styled party culture, and its rich kid–infused attitudes. There's truth to the satire. Queen's is one of the few universities in Canada that embraces generational legacy, and alumni include some of Canada's most elite businesspeople, scientists, and political leaders. It is, in other words, a perfect petri dish of white, wealthy privilege and modern university party culture. Considering its influential alumni, it's also the exact type of place you'd hope a "But, men!" narrative wouldn't thrive. Sigh. Sorry. Because here's Queen's other tradition: greeting frosh week young women with so-called "move-in" signs, scrawled on bed sheets and poster boards, that say things such as "Queen's fathers, say goodbye to your daughters' virginity!" and "Don't forget your knee pads!"

In early March 2014, Queen's became a violent anti-feminist battleground after a second-year student named Mohammed Albaghdadi formed the school's Men's Issues Awareness Society (MIAS). He told the student newspaper that he was stunned by the vitriolic reaction from feminists: "I was surprised. I genuinely thought I was in the majority point of view." He later added that he'd founded the society, in large part, to focus on false accusations of sexual assault. (It's worth noting here that the frequency of false rape reports is statistically thorny ground, with numbers ranging from the feminist-friendly 2 percent to the MRA-friendly 40 percent. Neither has been deemed satisfactorily true. Many people settle on the 8 percent statistic favored by the FBI, but the accuracy of that is debatable, largely because women who either don't report or withdraw their complaint under fear or pressure skew the numbers. Suffice it to say, however, false reports are not the epidemic of injustice MRAs pretend.)

That same year, feminist groups on campuses across Canada faced an MRA-led backlash for mobilizing against sexual assault on campus. The anti-rape campaign plastered posters bearing should-be-obvious-but-somehow-aren't slogans such as "It's not sex…when she's passed out" and "Just because she isn't saying no…doesn't mean she's saying yes." In response, anti-feminists created their own campaign, dubbed "Don't Be That Girl." Posters unhelpfully told women that lying about sexual assault is a crime and claimed women benefit from double standards (presumably some get-out-of-jail-free card activated with cleavage and eyelash batting). They played deeply on the stereotypes against women who report rape. One admonished women: "Just because you regret a one-night stand, it doesn't mean it wasn't consensual." Another, addressed to men, asserted: "Just because she's easy, it doesn't mean you should fear false criminal accusation." These twin finger-wagging narratives affirmed both that women lie and, also, that they should *want* to lie after engaging in casual sex — the shame! What a soothing balm for young men, some of whom, of course, welcomed messages like: "None of this is your fault," or "It's all her fault (because she's a slut)!" As Janice Fiamengo put it in an article commending the countercampaign, it's not fair that "no matter what a woman does—no matter how careless and irresponsible—she is always innocent."

Well, of her own rape, yes. The deeper problem here, though, is that for someone like Fiamengo these cases of sexual assault aren't rapes. They're *lies*. According to Fiamengo (and others), narratives against sexual assault punish men. They tell men—alone—not to engage in party culture. They tell men not to celebrate their sexuality. They shame and stigmatize *men*. Fiamengo and her cohort worry that men are failing, at the hands of women and feminism no less, and if we, as a society, really cared about men, we'd shunt aside conversations of women's rights and focus on saving our men. I'd find such arguments easier to stomach if they focused on the very real struggles facing men—especially low-income, queer, and racialized men—and less on attacking feminism and calling women lying, slutty criminals. But, hey, that's just me. Many others, particularly young men who feel they shouldn't have to navigate the pesky issue of consent while blitzed at a rad party, have gobbled up these arguments like a five-star meal.

It was no coincidence that Queen's MIAS students launched their men's rights group in the midst of this brewing anti-feminist storm or that the group invited Fiamengo, who had become a sought-after campus speaker, to talk at its first event. (Today, she is a bona fide men's rights star: when a student launched a human rights complaint against her in late 2016, Fiamengo's supporters raised more than $12,000 for her legal fees within days.) Queen's, while a remarkably fertile ground for such narratives, was not unique. Earlier that year, men's rights student groups at the University of Ottawa and the University of Toronto asked Fiamengo, whom the ultra-conservative *Toronto Sun* pointedly characterized as a "soft-spoken academic," to lecture against women's studies, feminism, and the work both did on campus. The response was furious: feminist activists pulled the fire alarm to interrupt her presentations (it didn't stop either presentation but did stall both) and protested loudly outside the venues. But, similar to their swift response to an anti-rape postering campaign, Fiamengo and her ilk were ready with counter-messaging. Predictably, it centered on pernicious stereotypes of women and feminism, and like many messages built on half-truths, prejudices, and fear, it worked.

By the time the Queen's event was underway, the men's rights movement had neatly snuggled into its underdog onesie. Feminist action was rebranded as not an effort to halt damaging and long-standing myths about women, rape, and sexual assault (I'll explore this in a later chapter) but an insidious effort to curb free speech. Fiamengo, exploiting the hairy-legged, bra-burning stereotype, called the feminist movement a totalitarian ideology that had no interest in equality, only supremacy. A *Maclean's* reporter who wrote about her University of Toronto talk called the protestors' actions "dramatic" and "childish"; its headline writer crowed that "free speech had prevailed." The reporter agreed that Fiamengo's critique of feminism—namely, that that the movement is empty, dishonest, and incoherent—is a fairly common one.

The idea that feminism is lying about its equal rights mission? Not outrageous. Not bizarre. Totally normal. We all know feminism is *really* about man hating, right? Increasingly, though, as the 2016 *Washington Post*/Kaiser survey showed, that is what we believe. Caught in this roundabout logic, feminists can't win. Any protest action is seen as proof of their secret agendas. That's not to mention the un-intentional side effect of shining an even bigger spotlight on men's rights events.

Organizers of the Fiamengo talk had booked an auditorium that could seat almost four hundred. How do you attract that many people? Brea Hutchinson, coordinator of the left-leaning Ontario Public Interest Research Group (OPIRG) in Kingston, knew the answer: conflict. From the beginning, Hutchinson tried to dampen the conflict. With about fifteen others, she'd created a "Not That Space" group that met in Grey House (one of the few shabby buildings on the Queen's campus and then home to both the Levana Gender Advocacy Centre and OPIRG) to *not* talk about the MIAS. Hutchinson urged fellow activists to remain silent, to not create the controversy the events had thrived on at other universities. In a mass email she wrote, "Give no reaction."

But that's not what happened. First, feminists tried to get the Alma Mater Society at Queen's to revoke the MIAS's official club status. Then they publicly urged administration to cancel the talk. "That's when things got intense," said Hutchinson. "We had drawn a line collectively that we were not going to let this happen. And it meant the Men's Issues Awareness Society had a reason to fight us."

On the night of Fiamengo's talk, campus feminists decided to host an alternative-spaces event at Grey House. More than one hundred people packed into the ramshackle building, where cupcakes, tea, and counselors were on hand. Organizers wanted it to be a friendly space, where women (and men) could talk about feminism, or not. It was an act of solidarity and resistance. It said: Here we are, together, in a place that still makes sense to us. Fiamengo's speech was being streamed in one room, but the idea was to make Grey House a place where feminism, not anti-feminism, got to define itself, a place where Fiamengo was not given credibility. But I wondered: Was it too late for that? Didn't this event show the two movements had become entwined? "We tried to create spaces where they weren't a thing," Hutchinson said, "which was a nice thought, but in practice it became, unfortunately, really untenable."

Online, those who spoke out against the MIAS were targeted and harassed. Grey House suddenly drew an alarming number of male visitors and passersby, all dressed in black. One woman involved in the center (she is still studying on campus and asked me not to use her name because of what followed), started to tally the phone calls and emails the center received from men (and some women). More than a dozen callers used fake names, assuring Levana volunteers that they wanted to get involved to help "save" women. None ever answered the center's follow-up invitations. Soon, Levana volunteers reported being followed. The woman I spoke to woke up to panicked phone calls from women at two AM, who feared that strange men were tailing them. Eventually, she was followed, too. Men drove by Grey House and yelled from cars. The woman, who had immigrated to Canada from a war-torn country, was shocked. "Coming here to Canada," she said, "it was the kind of thing that I never thought would ever happen…that normalization of violence against women."

And then it escalated. Danielle d'Entremont, a feminist on campus who'd vocally opposed Fiamengo's talk and had helped lead efforts to de-ratify the MIAS, left her house late one Wednesday night that March. When a strange man called her name, she turned, and the assailant punched her in the face multiple times, so hard that she lost half a tooth. In a Facebook photo posted after the attack, the left side of her face is puffed out, the trauma squinting shut her eye and enlarging her lip, making her cheek alarmingly red and swollen. "How's this for a no makeup selfie?" she asked. Police investigated but no charges were ever filed and, although anti-feminists had threatened her online, no formal connection could be made between the two events. Police felt obligated to make the public statement: "Regardless of a person's opinion on feminism, or equality for all, is the fact that no one deserves to be assaulted" — something we now, absurdly, need to be reminded about.

Men's rights groups seized the moment, chivalrously denouncing the attack and simultaneously suggesting — big surprise — d'Entremont was making it all up. Various men's rights groups, including one in Australia and the women-led Honey Badger Brigade, collectively ponied up $4,500 to reward anyone with information that could lead to an arrest. Attila Vinczer, leader of Men's Rights Canada, put up reward posters on campus. Yet even as they denounced the attack, they sowed doubt. The reward money they collected proved that no men's rights activist could possibly have attacked d'Entremont, or so they argued. Considering the already heated and threatening environment on campus, such a claim stretched credulity. Yet the obfuscation was effective. Wasn't this just another case of a woman being deceitful to get what she wanted? As another men's rights leader wrote on the organization's website: "My money is on the idea, and I don't think I am alone here, that it [feminism] is the kind of movement filled with people who may not really want this case to be solved; with people who think she is lying."

Lest we make the mistake of dismissing how dangerous and widespread these narratives have become in the short years since, let's briefly return to what Donald Trump said in the run-up to the 2016 presidential election after multiple women accused him of sexual assault: "Every woman lied." *Hell, he didn't even know them.* Trump claimed the women fibbed because they wanted to hurt his campaign. Was he mocked for this? Yes, of course. But he also won the election. Enough people (a lot of them, apparently, and many of them women) were eager to believe him. Because, as one Queen's activist told me multiple times during our interview, the sentiment that feminists are liars, that they're out to harm and undermine men, is everywhere. No wonder women are reluctant to call themselves feminists. The deeper questions are How did this happen and Why are women cheering it?

I was invited to Queen's in fall 2016 to do a talk on the importance of independent media. While there, I visited with Brea Hutchinson at Grey House. I wanted to know what the campus was like two years after Fiamengo's talk. Was men's rights activism thriving? Was feminism? We sat down on mismatched furniture in one of the space's casual meeting rooms. Outside, gray and white paint peeled from the wood, but a cheery, multicolored "Come in! Everyone welcome!"

sign that hung from the porch extinguished any spookiness. Grey
House was both shabby and cozy, certainly not the rich HQ of
women's privilege. Hutchinson told me that, so far, the 2016–17
academic year had been relatively quiet. The MIAS and feminists
hadn't clashed since the Fiamengo talk; in fact, she hadn't heard a
peep from MIAS at all that year. (And indeed, as of this writing, the
group's Facebook page seems to have vanished.) But, the Levana
volunteer would agree in our later interview, that didn't mean
nothing had happened. Thinking had shifted, and while the MRA-
feminist controversy might in many ways resemble a young sibling
rivalry—that's my toy! I want whatever she has! It's not fair!—there
were no "take-backsies" here.

Just that morning, I'd grabbed the satirical student paper *Golden
Words*, in which one of the male editors had written a column called
"Has Science Gone Too Far? Girls Now Have the Technology to Tell
Me to Fuck Off." It was supposed to be funny, I guess. But I mean,
come on, dude: "What ground-breaking research was developed to
allow women to come to terms with their agency and confidence to
say this? Even ten years ago, they would have giggled uncomfortably
and told me, 'No thanks, maybe another time!'" Around the same
time, Queen's hosted its first Worth Week, a social justice initiative
that was founded as *Women's* Worth Week (emphasis mine). It had
rebranded, organizers said, "to be more inclusive." A few years
before the rebranding, the campus paper had described the event
as "a celebration of women." That was wrong, said organizers. "Our
event aims to celebrate all individuals, regardless of gender, by
drawing attention to the importance of gender equality." Remember,
as the young college feminist told the *Washington Post*: "Feminism
isn't a political movement."

This is the same campus where, in 2016, a twentysomething—
presumably out to be the next, somehow cruder, *Girls Gone Wild*
millionaire—made the video "Drunk Times with College Girls:
Queen's Homecoming" ("girls" was later changed to "students"),

asking them if he could touch their "boobs." The creator of the video, which had been watched sixteen thousand times in less than three months, pinned his own comment at the top: "Don't take it out of context. If you can't handle it — go watch cat videos!" But what context, exactly? Queen's is also the same campus where school security has, in recent years, reported a distressing rise in prank calls through its blue light system, which is designed to prevent sexual assault on campus. They blamed the rise on engineering students who compete to get a "blue bar" for their school jackets, a process that involves going to blue light locations on campus, drinking a Blue Light beer, taping it to the pole, hitting the button, and then bolting. Apparently, you can also get a "true blue bar" if you damage the alarm. As Pam Cross, chair of Sexual Assault Centre Kingston, wrote at the end of 2012, the behavior is chillingly like the campus climate in 1989 "when some male students in residence responded to the No Means No anti-rape campaign by placing offensive signs in their residence windows. Those signs contained such slogans as 'No Means Harder,' 'No Means More Beer,' and 'No Means Down on your Knees, Bitch.'"

I don't want to pick on Queen's. Universities across Canada and the US are grappling with the same potent culture. At the University of Toronto, backlash against the feminists who protested Fiamengo's talk was both swift and violent. Men's rights groups put the women's photos online and encouraged surveillance. The first woman they targeted wrote about her experiences in the zine *Pineapples Against the Patriarchy*, produced by Queen's feminists to discuss men's rights action on their campus. "I was called Hitler's Barbie, Feminazi Bitch, Princess Cupcake," she wrote. "Walking around on campus and in the city became a difficult thing to do with what felt like an X marked on the back of my head." And then, the next year, someone with the screen name "KillFeminists" threatened to do exactly that. "Walk into a classroom and fire a bullet in the feminist professor's head," read the anonymous threat, "and proceed to spray bullets all over the classroom." The rest of the threat is even more gruesome and helpfully offers the location and price of where to get a gun in downtown Toronto. Police later deemed the threat "not credible," but students were understandably scared. Some called for the cancellation of classes, and for six months after the threat police wandered the hallways where women's studies classes were held.

Bonnie Burstow, an associate professor at the university's Ontario Institute for Studies in Education, did not cancel her classes, though she did tell students she'd support them if they didn't feel safe coming to class. She also told them this: "If feminists started canceling classes, they win. Whoever is sending around those threats wins." Burstow was not impressed with how the university handled the anonymous online encouragement to shoot her, her colleagues, and her students. At first, she told me, administration didn't even reveal the threats were against women. Instead, they used the term "members of the university community." Campus feminists confronted administrators and forced them to be transparent. But, shockingly, added Burstow, administrators never consulted any of the faculty's numerous experts on violence against women. "You might say they didn't want to alarm women. Well, that's also patriarchal. If our lives are being threatened we need to hear about it, and we need to figure out how we want to organize. Then *they* need to find a way to support *us*," she said. "I don't think anyone took seriously that this combines with other anti-feminist things we're seeing at the university. It was treated as an isolated case, and it wasn't isolated in the sense we're seeing more and more action of men's rights groups. These are people who are misogynists on a profound level. And you never know where that's going to go."

Men's rights groups have sprouted across Canada and the US. Women, people of color, and transgender folk are involved with many of them, in some cases acting as founders or co-founders, presidents and vice-presidents—belying stereotypes of the usual suspects. In a few short years, at least fifteen groups formed on Canadian campuses from coast to coast, and plenty of them faced their own battles with women on campus. Toronto's Ryerson University drew the attention of men's rights activists worldwide after its student union repeatedly denied the campus MIAS official club status, blocking it from funding or resources available to other student groups, like the Women's and Trans Collective. In response, the MIAS sued the student union in April 2016. The lawsuit, led by the group's president, a male fourth-year politics and governance student, and its social media executive, a female fourth-year journalism student, demanded the student union respect "freedom of expression" and give the MIAS club status. "[The denial] was contrary to the principles of natural justice and procedural fairness," reads the suit, "[and] was tainted by a closed mind and bias." The tense climate has led to a resurgent push — presumably resurrected from the horse-and-buggy era — for men-only universities. "Why not give men the chance to learn in male-positive spaces and be taught by teachers practicing male-positive pedagogy?" Fiamengo wrote in a September 2016 op-ed in the *Toronto Sun*. "I wouldn't want to be a young man attending a co-ed university today."

What a mess.

Elisabeth Eigerman is a curly-haired high school senior in Weston, Massachusetts. I spoke to her, along with dozens of other young women, throughout my three years researching this book because I wanted to know what drew — and repelled — young women when it came to feminism today, what issues they saw facing them and the movement itself. Her mom, she told me, with a laugh that dimpled her cheeks, was a women's studies major who had wanted to raise her daughter without gender. She was terribly dismayed to find her young daughter shouting, "Need man! Need man!" at a Barbie catalogue. Nonetheless, Eigerman grew into feminism and has gone on to write for feminist publications, including the Jewish Women's Archive website as its 2015–16 Rising Voices Fellow. When

I asked Eigerman whom she'd like to see more involved in the feminist movement going forward, her response was immediate and ebullient: "Men, please!" It's an answer I heard from many young women, who usually cited a variation of fifteen-year-old Michigan teen Enya Spaulding's argument. "It will encourage larger change by eradicating the idea that only women can be feminists," Spaulding told me, "which would open more minds to the idea of feminism."

I don't disagree. And neither, likely, would Eigerman. Like many feminists I spoke to, young and old, the eighteen-year-old argued that women's rights had done a terrible job of discussing how the patriarchy affects men. "When we're tackling social norms," she told me, pausing in between sips from a mug of tea, "we should really tackle social norms that affect boys." In a March 2016 blog post on the Jewish Women's Archive, she expanded on her views, explaining what drives teen boys away from feminism, hitting the proverbial nail on its proverbial head. "These boys grow up being told they're inherently sexist," she wrote, "and watch as feminism tackles minor issues." Modern feminist discourse, she criticized, treats all issues as equally problematic, expressing equal outrage over domestic violence (a reaction that she contends is justified) as it does over, say, super-air-conditioned workspaces (not so much). Boys see this and assume feminists are nitpickers with no real problems, she added. She stressed to me that she doesn't think the men's rights movement is the answer to tackling this disconnect, largely because it sacrifices focus on serious issues that affect men in favor of making fun of feminism.

Again, I don't really disagree. Feminism has done a not-hot job of advocating for men and boys; we were too busy fighting for women. But men do face gender restrictions and damning expectations under the patriarchy, of course. Namely, they're not supposed to do anything that seems remotely feminine. There are also places where race and class intersect. Though they do not uniquely affect men, they cause real trauma that can thread through generations. Indigenous and Black men, for example, face disturbing and disproportionately high rates of incarceration and poverty. These and many other issues demand more attention. They're also ones that have complex underlying, contributing factors—none of which, however, can reasonably be blamed on feminism.

I wonder, though, if women, particularly those "fence-sitters" who operate outside of politics, realize the unintended consequences of adding their voices to the "But, men!" choir. You'll get no arguments from me that society would be more equitable if we broke down gender should-bes, as in "women should be polite" and "men should be prodigious and hearty grunters." But is that what we are, in fact, doing? I have my doubts. Statistics on male suicide, for instance, are commonly trotted out whenever an argument for men's rights is put forward, highlighting the fact that men die by suicide at a rate four times higher than women. What is often not mentioned in this context is that women are three to four times more likely to attempt suicide and are hospitalized for attempts at one-and-a-half times more than men. Suicide is an important social issue, but it is not a zero-sum gender game. It's both misleading and dangerous to paint it as such, especially when it's used to put forth the idea that men lose while women gain at their expense (laughing diabolically while we do it).

Yet if the diverse rise in men's and boys' conferences (and not just those led by men's rights groups) is anything to judge by, the idea that men need special attention has certainly caught on. The results are mixed, and in some cases very strange. Across the US are, for example, a plethora of Christian-based men-only conferences with names like "No Regrets," "As For Me and My House," "Courageous," "Stronger," "Master's Men," and, arguably the most popular, "Act Like Men," an extension of the book of the same name, which preaches that men need forty days to achieve what's called "biblical manhood." The author of *Act Like Men*, James MacDonald, gruffly acknowledges that some people break gender stereotypes, but he clearly doesn't like it: "We also know the woman who swears like a sailor and changes the oil in her own car—but if she's your wife, that says more about you than it does about her." Mostly, his advice is that acting like a man means not acting like a woman. I'm not being unfair here; that's one of his primary rules, verbatim. Similar messaging is found in other Christian men's conferences. The slogan of Master's Men, held in Fresno, California, is "Iron Sharpening Iron."

Then there are men's health conferences—all great causes with somewhat constrained definitions of masculinity, mostly based on facial hair. Take the Southern Illinois Men's Expo, which featured talks from a urologist and an infectious diseases doctor, as well as a beard and mustache contest and Dr. Dan the Pancake Man, who promised to immortalize attendees' faces in batter (until they eat it, I suppose). The expo's logo featured the trifecta of modern masculinity: beards, bowties, and bacon. The 2017 Epic Men's Expo in Pennsylvania scrapped the health focus but did have a former Pittsburg Steelers linebacker as a guest and, of course, its own *epic* beard contest. Even the Movember Foundation, which does amazing work for men's health issues, started after its founders decided to see if they could bring the mustache back, launching the campaign with an email that said: "Are you man enough to be my man?" Somewhere one of these campaigns has, I'm sure, included an axe-throwing contest. If it hasn't already happened, I'd bet my beloved and extremely obese twelve-year-old tabby cat that it will soon.

Toronto's inaugural three-day Gentleman's Expo in 2016 (not to be confused with the Gentleman's *Club* Expo, which bills itself as "the ONLY national convention and awards show for the multi-billion-dollar adult nightclub industry") encouraged men to #BeBetter. Sponsored by Best Buy, Lincoln, American Express, and Clinique, the expo included a fashion show, beers, burgers, and guest talks from UFC fighter Georges St-Pierre, as well as former Toronto Maple Leafs heroes Wendel Clark and Doug Gilmour. It told men not to send unsolicited dick pics online and used busty "booth babes" to sell its products. The Concierge Club, an event-planning company in Toronto that supplies models to host your party, featured prominently. Talk about mixed messages: similar to their Christian counterparts, these conferences preach a rigid and even traditionalist-infused masculinity, albeit more Dos Equis or Don Draper than Jesus. Don't even get me started on the rise of International Men's Day, which, since 2010, has gained steam in both Canada and the US (the opening of Global TV's 2016 piece honoring the auspicious day: "Ladies, get ready to give your man some extra attention this November 19").

It's not all discouraging. My home city, Toronto, has, for the past few years, hosted the What Makes a Man conference. It's the flagship annual event for the White Ribbon Campaign, a worldwide movement of men and boys who are, as its mission statement says, "working to end violence against women and girls, promote gender equity, healthy relationships and a new vision of masculinity." The 2016 conference day featured prominent feminist activists on its panels, which included topics such as: "Men and Masculinity On and Off the Field," which tackled sports culture and its presentation of ideal masculinity; "Military Culture and Evolving Masculinity," an exploration of how that male-dominated culture has narrowed masculinity in harmful ways; and a panel on Canada's Missing and Murdered Indigenous Women crisis, a women-led conversation on how men can be better allies in pushing for much-needed answers and action. Interspersed among the afternoon's talks were video presentations of men sharing their experiences with masculinity while building on the idea of safe spaces for men, free from forced and constricting expectations of what, ahem, makes a man. So good! This is, no doubt, the type of action Eigerman and other feminists are talking about when they ask feminism to expand into men's issues territory.

Men's rights activists *loathe* the What Makes A Man conference, of course. More moderate MRAs complain that the conference and its attendees don't discuss the real issues men face; others prefer to call the men who attend "pussies." MRAs, after all, don't want to ally with feminists; they want to blame them. Unsurprisingly, they also ridicule White Ribbon founder Jeff Perera chiefly because he has focused his foundation on helping men end violence against women. In their spirited takedowns of any anti–violence against women organization, including Perera's, MRAs gloss over the complexities of violence, particularly intimate partner violence. In 2008, for example, men committed 99 percent of the intimate-partner violence reported by women, according to the US National Data on Intimate Partner Violence, and women committed 83 percent of the intimate-partner violence reported by men. In sheer numbers, this translates to 552,000 non-fatal violent incidents against women and 101,000 against men. Many men's rights activists use raw data like these to argue women are just as violent as men. When they do this, they usually neglect to add that numerous studies have shown a woman's violence in these cases, unlike men's, is often in self-defense, less severe, and rarely continues after she leaves the relationship.

This doesn't mean we should demonize men or ignore violence against men; it does mean context is essential. The data cherry-picking has gotten so bad that some researchers have taken to adding what are essentially direct academic disclaimers to MRAs in their papers. For example, one 2017 paper in the journal *Violence Against Women* noted: "We resist the anti-feminist misinterpretation of studies on female perpetrators of violence in which readers mistakenly assume that males and females commit [intimate-partner violence] at identical rates, with identical consequences, and in identical contexts." Another prominent longtime researcher on violence against women wrote a direct response paper to anti-feminists, addressing each of their criticisms of his research. At the end, he asked: "So, what's up with these authors? Why the comic book caricatures of the feminist analysis? Why the gross misrepresentations…? Why the single-minded focus on alleged evidence that women are as bad as men?"

These researchers might as well be asking a fish why it swims. None of it matters to anti-feminists. Just look at why they don't like Jeff Perera. To them, he is a feminist apologist and a hypocrite, largely because—and I'm not kidding—he once indicated he's a fan of Miss Piggy. When Perera tweeted approval of an MTV clip of the famous Muppet asserting she'd make a pothole out of any catcaller, MRAs frothed. He was promoting violence against men! Miss Piggy was an abuser! She probably, one commenter suggested, called fake rape after her famous "Hiii-yah!" Another responded: "[It] adds a new dimension to squealing like a pig." It's all so ludicrous—except we keep hearing this about real women, too.

If we can conclude anything, it's that this renewed focus on masculinity and men's issues is filled with contradictions and confusion. Which version of #BeBetter are men supposed to embrace? Are we really exploring and expanding masculinity, or are we using this exercise as the guise to reinforce pre-feminism gender roles? We're not just selling these shiny new Ken doll concepts to men, either. Women are the secondary (and, in some cases, primary) intended buyers. We're the ones who are supposed not only to "Need man! Need man!" but "Want man! Want man!" regardless of our age or sexual orientation. What an effective distraction. We are busy trying to parse what kind of behavior and beard make the perfect (gentle) men and we're simultaneously guilt-tripped for spending too much time on women's issues. The underlying message is apparent: Stop being so selfish, ladies. You've already made it. It's time to help make men great again.

At the end of our conversation at Grey House in 2016, Brea Hutchinson said something that at first surprised me, given her history of political action: "I don't identify as a feminist today." She was quick to expand, perhaps accustomed, by now, to disaster-managing people's shock. "It's not because I reject feminism but because I think feminism is a past practice and not a future practice. In feminist communities and dialogues, we're not open to contradictory opinions. We're not willing to hold that maybe we're not doing things right. Our understanding of power is incomplete," she said. "It means we have to review and revisit [our actions] and maybe listen to people who we don't like." She went on. "What does feminism mean today in 2016? It's a question I can't answer. For me, I can't answer." She added that her actions can be described as feminist, but that's she's not sure what the politic is anymore—or even if there is one. Can we say we're feminist if our actions aren't? And who gets to police that? But there's more: "Feminism has never really made much space for me as a trans woman. Feminism has never included my body or my experiences in any real way. So, I'm like, 'I'm going to step aside and let you guys have this.'" She looked at me tentatively.

But I was not shocked. The more I reported and researched, the more it made sense to me that some women didn't identify with the word "feminist" as a label, a movement, or both. And it made sense that one woman's feminism may look nothing like another woman's. The movement and the word were both, I was discovering, going through the most severe growing pains: crucial self-analysis, tough discussions, bad PR, brutal backlash, active exclusion and active inclusion, a new and contradictory rise in seeing both everything and nothing as political, an onslaught of mixed messages on what it means to be women and men and what it means to include men, the total normalization of anti-women narratives, love and hate and apathy, and on and on. So, yes, I understood why women shied away from the f-word, even as they worked to improve women's rights and equality, often doing a neat little linguistic sidestep with "I'm not a feminist, but . . ." What I still didn't understand was why women identified with the *anti*-feminist movement, or what, beyond endless kerfuffle over the label, it would mean in the long term. What was their end goal? How were these narratives reframing conversations and affecting polices? Before I could dive into examining the consequences, I realized I needed to hear what they had to say for themselves.

It was time to meet the women who hated feminism.

TWO

On the front lines of the new
women-on-women gender wars

4 How a feMRA is made:
In conversation with the leaders of today's rising women-led anti-feminist movement

At the end of June 2014, roughly two hundred men and women packed a shabby, wood-paneled Veterans of Foreign Wars hall located in a northern suburb of Detroit. As the fluorescent lights beamed down, giving cheeks, bald heads, and linoleum floors an unflattering sheen, the attendees, drawn from all corners of the world, hooted and hollered. This was the first annual International Conference on Men's Rights, and it was a long time coming. Self-righteous victory hung heavy in the air: for months, feminists had tried and ultimately failed to stop the conference. Nothing could dampen the triumph: not the bad lighting, or the hardback chairs, or the dumpy venue. Today, the (self-proclaimed) underdogs were on top. If they wanted to trash talk feminists, nothing could stop them now, and they knew it. As the three-day conference opened, Janet Bloomfield, a general of the women-led men's rights, anti-feminist faction, said of the hundreds of women who protested the conference: "Let those cunts fuck themselves up their own asses. Bring it, halfwits!"

Still, this wasn't how Paul Elam, head honcho of North America's most prominent men's rights activist (MRA) organization, A Voice for Men, had pictured the day when he announced the conference in December 2013. Elam is an imposing presence: a physically large man (in one A Voice for Men post, he assures followers that he'd hit a woman back if physically provoked, boasting that he's six foot eight and 285 pounds) and a loud, aggressive one, too. Judging by looks alone, he's a man's man. He had made much of its chosen location, initially downtown Detroit, calling it a poetic choice. "If we wanted to find a city that was an iconic testament to masculinity, we'd need look no further," he wrote on the group's blog. "It is a city teetering and struggling for its footing. It is seeking, like many men, to find its balance and its place in the world again." Elam booked the conference into a swank hotel, the DoubleTree by Hilton, its banquet hall resplendent with fresh flowers, plush chairs, and damask carpeting. It was symbolic and perfect, the right place for such a momentous occasion.

Except hundreds of people in Detroit disagreed: they stormed the streets, surrounding the hotel, mere weeks before the conference was supposed to take place. Protestors circulated a petition claiming the hotel would put itself "in bed with domestic terrorists" by hosting the conference. The men's rights movement is linked to the May 2014 mass shooting in which Elliot Rodger killed six and injured fourteen University of California, Santa Barbara (UCSB) students, including two sorority girls. Before the shooting, Rodger uploaded his 140-page "manifesto," in which he called himself an "incel" (a term those in the manosphere use to describe involuntary celibacy). He grew increasingly obsessed over said status, eventually claiming that "females truly have something mentally wrong with them" and that he wanted to kill both the men that "took the females" away from him, as well as the women who rejected him. Women were "foul bitches" for not having the "grace" to say hi to him. He blamed them for making him feel "worthless." He started throwing his drinks at couples who kissed in front of him, later trying a gun out for target practice and joining several online forums for men who were "starved of sex" and shared his "hatred of women." He hated (and named) men whom he viewed as more socially successful than him, planning a "Day of Retribution" to punish, torture, and kill women. Though he never called himself an MRA, many feminists linked him to the movement, citing the mirrored "I'm a nice guy and it's women's fault, not mine, that X, X, and X is wrong with my life" rhetoric. "Simply search the phrase 'MRA,'" said protesters in Detroit, "and you'll see the violence, hatred, bigotry, and misogyny that MRAs support."

Soon thereafter came the threats, or so A Voice for Men claimed. The group complained of anonymous letter writers who said they would disguise themselves as guests; feminist groups openly said they would storm the hotel. Hotel managers sent A Voice for Men an ultimatum: hire eight police officers to provide security, or get out. Staff wanted two officers in the lobby, three on the floor that held the conference, and three more patrolling the rooms. It would cost more money than A Voice for Men had budgeted for security, but the organization was used to playing the victim to its advantage.

The group immediately mobilized against the "feminist radicals," creating an online crowd-funding campaign that cast Bloomfield as its star. In the accompanying video plea, Bloomfield, a conventionally attractive, slim blond, abandoned her usually crass online persona, instead calling herself a wife and a mother who "needs your help." The feminists, she said, "want to silence me — no, they want to do more than that. They want to kill me." Alison Tieman, another feMRA, as female MRAs are colloquially known, took to her anti-feminist YouTube channel, eyes wet, stating: "Even discussing men's problems — this society can't handle it, can't tolerate it. How is that a patriarchy?" The women saved the conference. The campaign easily surpassed its $25,000 goal, raising more than $32,000. A handful of people were so moved by the pleas they donated $1,000 each.

Yet here everybody was in June at a different location anyway, cheering and buying T-shirts emblazoned with Bloomfield and Tieman's faces. It's unclear why the conference venue was changed when A Voice for Men was able to pony up the cash for extra security. In subsequent updates, Elam glossed over the details, intimating

it was his choice to move the conference. He claimed interest had
grown rapidly and they needed a bigger venue. Considering the hotel
has two ballrooms and seventeen meeting rooms, and the VFW hall
is just, well, a hall, it seems more likely the hotel wanted the conference gone, or that, despite all their bluster, the MRAs were spooked.
Ensconced within their suburban fortress, MRAs were able to jeer at
feminists all they wanted and control the message getting out.

No matter what work got done inside, though, the event's
biggest success was proving the might of the men's rights movement
beyond the fringes of the internet. Not only was it able to show that
its members existed in real life and not their mother's proverbial
basements, it also demonstrated it could quickly marshal itself to
raise cash, if needed. Instead of being something feminists could
laugh at, it suddenly became something worth being scared of—a
Halloween freak show turned next-door neighbor.

Even worse, perhaps, was that the MRAs demonstrated they could
secure a PR win. Sure, hundreds protested against the conference,
but hundreds also *supported* it, donating without attending, all buying
into the men-are-losing-because-of-feminists narrative. It was, in
essence, the same hate-filled and formulaic propaganda that has
always worked. With the venue crisis, the MRA movement had finally
found its lynchpin: charismatic women orators. Who better to tell
the world feminism should be dead?

Bloomfield and her cohort fascinated and repulsed me. In fact,
women who eschewed feminism in general puzzled me; they scared
me, too. Everywhere I looked women were saying no to feminism
and yes to weirder things, like becoming feMRAs. I feared that, if
their ranks kept growing, we were unwittingly heading for the ultimate patriarchal victory: women who'd willingly abandon the fight
for their own rights in favor of helping men superglue their royal
bottoms to the Top Dog throne. It was like the world's biggest guilt
trip. Women were convinced they should feel bad about feminism's
victories, ready to rewind our gains. FeMRAs seemed like cartoon

characters, but also ones that could suddenly come to life à la Roger Rabbit. I ping-ponged back and forth, unable to decide where I landed on the terror-o-meter. Should I feel threatened that these women could become the norm, or were they destined to live forever on the fringes of freak? I had to know more about what motivated them to—so adamantly—decide that while women had it all, men were hurting. Just imagine our lives if every women started to feel that way.

Oh, hell no.

The men's rights movement is fond of saying its members don't *hate* women. What a load of BS. Sure, I'll buy MRAs may love some particular women. But it's hard to see how a movement that's always fought to quash our rights could argue it *likes* capital-W women. That's akin to saying an abusive husband likes his wife. Whatever, buddy; that's not the point.

Like breadcrumbs along a fairytale forest path, the movement's origins can be traced back to the innocent-sounding A League for Men's Rights. Founded in the late 1800s in England, the league was a direct answer to feminism, "securing the legal and moral protection of men against the encroachment of women." Its founder, William Austin, told the *Weekly Standard and Express,* "I have looked carefully into the legal aspect of the matter and find that a woman has a much greater advantage when it comes to litigation about almost any matter over any man, rich or poor." The fledgling feminist movement, he added, meant men were always losing and women were always winning. His screed appeared in the *Weekly Standard* on May 14, 1898, under an advertisement hailing the new discovery of Dr. Weir's Porous Plaster, "a sure and certain cure for pains in the back and joints."

Thirty years later in Vienna, Sigurd Höberth von Schwarzthal founded another men's rights group called, in German, Der Bund

für Männerrechte (or, in English, The Federation of Men's Rights).
A divorced man with arched eyebrows and a moustache reminiscent
of two dead caterpillars, Höberth von Schwarzthal remains a men's
rights folk hero today. One of his more famous (or infamous)
statements is: "We love and honour the ladies, but we want to leave to
our descendants once more real mothers and wives, and to prevent
their being killed off by the alleged emancipation of the woman."
Bachelors, divorced husbands, and unmarried fathers comprised his
group. He insisted married men wanted to join, but their wives held
their coattails too close.

At the group's first mass meeting in 1926, its members showed
an unbridled distaste for the new feminist movement. "The feminist,
hysterical and degenerate cafe scribblers have helped cunning
woman to forge intolerable chains for men," one rally member told
newspapers at the time. "The man is roped before the family coach,
and on the driving seat sits the 'gracious lady,' and if he doesn't pull
till he drops, she swings the whip of legal paragraphs over him."

This sentiment persisted throughout the next several decades,
dominating various men's rights groups who opposed the increasing rights of women. Many groups took on the crusade against
alimony payments, saying they shackled men to the responsibility of
marriage but encouraged women to "become out-and-out adventur-
esses" — Höberth von Schwarzthal again. They demanded alimony
be repealed, or at the very least that women also be forced to pay it
(should the divorce be their fault) and that all legal punishment be
overturned for failure to pay (for men only). Even silent film star
Charlie Chaplin, whose second ex-wife, Lita Grey, supposedly demanded $1.25 million in alimony, reportedly joined the movement,
earning himself the admiration of today's men's rights activists.
On the whole, the movement called for equality, but only in the
broadest, most simplistic sense. If a woman killed her husband in
self-defense, for instance, she should be sentenced to the same jail
time as a male abuser who beat his wife to death. And so on and so

on, in a weird Chinese finger pull of logic: the more feminists talked about women's rights, the more MRAs screamed, "But, men!"

One of the earliest mentions of men's rights was in 1886, in *Putnam's Magazine*, a then contemporary competitor of *Harper's*. "*Putnam* is for progress. *Putnam* is for women's rights; but it is also for men's rights — for everybody's rights." That doesn't sound so bad, but the magazine's editors went on to entirely miss the point of equal rights, stating that since the man in marriage was like the "guardian and master" and the woman "a child and a servant" he was duty-bound to take responsibility for her behavior, even if her actions were atrocious and even if they were her idea. As an illustration of women's power for manipulation and penchant for wickedness, the magazine cited Lady Macbeth. Evidently, many late-Victorian women persuaded their husbands to commit murder.

Putnam editors woefully admitted they knew women "cared nothing for logic," appealing instead to women's "sense of justice and tender hearts" to cease abusing their newly won rights. Namely, *Putnam* wanted women to stop accusing their husbands of domestic violence and sending them to jail. How else, implored the magazine, did women expect "domestic discipline to be preserved"? The article went on for too many more pages, but it essentially boiled down to this: if the law declared that husbands must provide for their wives, and women benefitted, then men should be able to do whatever they wanted to ensure their wives stayed good and trouble-free. Punishing them for punishing their wives, then, was just plain unfair.

It's easy, and altogether desirable for our own sanity, to dismiss these loopy arguments as anachronistic. But modernize the slang and it all sounds alarmingly similar to the men's rights rhetoric of today. Men's activists carry signs that read things like "Our brothers and sons need protection from abusive wives" and claim that men are more likely to be raped and more likely to be attacked at night — full stop. Under the blanket of encompassing equality, all rational argument is smothered. It doesn't matter if statistics state that most attackers are men; it only matters that no situation is, technically, unique to women.

In March 2015, #LetsTalkMen billboards appeared in downtown Toronto with this misleading, half-true assertion: "Half of domestic violence victims are men; no domestic violence shelters are dedicated to us." The massive signs depicted a hunched-over Fabio character, fingers plugged into his ears, shrinking from a looming, screaming vampire-esque woman. (What a supernatural nag!) A Canadian Association for Equality (CAFE) logo branded the corner, showily using both the male and female gender signs. Critics have long regarded the CAFE as a men's rights group in disguise, and not a very good disguise (see aforementioned billboards). Tellingly, its advocacy is centered entirely on men's rights, and its mandate states it focuses on men and boys because "investment and support for educational and social programs stands at a level that is far from equal to the seriousness of the problem."

This style of rhetoric owes much to the first wave of the modern men's rights movement, which started in the 1970s. Activists during this time focused on the rights of divorced dads and the demasculinization of all things sacred and manly. MRAs wanted to preserve traditional roles for women and cringed at the idea of women with autonomy, women in universities, and women doing anything other than making babies, assembling sandwiches, and fetching cold brewskies. MRAs fed into men's resentment, often pushing it into violence.

We saw the first terrible glimpse of this in 1989, when, decades before cultivating UCSB shooter Elliot Rodger, the men's rights movement helped form another mass murderer: Marc Lépine. The self-proclaimed MRA used the movement's propaganda to write his own manifesto, complete with the line "I hate feminists!" Fueled by a burning bitterness toward high-achieving women, Lépine stormed an engineering class at the École Polytechnique in Montreal and murdered fourteen young women before killing himself. A shocked nation dubbed the tragedy the "Montreal Massacre" and quickly worked to explain it: Lépine was mentally ill. Gun control was too lax. It was a violent act, but not at all symptomatic of a larger culture of violence against women.

Feminists knew better. Anti-woman sentiment had been poisoning the air for years. The murders weren't isolated. They were just another version of ingrained violence against women. This could happen again, they warned. And it has. Lépine's messaging has lived on, repeating itself in mass-market MRA screeds and informing other murderers: men who kill their wives, men who kill women they don't know, and men who kill a lot of women because they hate them, like Rodger, who eagerly adopted MRA rhetoric. Similar to Lépine, Rodger's spree was dismissed as the work of a crazy man, as if he had worked up all that hate in a bubble. We're too ready to forget that the men's rights movement has been actively trying to reframe the conversation for years, purposely feeding antipathy, acrimony, and sexism. I don't doubt that some of these men are unstable: I once interviewed an MRA in a homemade superhero costume, surrounded by a Toronto SWAT team, who refused to leave the roof of a politician's office until he had secured a promise of improved rights for men. It's not an accident these men have found a home in the MRA movement, because the movement courts them.

With Elam, the movement has taken even bigger steps out of fringe territory and into mainstream conversation. Through Texas-based A Voice for Men, Elam has brought the men's rights movement online, connecting and unifying it, while at the same time working to shed its radical right-wing association. He remains inflammatory — in 2010, he named October "Bash a Violent Bitch Month" — but he was smart. In a true feat of doublespeak, he has endorsed the worst kind of locker room talk, calling it equality, and then using modern technology to foster it like a dandelion weed.

Under Elam, the MRA movement began to court women actively for the first time, not just bringing them into the fold but propping them up as its shrewdest, most well-known personalities. Elam must have known that with their involvement the MRA movement could more believably claim to support human rights, even if critics still called that support a front for its true misogynist core. Following this new push toward the mainstream, the wider movement adopted a Melba toast attitude toward equality: we're happily for men, but not angrily against anyone; we want rights for everybody, too! CAFE, especially, succeeded when it achieved official charity status in 2014. That same year, a week after the Rodger shooting, the organization coined Equality Day (or E-Day), a made-up occasion to, it said, "celebrate the gains made in advancing social equality."

This benign branding allowed CAFE to get pretty far in its celebration planning: it reserved an event space on Toronto Island, secured beer sponsorship, and even booked an (entirely male) line-up of Toronto indie musicians. But before the show could go on, feminists, and then media, caught wind of the concert. Soon everyone — except CAFE — claimed they'd been duped; nobody wanted their name attached to the MRA movement. Artists canceled, the venue canceled, and sponsors pulled out. CAFE volunteers ended up handing out pamphlets on the street instead, stationed next to the mall and a few fanatics who really loved Jesus.

For feminists, it was a happy ending. And yet I worry it won't always be this way; we can already see the shift. The MRA machine has directly powered some of the biggest campaigns and attacks against women's rights. It has funded legal battles against rape victims, using its deep pockets to launch dozens of civil lawsuits in the US that discredit women but boost their accusers; its legions comprised Gamergate's loudest, most dedicated factions (which I cover further in chapter six); and its anti–women's rights rhetoric has leaked onto our screens and airwaves and into locker rooms and campuses, and even our legislatures. In October 2015, an Idaho high school boy threatened to "kill all the girls" at his school after the cheerleading team refused to send him nude photos. This is no longer an anomaly. Thank you, men's rights movement.

What the movement wants is at once completely vague—to secure men's rights—and entirely simplistic: to end women's rights, sending us back to a world of kitchens and babies, what the movement sees as our traditional, rightful, and *honorable* roles. I don't think the question is whether MRAs will one day get their E-Day, or something like it, but, rather, how long until they do? How long will it take before they fully hide a culture of rape denial, patriarchy denial, abuse denial, and a general desire to return to 1952 behind the unobjectionable, huggable term "equality"? Not as long as I'd like, surely, which would roughly be around the time pigs fly and Satan's bundled in a parka.

This huge push to rebrand explains, in part, how we've wound up with Janet Bloomfield, Alison Tieman, and others, including Karen Straughan, the third star of the feMRA trio. But it doesn't *really* explain how three women came to support a movement that encourages men to bash a violent bitch, or why they cheered MRAs through Gamergate and the creation of an online game that encouraged players to virtually beat up feminist media critic Anita Sarkeesian, merely because she had the nerve to say video games could stand to be less sexist. Why have they repeatedly called women and young girls who are raped "whores" who deserved it, or spearheaded the counterattack against the anti-rape campaign on Canadian university campuses? Why do they think men's rights are a more pressing issue than women's rights, which they don't seem to think matter at all?

Janet Bloomfield is a gregarious stay-at-home mom who hates feminism. When she is not busy baking after-school snacks or cheering her young son and two daughters from the sidelines, she is often online penning vitriolic, click-baity criticism of the movement. In recent years, on her uber-popular, million-plus-hits blog, *JudgyBitch*, she has stated that underage victims in high-profile rape cases are "dumb fucking whores," and that single mothers are "clearly really, really shitty at making life decisions." She routinely calls women that advocate for their rights "little dumbass feminists." When I met her in June 2016, her newest campaign, #WhyWomenShouldNotVote, advocated for disenfranchising women. Two years earlier, *Salon* writer Amanda Marcotte called her one of the seven scariest women alive "working tirelessly to attack equal rights for women." Bloomfield loved it when her incendiary jabs went viral. "It's fun," she told me, laughing.

Born to a Seventh-day Adventist family in rural Alberta, Bloomfield grew up the only girl among three brothers. She lived on a hobby farm, worked to eat, and was generally fearful of her evangelical parents, whom she describes as "crazy and violent." She began to connect the dots of her anti-feminism later at the University of Western Ontario, where she completed an undergraduate degree in film theory. Much of the film criticism taught at the university, she says, took place through a women's studies lens. Bloomfield learned how contemporary feminist scholars saw the world, and she hated it. To her, feminist theory mandated that everyone would be better off if women were in charge. She thought of her mother, who she saw as much more violent than her father, and shook her head.

After graduation, Bloomfield had a lot of conversations lamenting her future. It was during one of these regular sessions she realized her biggest ambition was to be a wife and a mother. She wanted to create the happy, nuclear family she wished she'd had, but didn't—to paint herself into a Norman Rockwell. "You can't say that out loud," she said. "I was immediately met with criticism: 'You're wasting your life; you're taking such a huge risk; you should never rely on a man; you should never rely on *anyone*. You have to participate in the labor force.'" But Bloomfield was determined. Hedging her bets, she decided to pursue a master of business administration at the University of Victoria. She was, she told me in absolute sincerity, choosing her marriage pool. It turned out to be a smart choice. She met a man, also an MBA student, who was looking for a wife, "Not.

A. Girl. Friend," she stressed. She was happy. And whenever anyone criticized her choice to marry and stay home, she blamed feminism.

Then, shortly after her son was born, her father attempted to reconnect. Bloomfield had distanced herself from her parents, who divorced when she was still a child. He arrived at her door with two boxes. One contained income tax returns, showing that, contrary to her mother's claims, he had never missed a child support payment. The other was full of letters and cards meant for her and her brothers, but sent back by her mother unopened. Bloomfield forgave him. But she was furious that she'd missed what she saw as her window to properly reconcile. She took to Google: "How on earth did my mother have the power to do this?" As an answer, she found the men's rights movement and its strong belief that fathers are unfairly disadvantaged during divorce and custody disputes. Inspired, she officially launched *JudgyBitch* in April 2013. It quickly amassed fifteen thousand page views and enough buzz to attract the MRA movement's most prominent members.

Today, as head of social media for A Voice for Men, Bloomfield is a master of branding and development, though, more and more, she's been calling herself an anti-feminist first and a men's rights activist second. The distinction is subtle. In addition to fighting for men's rights, A Voice for Men preaches anti-feminism, calling feminists a "social malignancy" akin to the Ku Klux Klan. As a whole, the so-called "manosphere" is surely growing, steadily challenging the feminist conversation and building momentum to overthrow the movement's biggest victories, particularly progressive rape shield and child support legislation. Already, its members have played a role in the recent years' most successful anti-feminist campaigns, including the battle to weaken, or eliminate, women-friendly university policies on sexual assault.

After our initial two-hour phone interview, I still wasn't sure I understood her. I flew to meet Bloomfield on her close-knit, tree-studded street in Thunder Bay, Ontario. When I arrived at her house in a taxi, I discovered Bloomfield bent over her front garden, tending to a bed of zinnias, snapdragons, and daisies. She greeted me with a smile and an apology for her grimy hands. Bloomfield is a trim woman in her early forties, with an etched, tanned face and clear blue eyes. She was wearing a red "Make America Great Again" ball cap, snugly pulled down over her long blond hair. She is, as her hat attested, a huge fan of Donald Trump. (She also had a Trump phone case, emblazoned with the US flag.) Inside her house, framed children's artwork decorated the walls. Chocolate chip cookies cooled on a wood dinner table that could seat fourteen, but was, at that moment, providing a hiding spot for the family bunny.

Janet Bloomfield is not her real name, though it's how she's known to both her fans and her enemies. Initially, she kept her legal name secret to protect her family from her controversial persona; she's received regular death threats. A male MRA activist, affronted when Bloomfield objected to blow-up penises at an event, revealed her identity, and the public outing led to a letter-writing campaign against her husband, Tim, who is an associate professor and assistant dean in Lakehead University's business department. While the letter-writing campaign fizzled—as Tim said, he doesn't control his wife, or even really read most of what she writes on *JudgyBitch*—she still preferred to go by Janet Bloomfield. The pseudonym has become her brand, and because this is how she's known, it's also how I'll refer to her here.

In person, Bloomfield was a more thoughtful, less singularly offensive version of her online self. She reiterated the ideas she posted online but was prone to discuss them with more civility. For instance, one of her closest friends and neighbors was an Indigenous woman who described herself as a lefty and who disagreed with most of Bloomfield's political assessments (though she confessed to me over dinner that she also had reservations about where she fit into feminism). As I watched them debate climate change and unionization, Bloomfield suddenly exclaimed: "See, if we were online, I would have called you a cunt and you would have called me Hitler!" But as much as she lamented such knee-jerk name-calling on social media, she wasn't about to stop it.

Often a bundle of twists and contradictions, Bloomfield told me she can't support anything that declared it a woman's *duty* to be a mother and homemaker. She believes it should be a choice and that, if given that choice, most women would happily opt to stay home. She is strongly in favor of abortion rights, allowing that Roe v. Wade is "the absolute stunning achievement of feminism." She has rejected her evangelical upbringing and is not religious. Yet when I asked her to elaborate on why she believes women shouldn't vote, she argued that it was because they cannot be drafted, they make bad economic decisions (particularly when it comes to military defense), and they are too pro-immigration. Or, as she put it on *JudgyBitch*: "Women have had the vote in the West for almost 100 years, and all they have done is vote to destroy and destabilize the world men built for us, while protecting themselves from the blood consequences." She's since added a few exceptions to her rule, clarifying that women can earn the right to vote if they are in the military, mothers of sons, wives of men, officials, or elected by men. This would suggest submission, but like many of the feMRAs, she was also emphatically against the murkier corners of the men's rights world, such as the red pill movement.

"Red pill" is a geeky reference to the *Matrix* movies, in which courageous main character Neo took a cherry-colored pill and saw the world as it really was. These MRAs see themselves as Neo, and the real world as one feminists have ruined. Red pillers argue for a return to strict gender roles, in which men have sexual dominance over women in return for providing financial stability. Women should support them in all ways in return for the ability to "make house," which is all women really want anyway. Men who buy into the philosophy also claim women who say no to sexual advances don't really mean it: men should listen not to what they say but to what their actions show, which pillers invariably interpret to mean "yes." Bloomfield told me she believed such messaging tarnished the movement; women should always have choice (how very feminist of her). If the pillers weren't silenced, she feared, they'd drag the movement out of the reaches of the mainstream conversation and back into the dregs of internet message boards. None of the feMRAs wanted that.

When I told her I was surprised she would find something offensive, Bloomfield confided that much of her bluster on social media and *JudgyBitch* is, essentially, click bait. Bloomfield saw her extremism as part of spreading the anti-feminist message. Her decision to write outrageous headlines—"The world's most retarded feminist: I have found her" and "Why are feminist women so fucking pathetic?"—is a tactical one. Moments before, Bloomfield had proposed that women shouldn't have nuclear weapon codes because their periods make them emotionally unpredictable. Her website's headlines, Bloomfield said, while slicing through strips of bacon for the pizza we were making, are purposely written to grab attention. She laughed: The more riled-up feminists get, the more she pokes at them. While she admits her shouty tone may be too over the top for some readers, her hope is that *JudgyBitch* provides a portal into the diverse world of anti-feminism and that, when compared to her, its other stars may even seem more measured. A successful movement, she figures, needs both to flourish.

This tactic makes her even more frightening: she's a smart, savvy woman who has overcome terrible things in her life, but whose smartness, savviness, and tenacity have convinced her that feminism is no longer relevant for women—that, in fact, not to put too fine a point on it, feminism is harming women and destroying the world.

Unlike many of the men in the movement, Bloomfield also knows how to play the attention game against feminists and win. None of her myriad PR costumes—pundit, mom, daughter, wife, radical, conservative, liberal, activist, debater, businessperson, and so on—are that of an angry man. As much as feminists dismiss her, other women (and men) listen. It's like feminists are playing an impossible game of Whac-a-Mole; on the defensive, they can't possibly crush all the anti-feminists Bloomfield is encouraging to rise up. Some would inevitably hear her and ask: If she's saying no to feminism, why shouldn't I?

Bloomfield gives feminism its due for getting women where they are today but echoes the common anti-feminist sentiment that the movement has gone too far. "I believe in equality of opportunity," she told me more than once, "but I do not believe in equality of outcome." Like every anti-feminist I spoke to, Bloomfield argues that feminism, while once needed, has now built its message on the idea that women are perpetual victims. Anti-feminists also argue that feminism creates a moral panic around rape culture (which they don't believe exists) that in turn encourages man hating. Bloomfield contends that feminism limits women (in that it devalues mother-hood), sets them up for a life of misery (in that it was responsible for selling the myth that women "can have it all"); and does nothing to empower them (in that it stresses what women can't do, when, in fact, equality of opportunity meant they could do anything).

Many feminists and even members of liberal-minded media have tended to dismiss such criticisms as the rumblings of fringe online hordes. But those who dismiss the anti-feminist movement underestimate the dissatisfaction many women have with feminism's perceived messages, in particular the idea that it seeks special priv-ileges for women. (Take, for example, the Canadian Club panel, or the many comments from young Hollywood actors such as Shailene Woodley.) To many ordinary women who are followers of bootstrap can-do-ness, anti-feminism is like a clarion call that promises that, for once, the only thing that matters is their own hard work, sexism be damned. Bloomfield gave interviews to Gavin McInnes's *Rebel Media Show*, NBC's *Today Show*, and the *Dr. Phil* offshoot *The Doctors*. Everywhere her core message was the same: feminism is dangerously past its best-before date, and women now flourish better without it. Or, more to the point, as Bloomfield said: feminism is cancer.

Back in Bloomfield's happy home, this message played out over a post-dinner game of Jenga. A family friend had learned I was interviewing Bloomfield about anti-feminism and wondered what Bloomfield's youngest daughter, Jane, a whip-smart and impish seven-year-old, made of the word. (She has no idea what her mom does online, though Bloomfield has made no effort to shield her children from her views.) Bloomfield turned to her daughter: "What do you think the word 'feminist' means?"

Jane didn't miss a beat: "Girls who think they are better than boys."

"Do you think that's right? Are girls better than boys?"

"No, boys and girls are the same."

"The same but different," Bloomfield suggested.

"They're both human, so that's the same."

"Do you think girls can be soldiers?"

"If they want to."

"Do you think most girls want to?"

Jane paused. "Some do."

"Do you think some boys want to stay at home and be dads?"

Again: "Some do."

"Should they?"

Jane repeated that it was okay if they wanted to. Dads should care about their children. Bloomfield asked her daughter again what feminists think, and Jane repeated her earlier answer, adding that it wasn't fair for girls to think they're better than boys. "Where did you learn that feminists think that?" Bloomfield wondered. Jane responded with a crooked grin: "I learned from you, Mom." Her mom answered with a proud grin of her own.

For insight into how an effective feMRA is created, I could have easily picked any of the other female men's rights activists (what a mouthful) in North America. In the US, twentysomething Tomi Lahren catapulted to fame thanks, in part, to her feminist "takedowns" on the "Final Thoughts" segment of her show on Glenn Beck's network, TheBlaze. She believes the term "feminism" has been hijacked but, like Bloomfield and others, strongly advocates for women's empowerment, blurring the rhetorical line between anti-feminists, post-feminists, and the "I'm not a feminist, but…" crowd. She's called feminists "bitter" and the movement "a giant contradiction." "Women could rule the world," she's said, "if we stop dragging each other down," but she's also said that if, thanks to feminists, "the world is subjected to Lena Dunham's naked body," feminists should not be able to "pick and choose what type of women fit [their] agenda." Feminists don't criticize the damaging reinforcement of narrow body norms, Lahren asserted, but are jealous fatties intent on tearing down women with "hard bodies." She liked to use air quotes, flicking her fingers at "mystical women's issues," ridiculing the pay gap, birth control, maternity leave, and sexual assault. To Lahren and her followers, strong women aren't whiners. Strong women care about law enforcement and military readiness, economic growth and national security, and family values—as if none of those things align with the feminist movement.

In Canada, the ranks of female anti-feminist leaders include YouTube celebrity Karen Straughan, who, when I visited Bloomfield in mid-2016, had nearly 130,000 followers, and Alison Tieman, leader of the women-led MRA group called the Honey Badger Brigade (a nod to both the vicious animal and the viral meme "honey badger don't care," in which said vicious animal doesn't care what you think of it). Another high-profile woman in the anti-feminist movement is BC-based Lauren Southern, a fellow blond provocateur and contributor to Ezra Levant's Rebel Media platform. Then there's Diana Davison, who runs the YouTube channel Feminism LOL; she gained more than 42,000 followers by purporting to debunk the sexual assault case against Jian Ghomeshi, which she believes was a media- and feminist-produced hoax. On the establishment side is, of course, Janice Fiamengo, the English professor at the University of Ottawa and the anti-feminist who believes university rape culture is dangerous make-believe. Anne Cools, a former Liberal Party member and current independent, and the first Black woman appointed to Canada's senate, believes that feminism is a "personality disorder" and opened A Voice for Men's inaugural international men's rights conference with a galvanizing call to arms. "The cause that is before you and the things that you fight for are valid and just," she said, urging MRAs to remember they were at war.

Some of these women were once feminists. Take Theryn Meyer, a transgender woman and former president of Simon Fraser University's MRA campus group. "I used to be a feminist, and I was a fucking wreck," she told *Xtra* in late 2015. "I was eating up everything that feminism fed to me: that the world was out to get me, that the world was structured to not accommodate me." She admitted that while it's true she faced discrimination, she didn't hold with feminism's "constant harping" about it or what she saw as the message that she had no power to change it. Feminism might be relevant in the Middle East, a shadowy, backward place where, the anti-feminists allowed, women needed more rights. But here in a democratic West? Stop your crying, baby girl.

In the past several years, many of these women who challenged feminism have expanded their influence. When I started this research in 2014, Straughan and Tieman, both based in Western Canada, worked part-time jobs to make ends meet while they focused on their anti-feminism and MRA advocacy work. When I interviewed them again in 2016, both said they were more sought after and connected than ever. Karen Straughan's videos, in particular, routinely got hundreds of thousands of views, and sometimes more than one million; fans often stopped her in the street and at work. Her most popular video was called "Feminism and the Disposable Male," a critique of how feminism devalues men (in other words, feminists are all man bashers). The video has made the front page of Reddit multiple times and prompted requests for her to speak across North America.

Straughan is an unapologetic university dropout who punctuates her sentences with profanity and the word "right" — the last to such a degree that even those on MRA online forums have called her out on it, begging Elam to tell her to cut it out. Long before she became a professional anti-feminist, Straughan made a living writing and publishing "dirty books" for women. She formed a strong community around an online group of erotica authors. Swigging red wine and puffing an endless chain of cigarettes, she told me how, in 2011, a small but persistent number of men from the anti-feminist website The Spearhead began to troll a website she wrote for, leaving disparaging comments about the "feminization" of literature. Straughan eagerly joined the retaliation committee to comment-bomb the offending website. But she found too much with which she agreed on the offending website. Instead of flooding the site with pro-women messaging, Straughan turned coat.

"So often," she told me, "what feminists think is just completely woo-woo." She soon began to see feminism as a dangerous social movement that devalued both genders, and she decided it must be stopped. Three years after her inadvertent toe dip into the seas of anti-feminism, Straughan swapped her "dirty book" community for the wild world of women against women. At the inaugural men's rights conference, the T-shirt depicting her as a superhero sold out; she couldn't even find one to bring home to her boyfriend. As her popularity first spiked in 2014, and urged on by the same culture that had incubated Gamergate and the surging on-campus rape culture denialism, people started to stop her on the street. They pumped her hand like she was a war hero and told her never to stop the good fight. The recognition was weird, Straughan confessed to me, her voice briefly dropping velvet-soft in reflection before rising to barroom boisterous again, but it was also thrilling; her message was spreading, connecting. By our next interview in 2016, Straughan had been able to quit her part-time restaurant job thanks to increased revenue from her website's ads and public speaking demands; her talks routinely brought in $5,000 to $20,000 per engagement, though she joked she was no Anita Sarkeesian and sometimes she was lucky that her expenses were paid. She lives in Edmonton and is routinely recognized on the street, at restaurants and, recently, at the grocery store, where a man took a selfie with Straughan to show his girlfriend, who, he told her, "would get a kick out of it." She was even spoofed in an episode of *Bones* that focused on men's rights. "It's very, very different now," she told me. "And it's all positive."

The feMRAs all had similar theories of why women might abandon feminism and join them instead: feminism encouraged women to play the victim, always complaining about things they didn't have or ways in which they thought they weren't treated fairly, and women were, quite frankly, done with being victims. Victimhood was a lie, and they were done being lied to. In North America, women had access to the same rights as men, at least on paper; if they couldn't make it happen, it was their own fault. Feminists were "snowflakes," demanding special attention and melting under criticism. As Tomi Lahren claimed in 2017, feminists had "a victimhood mentality and a snowflake exterior." They were pathetic.

"The whole framing of feminism disenfranchises women," Alison Tieman told me. "Instead of building what they want, feminism teaches women-learned helplessness." Tieman runs the podcast and YouTube show Honey Badger Radio and quit her day job in 2016 to focus full-time on the Badgers. Midway through the year, the show was raking in around a minimum of $10,000 in monthly donations—enough, said Tieman, to keep her going and to also employ two other full-time and two part-time staff. She hoped that she could soon bring on some more people. She even offered Honey Badger merchandise: comic-book versions of the women on T-shirts, and stylized honey badgers on mugs, posters, and pins.

Whenever Tieman talks about why women have turned against feminism, she sounds like a self-empowerment wall hanging. A blend of pep talk and sermon, she preaches individualism, the power of creativity, and a can-do attitude. She believes being a woman in the West is the best thing to be. FeMRAs do women a favor by attacking feminism. To illustrate the lie of feminism, they often use the analogy of a frail, old, widowed aunt living alone. She lives in the safest neighborhood in her city, but an unscrupulous home alarm dealer targets her. He exaggerates the crime statistics in her area, and he harasses her constantly: she's a victim, she's a victim, she's a victim. The abuse in this situation, stresses Tieman, is so obvious. "We see it immediately," she added, "and yet this is what feminism is doing toward women." This is why her movement will never stop until feminism is dead. To feMRAs, they are setting both genders free.

The feMRAs' own con job is remarkable: convincing women to shun victimhood without actually doing anything to make us not victims. Of course, nobody *wants* to be a victim. Like, "Hey, please rape, harass, and objectify me, make me feel generally unsafe, and while you're at it, pay me less, limit my opportunities, and shut me out of lucrative industries! K THX PATRIARCHY BYE!" Just no. By definition, victimhood ain't fun. Yet our fundamentally unequal status in society means women are daily victims in so many ways, all of which the men's rights movement reinforces. Let's not forget it works to exploit human frustration; let's not forget how powerful and potent legitimizing hate can be; let's not forget Marc Lépine, Elliot Rodger, and those like them; most of all, let's not forget that we live in a society primed to believe the lie that equality means men need more rights and women fewer.

The feMRAs are wrong. Women can be angry victims. We can be strong victims. We can be victims on a rampage of change. What we can't afford to be is women who sweep our victimhood under the proverbial rug and, in pretending it's not there, forget the mess. Because whether we choose to see them or not, the dust bunnies of patriarchy are still screwing us. That's why we need feminism: to reach a place in which women aren't 24/7 victims of sexism.

The more I met feMRAs, or got stuck in the Tumblr vortex of movements like Women Against Feminism, the viral women-and-girl-led selfie-meets-anti-feminism campaign, the more I felt like I had caught a perpetual flu. If this is what post-feminism looked like, then I didn't want anything to do with it. For all its talk about empowering women to achieve their goals, the men's rights movement has done little to encourage women to support each other, preferring to wedge a vampire-sized stake between them. It assumes the status quo is that way for a reason. That's an insidiously dangerous assertion, least of all because it's so easy to agree with.

Here's an example of how this works. Straughan told me such low numbers of women are in STEM simply because women aren't interested in science, technology, engineering, or math. It was the same reason why, she argued, there are more women in other professions, like teaching and cleaning. Men prefer to put up drywall, and that's okay. Straughan knew this, she said, because she has always been the type of woman who was more comfortable with men—you know, because she could never adapt to all those weird affects and catty behavior that embody womanhood. "How far are you willing to push people to do things that they otherwise would not do?" she cried. "If everybody has the same choices, and they're happy with those choices, then what injustice has been done?"

And that's why MRA logic works: it tells us to do nothing. It doesn't matter that the movement's criticisms might have some validity, or that its monsters might not actually be monsters. This is why we should be afraid of what it's selling. As much as it tries to paint itself as forward-thinking and visionary, the MRA movement isn't really presenting us with any alternatives for a *new* world. It's demanding, instead, that we accept the current status quo as the best possible outcome, nay, *the* most *natural* outcome. They're like the Houdinis of discrimination and hate, conjuring up amazing illusions. Underneath it all, though, the message is essentially: Let's keep things unequal for women, so everybody wins!

Um, what?

At the end of my first conversation with Bloomfield, she had told me A Voice for Men was preparing its war chest, a fund to launch legal challenges against all the things feminism has wrought. "We are at the consciousness-raising stage," she said, "and we are moving at light speed." Then, I would have been tempted to dismiss the boasting as wishful thinking. Now, with women as the face of its movement and Donald Trump as the American president, I am convinced we no longer can, or should. As Bloomfield talked about all the rights the organization would fight once it raised the money, my mind drifted back to high school. It struck me that, for all their eloquence and research-heavy arguments, the feMRAs sounded a whole lot like the boys I knew then, all full of machismo and black-and-white derision whenever the f-word dropped, like a stone, into the conversation. Suddenly, I knew what the world would look like if the men's rights movement won: not a utopia of base equality, but a planet full of teenaged boys.

5 The domestic wife: The problem with retro revival, the new motherhood, and the glamorization of pre-feminist gender roles

"America doesn't value the caretaker," Kerry Dolan, a mother of three, told me. In 2014, after her own experience re-entering the workforce, Dolan founded OptIn, a US-based organization that helps women return to work and also advocates for more women-friendly labor policies. While society may have drawn little heart doodles next to the *idea* of motherhood (as Ivanka Trump proclaimed in a campaign video for her father, "The most important job any woman can have is being a mother"), it has, in practice, done little to help women. Dolan characterized Trump's six-week maternity leave campaign pledge, not yet enacted when we spoke, as "not enough"—not enough to stop women like her from feeling like they have to leave their jobs when they have children, not enough to eviscerate the guilt. She lamented that women have not "moved the needle at all" and, more than once, sadly asserted, "Women don't support women." Women must band together to change workplace culture and to advocate for flexible, progressive polices, she said, because "we don't have time to go backwards." She wanted her twin daughters to have better options than she did, to not have to choose. She believed once women saw the power in what they could accomplish together, many things would change. So I was surprised when she later hesitated and said, "I don't see myself as a feminist," in large part, it seemed, because she saw herself first as a mother.

In all the great women-on-women wars, none has more controversy power than Stay-At-Home Mom versus Working Mom. Or—if you really want to bring out the big nukes—Stay-At-Home Mom versus Childless Career Woman. Working Mom and Childless Career Woman are presumed to be on Team Feminist: the former is often characterized as frazzled, unavailable, miserable; the latter as frigid, secretly unfulfilled, mannish. Both are usually stereotyped as selfish. That neither may have ever uttered the f-word hardly matters.

"No woman should be authorized to stay at home to raise her children," feminist hero Simone de Beauvoir proclaimed in a 1975 interview with fellow feminist icon Betty Freidan. Since then, feminism's detractors have commonly and unfairly depicted the women's rights movement as both anti-mom and anti-housewife. So when *New York* magazine published its cover story "The Feminist Housewife" in March 2013, nearly forty years after de Beauvoir's assertion, national conversation didn't just spark, it exploded.

On the cover, the article's main subject, Kelly Makino, wore a green polka dot apron, a purple T-shirt, high tops, and striped Capri leggings. She held up a feather duster, her arm cocked at a V, and underneath her straight-edged Bettie Page-esque bangs, she appeared to be smirking. Makino, a university-educated, thirty-three-year-old, married mother of a five- and a four-year-old, had chosen to opt out of the workforce and be a full-time mom. The magazine sold her choice as the trend of "feminists who say they're having it all—by choosing to stay home." Makino, who told *New York* journalist Lisa Miller she was "a flaming liberal" and a feminist, spoke in pure click bait. "I want my daughter to be able to do anything she wants," she said. "But I also want to say, 'Have a career that you can walk away from at the drop of a hat.'" And this: "I'm really grateful that my husband and I have fallen into traditional gender roles without conflict." Oh, and this: "Women are raised from the get-go to raise children successfully. When we are moms, we have a better toolbox," a fact she attributed to young girls playing with dolls. Oh, be still in your grave, Simone.

Reaction was both heated and congratulatory. And there was a lot of it: more than four hundred responses online. Many of the comments were supportive: "Kelly Makino is very brave, along with the other stay-at-home moms, to go against what our society is viewing as normal today and to agree to stay at home." Others were cautious: "There is no question that women pay a price for taking time off—even if they stay current in their field. I think women need to carefully think about the career-altering consequences of their choices." And a few asked why the stay-at-home question was only posed to women and taught to daughters. "Furthermore, even if we don't give this dung a good flush, why does Makino only want to tell her daughter [to have a career she can walk away from]?" one asked. "Why is her son not awaiting the same lecture?" Some even thanked the feminist movement for giving them the *choice* to stay home while simultaneously dismissing feminism as old fashioned: "We have achieved the right to live our lives to the best of our ability, whatever that may be. I do not feel the need to participate in the battle of the sexes until the bitter end."

Elsewhere, feminist website *Jezebel* called the feature "such bullshit." *Slate* called the headline "alarmist." A contributor to *Forbes* unfavorably compared women like Makino to Phyllis Schlafly, organizer of the 1970s Stop ERA campaign, and warned of economic destruction: "'Retro Wives' can bring the American way of life to a grinding halt." Lisa Miller was invited on *CBS This Morning* and MSNBC's *Morning Joe*, where she talked about the concept of leaning out—women who slow their careers and embrace domesticity. She called her story, at its heart, an economic one. "In a world where our financial futures are uncertain, and we don't know what's going to become of us, and you're not making that much money, and you got two little kids, and your husband is working all the time," Miller told the *Morning Joe* panel, "it makes sense to lean out and focus on the home sphere."

But does it? In economically perilous times, is the best that we can really hope for a clumsy resurrection of tired old gender roles? I'm not saying that motherhood and feminism can't coexist: they *do*, and we need to find better, more equitable solutions so that men and women can both achieve happier work-life balance. That's pretty hard to do when we're not only fighting zombified versions of old anti-feminist stereotypes but also pretending they're the answer.

What's worse: we've been here before; it really is the unkillable trend. A decade earlier, the *New York Times* provoked an uproar when it featured a young, chic, white woman on its cover. She was dressed smartly in a white shirt, sitting cross-legged with her baby in her lap. Her brunette hair fell in a curtain as she looked calmly off into the distance, ignoring the orange ladder behind her. She floated on the two-part headline, which asked "Why don't more women get to the top?" and smugly answered, "They choose not to." Indeed, the *New York Times*, America's "paper of record," is so infatuated with the opt-out storyline that in 2006 one TV journalist described the supposed trend as "the *New York Times'* bizarre and suspiciously predetermined editorial effort to talk women out of working." The deluge of coverage prompted Joan Williams, Jessica Manvell, and Stephanie Bornstein, researchers with the Center for WorkLife Law at the University of California, to analyze 119 print news stories published from 1980 to 2006 on women who leave the workplace. The resulting study, "'Opt Out?' or Pushed Out?: How the Press Covers Work/Family Conflict," found that the opt-out storyline dominated coverage with an overwhelming focus on "psychological or biological 'pulls' that lure women back into traditional roles, rather than workplace 'pushes' that drive them out."

Meanwhile, Kelly Makino quietly re-entered the workforce shortly after becoming the poster mom for feminist housewives. She's since called the *New York* article — the same one that many commenters said accurately reflected their lives, or at least their fantasy lives — "Disneyfied" and "edited to fit an agenda." In an interview with OptIn, Makino remarked that having a job when her children were young was too expensive. After things like child care, dry cleaning, and take out, the profit margin on her $60,000 salary wasn't more than $18,000, or $1,500 per month. So home she went. Of course, it wasn't that easy, and she returned to work once her children were at school full time. She discovered, like many women, hurdles in the back-to-work path, including explaining the gap in her resumé to employers and a salary that, she said, will never recover. Why did she decide to re-enter the workforce? "I really psychologically needed to be in the workforce and at the office," she responded. A woman could want to be more than one thing! Who knew?

As the reigning queen of anti-feminism, Janet Bloomfield is emphatic that women don't *need* to be mothers, and mothers shouldn't be forced to stay at home. That's ludicrous; to her, anti-feminism is about empowering women to make their own choices. But she does believe that, if the stigma of feminism were erased, most women would *want* to stay at home and be mothers, just like most men would want to work. The worst thing feminism has done, she told me, is to sell women the lie of "having it all" without following through. That's because, according to her, it can't. She'd likely agree with Carrie Lukas, the managing director of the conservative-leaning Independent Women's Forum. In her book *The Politically Incorrect Guide to Women, Sex, and Feminism,* Lukas wrote: "Feminist groups like to pretend that women can have it all without sacrificing time with their families. This is false and most women know it." So: women + independence – family + work = ☹. The chain of logic here—if you want to call it that—is that feminism pushed women out of the house and into the workforce and women are not happy in the workforce, ergo it is feminism's fault that women are miserable.

Here's a sampling of what Bloomfield had to say about feminism and motherhood: "I don't want to be defined as a wholly independent person," she wrote in a May 2015 post defending the so-called "wife bonus"—a year-end chunk of cash given if a woman excels at performing her wifely duties. "I am a wife, a mother, a sister, a daughter, an aunt, a niece, a neighbor, a writer, a blogger, a citizen . . . Only feminists are foolish enough to believe that being free from all obligations and responsibilities towards others constitutes 'freedom.' It constitutes annihilation." In a post about stay-at-home mothers, she wrote: "Obviously that is the best possible gift a husband can give his wife: the opportunity to fulfill her most basic obligations as a mother." Similar sentiments to Lukas's and Bloomfield's are abundant, especially on the site Women Against Feminism. From one smiling young woman in a garden: "I don't need feminism because I don't want to be judged for my choices and hear that a career is more important than raising kids and making a man happy." Another young woman, with a penchant for capital letters, holds an adorable baby: "I Don't Need Feminism because…MY DAUGHTER IS A PRIVILEGE; NOT A CHOICE." And this woman with her cutie-pie kid: "I don't need feminism because being a stay-at-home mom is better than having someone else raise my child."

You get the point. If we're being simplistic, we might boil down the anti-feminist message to: Don't tell me to get out of the kitchen, woman! If we're being really dopey, we might even mutter something about Stockholm syndrome. I encourage us to think past both knee-jerk reactions. Much of what these women express (inflammatory as it may be) dovetails with wider ambivalence about the role of mothers and work. In 2014 the Pew Research Center reported that the number of stay-at-home mothers in the US had risen to 29 percent—a number that represented a soft rise over the past dozen years, after decades of decline. Roughly two-thirds of those 10.4 million women were women like Bloomfield: married moms with breadwinner husbands. "The recent turnaround," wrote the report's authors, "appears to be driven by a mix of demographic, economic and societal factors, including rising immigration as well as a downturn in women's labor force participation, and is set against a backdrop of continued public ambivalence about the impact of working mothers on young children." Essentially, we still can't seem to make up our minds about where women *belong*.

At nearly 80 percent, the vast majority of Americans — thankfully — say they reject the idea of women returning to traditional roles. Yet when you get down to the nitty-gritty of what that means in practice, their views don't always square. In another Pew report, nearly three-quarters of survey respondents said women's gains in the workplace made it harder to raise children; fully half said women at work made it harder for marriages to be successful; and, counterintuitively, more than a quarter said it made it *harder* for families to earn enough to live comfortably. Dig deeper, and you'll discover that though more than 70 percent of people believe a working mother can establish "just as warm and secure a relationship with her children" as one who stays home, more than half of the Pew respondents also believed children were better off if mothers, specifically, stayed home. Only 34 percent agreed children would fare as well with a working mother, though it's also worth mentioning almost 75 percent said it made no difference if fathers worked. So, no, we don't want women to go back to traditional roles, except for all the ways we kind of do. Talk about having it all.

Things aren't nearly as clear-cut as we'd like to believe. It's misleading to attribute the uptick in stay-at-home moms to simple choice — i.e., that moms are choosing to slot themselves into traditional family structures. The recession in 2008 contributed to a growing number of stay-at-home mothers (6 percent in 2012, compared to a scant 1 percent in 2000) who say they haven't *opted* out of the workforce; they can't find a job. Moreover, theorized Pew researchers, with incomes so stagnant for those who aren't college educated (the same women who make up the bulk of stay-at-home mothers), the cost of child care weighed against low wages likely factors heavily into the decision to stay home. In their report, "'Opt Out?' or Pushed Out?," the WorkLife Law authors noted that the predominant opt-out theme reassures everybody that nothing needs to change. "Perhaps the most damaging part of the Opt Out story-line is that it excuses gender discrimination under the rubric of 'choice,'" they wrote. "There is another story to be told, far different from that of educated women blithely 'choosing' to stay home: that women are not pulled out of the workforce by their biological need to care for their children but are often pushed out by maternal wall bias and discrimination against mothers at work."

Today, "full time" in professional and managerial jobs means working upward of fifty hours (and often more) a week. Such hours are not exactly conducive to being home for dinner, taking your sick kid to the doctor's office, or the multitude other demands of home and child care. Studies show a "two-person career" is required to succeed in such workplaces: the ability to have one spouse stay at home who can take care of every other aspect of life. Usually, that stay-at-home spouse is the wife. Yet careers among college-educated women — those most often painted as opting out — are often non-linear. Several studies have shown that highly educated women only take off 2.2 years, on average, to care for their children.

Unfortunately, that belies a more depressing reality, which is that a non-linear career path can often mean self-limiting opportunities — what the report's authors call trading in a good job for a bad one. According to Sylvia Ann Hewlett's report "The Hidden Brain Drain: Off-Ramps and On-Ramps in Women's Careers," published in the *Harvard Business Review*, nearly 40 percent of women said they took a job that had few responsibilities and a lower salary than they were qualified for so they could achieve a work-life balance. Hewlett, who is the co-director of the Women's Leadership Program at Columbia Business School, also found that 36 percent of women elected to shift to part-time work, 25 percent reduced their hours within their full-time jobs, and 16 percent declined promotions. Of the 93 percent of women who want to return to work after veering off the career ramp, less than three-quarters succeed, and much less than half of them return to full-time, mainstream jobs.

What's worse is that these opt-out stories largely feature white, affluent women with secure, high-powered jobs. They're a small slice of the demographic pie at 8 percent and an odd place from which to draw conclusions about an entire, diverse segment of the population. Consider also that women with higher education and thus more economic opportunity are actually more likely to *remain* in the workforce because they have the support. Entirely erased are the experiences of women of color, gay and transgender women, non-college-educated women, shift workers, single parents—and it goes on and on. Those in precarious jobs often cannot afford daycare at all, and many are one sick child away from being fired. When that happens, they are pushed out into untenable situations that may mimic the newly vaunted traditional family structures but are in no way desirable. How can we possibly begin to remodel our workplace policies if their stories remain silent?

Rather than signaling a total return to traditional values, the "'Opt Out?' or Pushed Out?" authors concluded that the decision to leave the workforce reflects "a clash between newly intensified ideals of motherhood and newly intensified ideals of a worker, all-or-nothing standards that have only taken shape in the past few decades." In other words, so long as work culture reflects an amped-up breadwinner model and mothers are pressured to "know best," women will find themselves pushed into their corresponding stay-at-home role, even if it doesn't quite fit. And while choice and the effects of workplace discrimination are not mutually exclusive, acknowledged the authors, one big problem remains: this complexity is not at all reflected in media. What emerges instead, argued Arielle Kuperberg and Pamela Stone, in their own 2008 study of opt-out coverage in the media, is a new kind of feminine mystique. "In this new mystique, as our results illustrate, the role of mother has displaced that of wife," they wrote, "and the decision to stay at home is distinguished from the old version by being couched in a discourse of choice and feminism."

We'll get to more on how discrimination at work operates, and how violently it's entrenched, in the next chapter, but here's what you need to know for now: research shows that this new framework of choice creates a vicious cycle in which discrimination against women at work is consistently underplayed and, therefore, maintained. In a 2011 paper published in *Psychological Science* called "Opting Out or Denying Discrimination?" researchers discovered that many of the women they interviewed favored a "choice framework" to describe their reasons for leaving the workforce. No surprise there. Slightly more disturbing: those who used the choice framework were also more likely to report increased personal well-being (good for them!) but less likely to recognize the structural barriers and discrimination that limit women's advancement at work (ugh). Mega disturbing: even a subtle exposure to choice narratives in the media increased respondents' belief that workplace equality is a done deal. To test this, researchers had respondents fill out a survey about "social issues" that included questions about women in the workplace. Each participant sat in a cubicle in which one of two mock posters advertised a book written about mothers who'd left the workforce. The images used in each poster were identical: a smiling mom seated at her work desk, laptop open in front of her, a phone in one hand, and her little munchkin in the other. One said: "Women at home: Women's experiences away from the workforce." The other: "Choosing to leave: Women's experiences away from the workforce."

Those who completed the survey in the cubicle with the latter poster were more likely to view a women's workplace departure as a choice, skipping right over the complex underpinnings of that decision. And if that's what happens after being exposed to one poster *for three minutes*, you can imagine how the deluge of opt-out media stories has influenced our collective thinking. (One exception to the second control group: women who identified as feminists were more likely to acknowledge workplace discrimination as a factor in opting out.)

The nostalgia narrative just keeps feeding itself, growing bigger and more powerful, defiantly blotting out the complicated diversity of women's experiences. As for the implications of this, researchers suggested that seeing women's interrupted careers as a personal, empowered choice, rather than one based on many underlying factors, could "prevent women from advocating for each other as they navigate their professional lives." Such biases, agreed the WorkLife Law researchers in their report, can often pit women against each other, ultimately giving the impression that working women with children, working women with no children, stay-at-home mothers, unemployed women and mothers, and even working women across job types and industries have no common goal.

What we're left with is a converging narrative in which both anti-feminists and post-feminists argue that feminism has done its job by securing women the "choice" to stay at home. To them, fighting for better treatment, more representation, and increased family-friendly policies in the workplace are tipping the scales too far the *other* way. Feminism is seen as turning women into men; as disparaging stay-at-home mothers; as forcing women into roles they don't necessarily want. Women see or experience firsthand the stress that comes from juggling work and life and blame feminism for putting them there. It doesn't help that modern feminism has largely chosen to address the stay-at-home issue by pretending it doesn't exist at all, pointing to studies that show there is no mass exodus of working mothers. "This response is convincing as far as it goes," wrote the "'Opt Out?' or Pushed Out?" authors, "but it overlooks the elephant in the room: the effect of children on women's employment may not have increased over time, but it is substantial." Substantial enough for some women to feel like staying at home is the best option—if not exactly their unencumbered choice.

We all stand to gain from addressing the complexities of family work-life balance. But anti-feminists and men's rights activists don't deal in complex; they deal in simple. The worst lie that anti-feminists have sold isn't that feminism has brainwashed women into wanting careers and spurning motherhood, though that one's still pretty bad. *Did ya hear? Feminists hate kids and their own mothers, too!* No, the worst lie—the one that hurts everybody, and the one that *New York* and the *New York Times* before it sold as a fantasy—is that staying at home is the simple solution that most women *want*, for which they are even biologically programmed. And the longer we believe and promote the narrative that most women all want the same thing, and in particular the thing they're most traditionally supposed to want, the harder it will be for us to gain the social and structural support to achieve whatever "having it all" means to us, whether it's at work, at home, or both.

In our collective imaginations, the 1950s are often painted as a bucolic wash of gingham dresses, carefully set hairdos, and baked-from-scratch brownies. The happiness of nuclear families is implied, if not entirely believable. "Contrary to popular opinion, *Leave It to Beaver* was not a documentary," historian Stephanie Coontz quipped in *The Way We Never Were: American Families and the Nostalgia Trap*, a book that was first published in 1992 and, tellingly, updated and rereleased in 2016. That year's vitriolic presidential election plucked at many modern-era hell-in-a-handbasket fears. On T-shirts, ball caps, hoodies, and buttons, Trump promised to "Make America Great Again" (in fact, Trump trademarked the phrase six days after Barack Obama won the 2012 presidential election). Trump implied, and sometimes even outright stated, that the golden time of "greatness" was in the 1950s—that time when, as Trump told the *New York Times* in March 2016, "we were not pushed around, we were respected by everybody, we had just won a war, we were pretty much doing what we had to do, yeah around that period." But, as Coontz warns, invoking this nostalgia is dangerous, and not in ways you might expect. Though critics of the nostalgic urge often nod to the restrictiveness of the 1950s Mommybot role, the problem runs deeper: we're extolling a lifestyle that never existed.

The resurgence of feminism in the 1960s is often blamed — or cheered — as the catalyst that ended the happy housewife but, in truth, women found the strict gender divisions suffocating long before women's libbers marched the streets. The idea of a successful nuclear family was often predicated on the wife's ability to be the nurturing organizational hub of the home. Contrary to the 1950s myth, however, many women did work, both because they wanted to and because a second income then, like now, was needed to buy the "extras" that every happy family was supposed to have: the suburban house, the car, and the TV. At the same time, women found their roles outside the house drastically, and forcibly, minimized. When women entered the workforce by the thousands during the war effort in the early 1940s, a full 95 percent of those who were undertaking their first jobs said they expected to quit at the end of the war. But, as Coontz notes in her book, that figure had nearly flipped by 1945, at which point almost an equal majority wanted to stay at work and not abandon their independence, responsibility, and income. Many of them did.

Well, they tried.

After WWII ended, and men resumed regular employment, management purged women from high-paying non-traditional jobs, essentially relegating them to the labor-force version of "women's work." And while two million more wives worked in 1952 than at peak wartime production, writes Coontz, those jobs were designed to encourage women to define themselves in terms of home and family. Think low-paying, low-responsibility work that mirrored their wifely expectations at home. The media called married working women a "disease" and a "menace." Say bye-bye to ambition, aspiration, and your own needs. "In consequence," writes Coontz, "no sooner was the ideal of the postwar family accepted than observers began to comment perplexedly on how discontented women seemed to end up in the very roles they supposedly desired most." Talk about immediate nostalgia. Historical research reveals the cracks showed in the nuclear family myth even as it was being created, but we just kept building. What's that, Bob? There's a crack as big as the Grand Canyon in the foundation? JUST CEMENT OVER IT! NOBODY WILL NOTICE!!!

Essentially, women gamely attempted to cement over their anxieties and fears. From 1958 to 1959, women's consumption of tranquilizer pills, colloquially known as "mother's little helpers," jumped to 1.15 million pounds from (a still astonishing) 462,000 pounds. A few years later, the Rolling Stones would riff on the concept in a song of the same name, ridiculing the widespread use of tranquilizers among housewives and, rather richly considering the messenger, warning of overdoses. Advertisements for the drugs themselves better revealed the clashing tensions between the expectations for a happy home and the realities for women. One ad for the popular drug Dexamyl, both an amphetamine and a barbiturate, showed a woman happily vacuuming in what appeared to be rays of sunshine. Just one capsule, it promised, provided day-long therapeutic effects. Vacuuming would become *transcendent*! Another showed a woman peacefully sewing but addressed the prescribing physician: "To help you transform a tense, irritable, depressed patient into a woman who is receptive to your counsel and adjusted to her environment." A third was more clear-cut: "To help the depressed and anxiety-ridden housewife who is surrounded by a monotonous routine of daily problems, disappointments, and responsibilities." "That's Dexamyl," a housewife might have said affectionately, "always helping!"

In her book *Modern Motherhood: An American History*, Jodi Vandenberg-Daves quotes from the diaries of a woman who had seven children between 1950 and 1960. Bright, lonely, and over-whelmed with guilt that she was "not a very good mother" because she "seem[ed] to put almost everything before her children," the woman went on Dexamyl in 1959. "Took a pill," she wrote, "and made the work fly." Even softer drugs like Anacin got in the game. In a 1968 ad, a woman looked vacantly off page over the words "Making beds, getting meals, acting as the family chauffeur—having to do the same dull, tiresome work day after day—is a mild form of torture." Right on, Anacin! But then: "These boring yet necessary tasks can bring on nervous tension, fatigue and what's now known as 'housewife headache.'" A pill would make women "feel better" and have "a brighter outlook." So just so we're clear: contemporary 1950s and '60s popular culture and mainstream media readily acknowledged the drudgery of the roles it expected women to perform. Its solution to these unachievable, misery-making expectations? *Drug the women.* It's enough to make me want to say, "Pass the Dexamyl, please."

It seemed that women couldn't win. Expert advice reminded mothers that the future of their children and the actual world depended on their ability to mother well and keep their families content. Bad mothers were blamed for a whole host of things, including communism, juvenile delinquency, homosexuality, men who raped women, anorexia, various mental illnesses (including schizophrenia), and even autism—the last of which spawned the term "refrigerator mothers." What made a bad mother? Everything, pretty much. For a role that was seemingly venerated as women's "natural" place, women were told a hell of a lot that they were getting it all wrong. Bad mothering, or "momism," as it was called, was attributed to both too much motherly love and too little. Betty Crocker, God of Cakes, help the woman if she spent too much time taking care of her kids at the expense of taking care of her husband, too. To make it more unachievable—because, of course, yes, it can get worse—women were also warned against being too wifely. In modern parlance: they shouldn't be so thirsty for it. *Playboy* warned men against gold-diggers and parasites. Revealingly, while 60 percent of women told a 1960 Gallup poll that they deemed their marriages happier than that of their parents, 90 percent of them also said they hoped their daughters' lives would be different than theirs.

Now their daughters want *their* lives. Or, more precisely, what they think their lives were. "We are tired of the moniker of 'housewife' being a derogatory word," writes Bethany Herwegh on her website, The Glamorous Housewife. "There is nothing wrong with taking pride in your family and home and it is high time we take this word back." Rules of her new definition include a woman who not only "takes pride in her role as the CEO of her household" but also "understands perfection is boring." Herwegh has credited feminism with giving her the choice to be a housewife (more on that in a minute) and said she was inspired to start her website (which now has several staff) after "letting herself go." Meanwhile, New England-based Holly Connors, the woman behind the blog *Modern Day '50s Housewife*, told me that she believes "parts of the feminist movement have hurt our society" and she wants women to know they can leave their careers to be mothers and housewives. Her goal is to re-teach the "lost art of being a family matriarch," and while her feelings on the f-word are mixed, she largely blames feminism for the supposedly tarnished view of housewives now, asserting that women had to rescue the term not only from the past but also from the backwater trenches of the women's movement.

I'd stumbled across Connors's blog while researching the "modern housewife" concept. While she didn't bill herself as an anti-feminist, the blog's rhetoric felt like a less profanity-laced, more buttoned-up cousin of Bloomfield's *JudgyBitch*. (Indeed, Connors told me her Facebook group is like "afternoon tea time," whereas Bloomfield's online community has more of a UFC cage match vibe.) On her manifesto page, Connors refers to an italicized "they" as the people who very nearly ruined her life by turning her into a successful career woman. To Connors, "they" included her teachers, school counselors, and "the women who came before me, who fought hard for equal rights and for the freedoms that I would never

have had if it weren't for them." All of them, she wrote in her manifesto, convinced her she couldn't be what she wanted to be: "an
amazing wife and a mother." At seventeen, when she became pregnant and gave birth to her daughter, they admonished her, telling
her to keep pushing forward with her career.

A list of other things Connors seemed to blame the catchall
"they" for: her first divorce, her failing second marriage, her long
hours and general unhappiness at work, her eventual dabbling
in drugs and drinking, and her thoughts of suicide. Only defying
supposed expectations, quitting her job, and becoming a housewife
fixed these things, she wrote. Elsewhere on her blog, she echoed
the philosophy of Laura Doyle's "surrendered wife" movement
(Doyle published a book of the same name in 2000): the idea that
to achieve marital bliss a woman must relinquish "control" of her
husband (i.e., stop nagging him) and also hand over decisions on
household finances, etc.

I needed to know more — and to also maybe barf a little bit, I
wasn't sure — and so I asked Connors how empowerment, feminism,
and being a housewife all fit together. "I am glad feminists exist and
have made my life as a woman easier, in some ways," she told me.
"The right to not be abused, for example, is huge. The right to say
no and not be raped by a husband is also huge. Those things and
other examples like them are all human rights that should have
always existed. They fought for them and for that I am appreciative.
And I appreciate the option to be able to choose to work outside of
my home. So, so, so important. Having rights is huge. Yes. But there
is also a part of me that still resents that feminism has changed the
world in many other ways. It used to be possible for a woman to
choose to stay home and be the one to raise her own children."

That's not possible now, she contended, largely because for many
people two-income households are now necessary, something, she
suggested, for which feminism is also at fault. For Connors and
others, like Bloomfield, this particular blame-it-on-feminism criticism

is built more on personal conviction and sworn-to anecdotes than it is on fact. The general lack of structural support for mothers, and more broadly speaking, women, points to definite discrimination. It seems counterintuitive to blame feminism—at least to me—but not to Connors. "For many, staying home is simply not an option and they are forced to have their children raised in daycare centers. That would never have happened before. Our country just wasn't programmed that way. In their attempt to help, [feminists] hurt. But what bothers me most is that they don't care. They look at women who want to be stay-at-home moms with disgust. How is that right? How does that jive with their fight for a right to pursue any path they choose? Why is my choice not okay?"

When I asked Connors how popular her blog is, she told me that when she's posting regularly, she gets between sixty thousand and eighty thousand hits every month. When she's not posting at all, it settles to twenty-five thousand hits per month. I'm not surprised. Her "Back off, judgy pants" views are common among many of the women I spoke to who are ambivalent about feminism, or outright hostile. She resents women who question her decision and often tells others that her husband "rules the roost." Things would be better, she added, if feminists stopped speaking out for all women and went on their merry way.

Ah, the power of nostalgia. Coontz told me that she has sympathy for those who yearn for their cherry-picked versions of the past. The same year *The Way We Never Were* debuted, US vice president Dan Quayle made national headlines when he slammed fictional character Murphy Brown's single parent lifestyle: "It doesn't help matters when primetime TV has Murphy Brown, a character who supposedly epitomizes today's intelligent and highly paid professional woman, mocking the importance of fathers by bearing a child alone and calling it just another lifestyle choice." Media soon styled Coontz as something of an anti-Quayle. "I spent the next year doing two or three radio interviews a day. It was just wild," she told me. "And I learned something in a hurry on those talk shows. The show would start and the interviewer would ask me, 'Should we go back to the 1950s?'" And Coontz would tell the interviewer no and list everything that was wrong back then. Inevitably, she would then field callers who would berate her for not knowing anything. So she sat down and listened to the tapes, and she soon realized that people must have thought she was discounting their pain, that her mind knew better than their hearts. Basically, they thought she was a snob.

She changed her tactic and began opening her interviews with a story in which her mother tore a strip off a librarian for refusing to loan a young Coontz *Of Mice and Men*, ending with, "You let my daughter check out anything she wants!" But in 1992 would Coontz herself have said that if her son wanted to check out anything at the video store? No way. So yes, some things about the 1950s she missed, too. Yet if you weren't one of the few who benefitted from that time, turning back the clock was a very bad idea indeed. "I'm more sympathetic than I used to be to what makes people pick and choose something from the past that they think they can hang on to," she told me not too long after Trump won the 2016 election. "They actually do miss it, but they often forget that if you actually went back to that, you'd have to take the whole package deal, much of which they've rejected." She now believes that our modern era's mid-century nostalgia—the sentiment that Trump capitalized on in his election win—is as much a critique of the present as it is a romanticization of the past. But here's the bottom line: "It's a dangerous critique that leads us into thinking that we can recapture the past"—and then trying to do just that.

Like Coontz, I sympathize with these women who yearn for supposedly simpler times. But it's worth mentioning here that extensive studies have shown that *working* women today spend as much time in interactive child care—activities like reading to their children, helping with homework, and playing—as did the housewives of yesteryear, and today's modern housewives are not necessarily happy.

Marriage and family therapist Celeste Catania-Opris gave her practice the tongue-in-cheek name Therapy for the Modern Housewives of South Florida. Her clients don't actually describe themselves as modern housewives, she notes, but "they'll come in and say, 'Sometimes, I feel like it's all on me. I have to do this. I have to do that.' They'll discuss the issues without saying, 'I'm a modern housewife.' But I think the name appeals to them. It resonates." Shortly after Catania-Opris got married, her best friend asked her, "What do you plan to do with your life now?" When Catania-Opris responded that she might have children—although she wasn't sure—her friend responded with disgust, "You're going to be a housewife." At the time, she heard a lot of disparaging remarks about housewives, including from the women themselves. It was the "just-a" syndrome, as in: I'm just a mom, I'm just a housewife. "Meanwhile," said Catania-Opris, "the jobs and the responsibilities of a modern housewife are to do it all."

To her, a modern housewife is a mother who, whether she works outside the home or not, is caught in all the expectations of what she thinks she's supposed to be. She feels guilty all the damn time. Because she feeds her daughter Cheetos. Because her son isn't enrolled in enough extracurricular activities. Because. Because. Because. "I would define a modern housewife as someone who puts everyone else's needs in front of herself. Your kids' needs, your spouse's needs, and then you put yourself at the end," she told me. "Pressure is the key word in all of this. There's so much pressure. And to live up to that standard." Many of her clients, she added, come in depressed, anxious, and feeling inadequate. They think they're the only ones. She validates those feelings. Yes, it is hard to work forty hours a week and come home to take care of your children. Yes, leaving your career to take care of your children can cause mixed feelings. Yes, it can feel lonely to be a stay-at-home mother. Once those feelings are normalized, she said, a lot of the anxiety can float away.

But one thing Catania-Opris said completely freaked me out.

When I asked her if she had clients who had left the workforce, even though they loved their jobs, because they were conflicted about child care duties, she answered with an emphatic yes. "One of my recent clients said to me, 'I worked so many years. And I'm not saying I don't love my husband. I'm not saying I don't love my children.' But she said, 'What's my purpose? What am I supposed to do?'" The woman felt terrible for admitting her doubts, added Catania-Opris. Guilt gnawed at her, and she admitted that she'd never, not once, expressed those feelings out loud before. "She went to college. She worked very hard for so many years. Then she gave it up. She *sacrificed*. It's a sacrifice that a lot of women make, and they sacrifice themselves as well." Surely, women with children must have better options than to feel like they're sacrificing their identities, throwing pieces of their internal selves overboard like flotsam and jetsam. No wonder so many of us feel like we're adrift.

The idea of "having it all" can seem elusive. As I write this, I'm thirty-two and part of the nearly 50 percent of women in my age range who are childless. I am still woefully unsure whether I even want children. But I would be lying if I said I'd never thought about it: my internal pendulum swings to *yes* every time I see a friend's chubby-cheeked child, and then back to *no* when I visualize that month's deadlines and work obligations, which together are basically a fragile and always teetering tower. I'm afraid having a child would knock down that tower. Game Over. My point is that I'm anxious about doing motherhood right and I'm not even a mom. So I understand why many women want an easy guarantee. But blaming feminism for mucking it up obscures the real challenges with past family values and roles. Namely, that they *never* worked. The simple truth is that we can't all do it all. If we wholesale embrace our fictional version of the past, we also embrace its very real problems, and we're already busy struggling with *that* legacy.

Let me just say it here, so we can move on: I'm not in favor of anything that demonizes or undervalues women. Period. What worries me is the concept that feminism ends with the supposed choice to not work. *Hooray! Thank you, Feminism, and happy retirement! Bring out the balloons and streamers! Make them pink because we can!* Look, I appreciate that feminism is getting some ostensibly good vibes here, but let's not kid ourselves (groan): this is its own brand of nostalgia, one that recalibrates the decision to opt out of the workforce as an empowering one and, also, feminism's ultimate end goal. Yet feminists who fought for motherhood rights in the 1960s and '70s didn't ignore the constraints under which many women made those choices, and neither should we. It's not a matter of pitting women's experiences against each other—that forever recycled "good mom" versus "bad mom" battle. It's a matter of reimagining gender roles and the family in a way that makes things better for everybody. But how on earth are we supposed to do that if we think feminism has already won, or, worse, that it's gone too far?

Let's pause for a moment and discuss that awful, ubiquitous phrase "having it all." Though the term is tethered to feminism, we can actually thank former *Cosmopolitan* editor Helen Gurley Brown for this particular devil (and for teaching us so many ways to please our man!). The term first appeared as a marketing pitch at the tail end of the 1970s, and then in 1980 in the title of a book that offered practical advice on managing a home and a career. But Brown's 1982 book *Having It All: Love, Success, Sex, Money, Even if You're Starting with Nothing,* and its prominent spot on the *New York Times* bestseller list, spat the phrase into the popular culture and the pages of aspirational women's magazines. "There is, then, no small absurdity in the fact that Brown's vision omitted children," wrote Jennifer Szalai in a 2015 *New York Times* article about the term's origins. It's not that Brown didn't care about children; it's that she had none. Szalai also noted that Brown also detested her book's title, pleading with the publisher to name it something that didn't make the author sound like "a smartass all-the-time winner from the beginning." (So maybe thank Brown for *that* effort instead.) Yet both the term and title have stuck. Conservatives have deliberately morphed "having it all" into a weapon to undermine those who step too far outside traditional roles and who advocate too loudly.

In fact, feminists who fought in the 1960s and '70s wanted to improve *all* women's lives. Second-wave feminists who rebelled against their socially mandated roles chanted "There are no individual solutions!" when they marched in the streets. Even Betty Friedan, the co-founder of the National Organization for Women who wrote in *The Feminine Mystique* about the "problem with no name," wanted *better* treatment for housewives, not to abolish the role, as many anti-feminists claimed (and claim). That infamous quote from Simone de Beauvoir is the product of some serious tension between her and Friedan. In the introduction to their 1975 interview, Friedan wrote that she wanted a conversation with someone "older, wiser" about her "fears that the women's movement was coming to a dead end." She spoke with de Beauvoir in Paris, through interpreters, in a salon decorated with a cluttered "Bohemian elegance": tapestries, porcelain cats, shawls, statues, pillows, pictures, and memorabilia of de Beauvoir's travels all over the world. Her idol was more prim than Friedan had imagined.

Later, Friedan cautioned against meeting your heroes. "The comforts of the family, the decoration of one's own home, fashion, marriage, motherhood—all these are women's enemy, [de Beauvoir] says," Friedan wrote retrospectively. "It is not even a question of giving women a choice—anything that encourages them to want to be mothers or gives them that choice is wrong. The family must be abolished, she says with absolute authority. How then will we perpetuate the human race? There are too many people already, she says. Am I supposed to take this seriously?" It's clear the two did not agree much on anything. Consider the exchange that prompted de Beauvoir's oft-recycled quote:

FRIEDAN: But don't you think that as long as women are going to do work in the home, especially when there are little children, the work should be valued at something?

DE BEAUVOIR: Why women? That's the question! Should one consider that the women are doomed to stay at home?

FRIEDAN: I don't think they should have to. The children should be the equal responsibility of both parents—and of society—but today a great many women have worked only in the home when their children were growing up, and this work has *not been valued* at even the minimum wage for purposes of social security, pensions, and division of property. There could be a voucher system which a woman who chooses to continue her profession or her education and have little children could use to pay for child care. But if she chooses to take care of her own children full time, she would earn the money herself.

Not exactly the stuff of feminist conspiracy, especially when you keep in mind that Friedan's views guided the movement in America. Ruth Rosen, a feminist historian and journalist, tackled the rewriting of "having it all" in her 2012 essay "Who Said 'We Could Have It All?'" Not feminists, she argued. "The belief that you could become a superwoman became a journalistic trope in the 1970s and has never vanished. By 1980, most women's (self-help) magazines turned a feminist into a Superwoman, hair flying as she rushed around, an attaché case in one arm, a baby in the other. The Superwoman could have it all, but only if she did it all. And that was exactly what feminists had not wanted," she wrote. "Millions of women cannot afford to care for the children they have, work dead-end jobs, and cannot begin to imagine living the life of a superwoman. These are the women that the radical women's liberation movement addressed and for whom they sought decent jobs, sustainable wages, and government training, social services and child care. These are the women who are stuck on the sticky floor, not held back by a glass ceiling."

We love to look at high-achieving women, those modern Superwomen, and ask, *If she can't keep her shit together, who can?* The backdown-the-ladder-and-into-the-kitchen conversation is so much *sexier*. Take Anne-Marie Slaughter, the first woman director of policy planning at the US State Department. Her 2012 *Atlantic* essay, "Why Women Still Can't Have it All," detailed her decision to leave government because of, as she put it, "my desire to be with my family and my conclusion that juggling high-level government work with the needs of two teenage boys was not possible." It quickly became one of the *Atlantic*'s most read articles, ever, racking up close to three million hits online and spawning reaction pieces across the internet. Though Slaughter was arguing for better support and social policy, some interpreted her message as, *Ladies, don't even try to have both a time-consuming job and children. Marie Claire* even asked Slaughter's former boss, Hillary Clinton, what she thought about the article, and her response caused a mild uproar: "Some women are not comfortable working at the pace and intensity you have to work at in these jobs . . . Other women don't break a sweat"—an upper-echelon conversation if ever there was one. But in her later book, *Unfinished Business*, Slaughter acknowledged the need to expand the conversation—a distinctly less grabby headline. *Let's all band together for equality? Pffft. Too much work.*

But radically changing the way we view domestic and employed work helps everybody, including men and other people who are not mothers. The way mothers and fathers spend their average week has drastically changed since the 1960s, according to the 2013 Pew

Center study "Modern Parenthood," an analysis of data from the American Time Use Survey that focused on how couples with children under eighteen spend their time. Though neither mothers nor fathers have surpassed each other in the so-called traditional realms, mothers now spend twenty-one hours, on average, working outside the home (as compared to eight hours in 1965), and fathers now spend seventeen hours a week engaged in housework and child care (compared to a scant 6.5 hours in 1965). What's more, a Council on Contemporary Families (CCF) 2015 report discovered that, before children, working men and women who cohabitate share household responsibilities equally while also working roughly the same hours each week (men worked three hours more).

After the birth of a child, however, during the critical transition to parenthood (before babies reach twelve months), women added twenty-two hours of child care to their work week while doing the same amount of housework and paid work as they did before, extending their total workload from fifty-six to seventy-seven hours each week. Men added fourteen hours of child care to their work week but did less housework, extending their workload to sixty-nine hours each week, a disparity that, researchers warned, could lead some women to leave the labor force. If they do, the scale could tip even more: men's work hours tend to rise once women stay home, and 90 percent of men who end up working fifty hours or more report they wish they could work less. About 50 percent of both working men and women say they have a difficult time juggling work-life balance, and nearly half of fathers worry they don't spend enough time with their children.

Interestingly, and contrary to what you might guess, childless single men and women do not report spending equal amounts of time on housework. Single women sans children spend twice as much time cooking, cleaning, and doing laundry than do kiddie-free single men. Clearly, such women are not beholden to men; I'm not sure that was ever the right argument. It's our own unshakable interpretations of what femininity means that has trapped us, held in check with a force-fed steady diet of mass media and anti-feminist sentiment. In her briefing for the CCF explaining the complexities of interpreting changing household patterns, Liana Sayer wrote of all the single ladies who were not up in the club but at home doing laundry. "It underscores the ways that 'doing gender' structures identities, as well as interactional dynamics in couples, social norms about femininity and masculinity, and institutions," she wrote. "In other words, some of the differences in men's and women's household activities may not stem from unfair interpersonal power dynamics but from entrenched individual and cultural beliefs about 'essential' qualities of being a woman versus being a man."

You don't have to be a feminist to see how breaking down those gender norms might benefit all of us. But it probably helps.

❧

Kate Reddy is a married finance executive with two young children. She loves her job, even if it means she's still awake at three AM, making to-do lists in her head; her daughter is resentful and won't hug her when she returns from a business trip; and her two-year-old son's first words were (of course!) "Bye-bye, Mama"; even if she's judged by her in-laws, her bosses, and the stay-at-home mothers who, presumably, spend six hours at the gym every day and are "perfect." If this sounds like a clumsy Hollywood take on our fretful obsession over modern work-life balance, well, that's because it is. Based on the novel of the same name, 2011's *I Don't Know How She Does It* stars Sarah Jessica Parker trying to check off all the boxes of "having it all." A quick glance at Rotten Tomatoes reveals the flick was universally panned, with critics and audiences both giving it two thumbs way, way down. People hated it both for having a "feminist" agenda and for its "hopelessly outdated viewpoint on gender."

Having dug deep into the research, though, I had to wonder if both were wrong. Despite its hokey Hollywood makeover, a high-powered career woman in a rigidly traditional workplace, being unable to successfully juggle all her work-home obligations (and desires!) seemed pretty spot-on. It was the movie's treatment of Kate that bothered me. In the end, she demands a more flexible work schedule and is immediately granted it, which is truly the stuff of Disney fairy tales, and then she runs through the newly falling snow to meet her husband at her daughter's school, interrupting a conversation about how she's never there, to apologize profusely for her work schedule. "I know I drive you crazy," she says. "I am so sorry about everything." The movie ends with her hubby promising to do a little more, but not before we get a very *Sex and the City* monologue, in which Kate tells us "somehow, some way, some day things have to change" (heavy-handed, but eff yes, they sure do, Kate!) and also "trying to be a man is a waste of a woman." (Noooo, Kate! Abort! Abort! Step away from the stereotypes!)

In an especially ill-considered form of self-torture, that same night I also watched 2016's *Bad Moms*. In this one, the exhausted, do-it-all protagonist, Amy, has put so much pressure on herself to be a good mom that she's cracking. Indeed, one 2012 Families and Work Institute Study showed that (non-fictional) women are often stressed for time because they have unrealistic expectations of how much they can get done in a day and feel squeamish about delegating. The predictable plot includes an outrageous battle for the PTA presidency, a self-correcting narrative when Amy goes too far into "selfish" territory (her kids angrily abandon her to stay with their childish father), and, given that, a slightly contradictory lesson at the end that affirms mothers should loosen up on all the judgy judginess and cut themselves, and each other, some slack—but not too much. "Moms don't quit!" one of Amy's friends tells her at a low point. "Quitting's for dads!" another retorts. Excuse me if I don't laugh as this retrograde joke further undermines any progressive messaging the movie hoped to project.

Here's the thing: *Bad Moms* was the first R-rated movie that year to gross more than $100 million in North America (it came out at the end of July). Motherhood and how to do it right is what media likes to call an "evergreen" topic, a story that can keep getting recycled and recycled and never becomes stale. The right-wing and anti-feminist movements may not have convinced North Americans that women belong at home (yet), but they have made considerable headway in framing the conversation as one that pinpoints women's expanding rights and roles as the center of the contemporary work-life dilemma. For decades, we've played on women's anxieties, gamely latching on to whatever answer requires we do nothing to break structural inequality or rewire the workplace. *Moms want to stay at home! They're happier that way! Dads like to work! They're happier that way! Everybody, SMILE!*

It's like we're swimming in a big bowl of rhetorical Jell-O, weighed down by sticky and false narratives, unable to get anywhere. And this is only one half of the story. If women are being *pushed* out of the workforce, what else is doing the pushing?

6 One at the top, five million at the bottom: How we sold ourselves the equal-opportunity lie and grew the violent push to keep women out of the workforce

Eron Gjoni was a twenty-four-year-old blogger and gamer when, in August 2014, he decided to air whole baskets of relationship dirty laundry on the internet. It stunk. Gjoni posted the chronicle of his entire relationship with indie game developer Zoe Quinn, whose crime was apparently having the audacity to cheat on him (allegedly). He meticulously detailed his perceived wrongs on a website he created entirely for the purpose of bizarrely bashing her. Gjoni accused Quinn of sleeping her way to good reviews for her game, *Depression Quest*, which explored mental health. Quinn, he alleged, set back the cause of women in gaming. Gamergate (GG) was born.

The internet army (gamers on Reddit, tech blogs, 4chan, and other gaming sites) rallied against Quinn. They doxxed her, publishing her personal contact information, including her address and phone number, to spur harassment. They hacked her computers and sent naked pictures of her to her dad. They called her with threats of rape and death. And they blamed her for all of it, saying what they were doing was all in the name of good journalism. GGers claimed that exchanging sex for favorable reviews was endemic in the video game journalism beat and yet another reason for male gamers to hang the "No Girls Allowed" sign on the big boss door. It was later proven that none of the men Quinn was accused of having sex with in return for good reviews had, in fact, even reviewed her game, but GGers tended to ignore that.

As Gamergate gained momentum, it continued to hide behind its "ethics in journalism" mandate. Its members repeatedly and uniformly derided feminists and anyone else who spoke out against it while at the same time denying it hated, or harmed, women, a claim easily disproved by anyone who possessed even the most rudimentary Google search skills. Basic facts didn't matter; messaging did. Again and again, proponents claimed they just wanted women to stop sleeping their way up the industry, to stop being supposed PR shills, to "respect themselves." None of that was anti-woman, according to Gamergate proponents, who universally blamed feminists for the movement's violent reputation. Feminists were misrepresenting and diluting their message, GGers claimed, *but that wasn't what it was about, man.* Some men in the technology industry promoted the harmful message, including one Montreal-based Ubisoft game developer who tweeted regularly in support of Gamergate, a move that its members call refreshing: "I find it *very* clear that Gamergate is not a hate group. That's a lazy smear tactic and an obvious lie."

It's worth mentioning, too, that like many anti-feminists, Alison Tieman and Karen Straughan are proud GGers. In 2015, for instance, the Calgary Expo kicked out both women, along with the other members of the Honey Badger Brigade, because the group promoted Gamergate at its booth. On their fundraising campaign page, which crowdsourced nearly $10,000 to send the Badgers to the expo, the women explained their "stealth" mission. "As men's issues advocates and defenders of a creator's rights to create unmolested, [this is] what we have to say to the nerds and geeks and gamers," they wrote. "You are fantastic as you are, carry on." In other words, *Feminists, stop whining!* Once at the expo, the Honey Badgers hung a huge "Stand against censorship" banner depicting a group of animated honey badgers waving a flag with the GG logo and the word "ethics." In response to getting the boot, the Honey Badgers sued the expo and the website Mary Sue, which covered the incident, claiming discrimination. (For a movement that decries feminism as a bunch of whiners…well, pot meet kettle.) Super-duper-conservative news website Breitbart covered the incident, and everyone from Christina Hoff Sommers to Milo Yiannopoulos, the originator of "feminism is cancer," tweeted support. (Yiannopoulos has since suffered a spectacular fall from right-wing grace; conservatives had no problem with his racism and misogyny but drew a line when he endorsed sexual relationships between adult males and adolescent boys.) In the end, the Honey Badgers raised $30,000 to support their lawsuit, hiring disbarred Ontario lawyer Harry Kopyto. They claim to be going to trial in November 2017.

At the time of the expo, I was editor of *This Magazine*, one of Canada's oldest independent, politically progressive publications. We published a feminist call-to-action issue, saying "F*@K THAT!" — right on the cover — to all the women-centered BS we were witnessing. Among many articles, we published an essay in which the writer questioned the real cost of the hyper-misogynistic social media harassment campaign to get women off social media, off the internet, away from video games, out of the tech industry, and also, preferably, raped and/or killed. Within hours of the piece going live, our website crashed. Rumors circulated that Gamergate had done it, but we could never confirm it. The essay's writer sent me an email saying she was "getting massacred" online for daring to argue it was impossible to know how many girls and women GG's harassment campaign had forced out of tech: surely the number must be unfathomably large. Our harassers called us, well, harassers. They said we'd lied, that we'd besmirched their reputations by saying what they'd done was terrible. They'd only been telling the truth, they countered: women didn't belong in technology. Our writer received the first threat. Incensed Gamergate supporters published her home address, along with her number, to teach her a lesson to never, ever speak out again.

In the months that followed Gamergate's rise, many women who decried the movement were doxxed and physically threatened. One developer, Brianna Wu, was forced to leave her home and go into hiding. She received her first death threat in October 2014 after venting about sexism in video games in her weekly podcast: "You cannot have thirty years of portraying women as bimbos, sex objects, second bananas, cleavage-y eye candy. Eventually it normalizes this treatment of women." The tweet in response: "Guess what bitch? I now know where you live." It was followed by another that revealed her home address. "Your mutilated corpse will be on the front page of *Jezebel* tomorrow." Wu and her husband fled their home that night, crashing on friends' couches and in hotels for a month, never feeling safe. In the following year, she received another one hundred death threats. They still roll in with regularity.

When Wu later wrote on a feminist website that Ohio's attorney general wasn't seriously responding to a subsequent phone threat to "slit her throat," he released a public rebuttal, saying the attention her story garnered "wasted time and resources" at his office. He wasn't the only one who dismissed the threats. A number of high-profile Hollywood stars, university academics, and CEOs of big-name tech companies spoke out in support of Gamergate, calling the threatened women liars and attention grabbers who wrongly skewed the movement's message (whatever it was). If that message had been misrepresented, however, the one to women and girls was clear: *The tech industry is not for you.* Also: *Shut up.*

It's tempting to dismiss those who believe in Gamergate as few and kooky, even if they seem like a maelstrom online. I mean, one of the men who threatened us online wore a pirate hat. It's equally tempting to say that what happens online doesn't touch people beyond the internet, that whatever hate is spewed on social media is trapped and contained, like the pit of a peach. Moments like the one we experienced at *This* show that's not true: the whole fruit is rotten.

Though women (including women of color and LGBTQ-identified women) at all types of work across all industries face discrimination and violence in the labor force, I chose to open with Gamergate because it is the most explicit example. This is an especially dismal thought when you consider, also, that the STEM fields are at the forefront of our modern economy. The threatening campaign of harassment, violence, and silencing is not only real but entrenched in the technology world, especially in video games. It existed long before Gamergate and, unless we do something about it, will persist long after.

Take Brenda Bailey Gershkovitch, who as a kid spent all her babysitting money at the arcade. Together with a crowd of boys and girls, she played Centipede, Asteroids, Pac-Man, even "stupid Ms. Pac-Man." She received her first rape threat in 2010 when she and her co-founder announced the launch of their Vancouver-based studio, Silicon Sisters, which designs video games specifically for girls and women. Its first game, *School 26*, is a worldwide bestseller, with more than one million downloads in thirty-six countries.

Gershkovitch told me the trolls focused on her simply because she wanted to build games for girls. It's not something she likes talking about. She said she didn't show anyone the threats, opting for the "don't feed the trolls" approach. Such an approach is, essentially, a grown-up version of the same advice parents have, for decades, given bullied children: ignore them, and they'll get bored of picking on you. The other approach, in which you invite the trolls over for a big buffet, fulfills the fantasy of every bullied child on that same playground: fight back. The latter option is the one our *This* writer chose, and also the same one many prominent feminists and other Gamergate targets have picked. It's grueling, exhausting, and can consume your days. It can come with IRL consequences, as one *This* reader from the US told us: "I have enjoyed my own bouts of being called a whore, a bigot, and all sorts of other names simply for expressing the view that video games could stand to evolve beyond the old, tired, sexist tropes currently so prevalent." She added that she often tried to protect other women, including her daughter, from Gamergate attacks. In return, they hacked her computer.

In other words, as any bullied child will tell you, both approaches suck. If someone wants to make your life miserable, they will. Gamergaters seem to have nothing but time, patience, and perseverance in their campaign to rid the tech world of feminists and, by extension, women. Gershkovitch may have taken the "soldier on" approach, but she knew the stakes. She was careful to add she has tremendous respect for the women who've spoken out against the onslaught of Gamergate, in particular Anita Sarkeesian, a feminist video game critic who runs the popular YouTube channel Feminist Frequency, where she dissects how women are portrayed in video games. In 2012, long before Gamergate was coined, anti-feminists targeted Sarkeesian for running a successful Kickstarter campaign to fund her then-new "Tropes vs. Women in Video Games" series. She'd since become their Public Enemy No. 1. "I'm going to send her a huge fruit basket," Gershkovitch told me, not quite joking, "to say that the shit that you're taking is for all of us and I appreciate it."

Sarkeesian fled her home that fall, too, as did Zoe Quinn. Sarkeesian was forced to cancel her talk at Utah State University after a deluge of threats. Among them was one from a writer who claimed to be a student at the university and threatened a mass shooting if Sarkeesian's talk went ahead: "I will write my manifesto in her spilled blood, and you will bear witness to what feminist lies and poison have done to the men of America." It wasn't the first death threat Sarkeesian had received, but it was the first time she canceled an event as a result. This time, she said, she wasn't confident police and the university had done enough to secure her safety. Utah is a concealed-carry state, meaning those with a gun permit are legally allowed to conceal their weapons. While the university hired extra security and promised to do a bomb sweep, it refused to install metal detectors or ban guns on campus. People had rights, after all. GGers later called the threat a hoax that feminists blew out of proportion, but it's hard to see how you can reasonably laugh off death threats. (*Law & Order* later turned Quinn, Wu, and Sarkeesian into a composite character and aired an episode that mirrored their collective ordeal.)

Let's pause for a moment here and let this all sink in: Sarkeesian and those like her were all feminists in gaming who vocally argued that women in the technology and gaming industry deserved to be treated better—and for that, Gamergate decided, they deserved to die.

Sarkeesian and Quinn both later revealed they had folders on their computers called "The ones we lost." In them were digital records of all the girls who'd written to them saying they were too afraid to become game developers now; some of those girls were as young as twelve. The restrictive culture had suffocated them out. We have no idea how many girls and women Gamergate has scared away. It's too soon to know. What we *do* know is that the industry can't afford to lose more women; the numbers are already depressingly low. The knowledge that Gamergate and the man-is-might culture it celebrated were succeeding in whittling that number down even further is almost too terrible to confront.

Women who speak out against the tech world have been taking that shit for a long time. In March 2013, Adria Richards, a developer evangelist for email delivery firm SendGrid, tweet-shamed two men sitting behind her at PyCon, the largest annual gathering for techies who use and develop Python, a computer programming language used by organizations such as Google and NASA to write code. While a woman presenter was speaking, the two men had made jokes about "big dongles" and "forking" (technology terms used out of context, in this case, to refer to male genitalia and sex, respectively) in direct violation of the conference's code of conduct. As the woman speaker thanked the event's sponsors, the men apparently giggled: "You can thank me; you can thank me." Presumably, they meant with a sexual act, though I don't want to guess which one they'd like "thank you" to have been.

Richards said: "I realized I had to do something or [that girl] would never have the chance to learn and love programming because the ass clowns behind me would make it impossible for her to do so," she later said. She publicly called out their conversation, took a photo of the two, and tweeted it using the expo's hashtag. She then tweeted at staff, asking them to do something about the men, and sent another tweet with a link to the conference's code of conduct. Shortly after, organizers escorted the men out. One was later fired, and the male technosphere unleashed its fury on Richards, posting both death and rape threats on Twitter and Hacker News, a respected industry discussion forum. 4chan users also targeted SendGrid with a DDoS (distributed denial of service) attack, shutting down the company's website in a baldly stated mission to "ruin her [Richards'] life." In response, SendGrid fired her. As a developer evangelist, it was her job to help the company achieve a critical mass of users for its product, and SendGrid said the controversy prevented her from being effective in her role.

In his 2015 book, *So You've Been Publicly Shamed*, journalist Jon Ronson interviewed Richards and one of the men who'd been fired—one who'd managed to keep his name secret. When Ronson asked the man what lessons he'd learned from the shaming, the man responded that he's less friendly and more distant with female developers. When Ronson asked him to give an example of how he talks to female colleagues, however, the man replied: "We don't have any female developers at the place I'm working at now. So." He'd found a new job almost immediately. At the time Ronson interviewed her, Richards was still unemployed.

The tech industry is littered with stories like these, ants all swept under the rug. Yet when Gamergate blew up the internet, much of the media talked about it as if it was the start of sexism and misogyny in the sector, imagining, perhaps, that everything before this was hunky-dory. That wasn't quite true, but it *was* the big reveal—like the *Wizard of Oz*, except in reverse. Instead of finding out a harmless old man was running the show, women discovered it was indeed Oz, the great and terrible. We've been plunged into a horrific Technicolor dream, so surreal we don't want to quite believe it's real.

In many ways, Gamergate has become a catch-all term for the rampant misogyny against women in technology. As it metastasizes, it's become many things: a great, malignant series of events; a movement of people who believe feminism is ruining video games and technology; a vicious campaign against any woman it deems responsible for said plunge into hell; and, also, arguably a place where casual hate against women is not just legitimized but watered and tended, like a garden. If you're like me, it's also a nightmare, a glimpse into a sadly probable future, one in which few little girls will learn how to code or make video games or even spend their afternoons like I did, cross-legged, glued to the TV, fingers finely dusted with neon-orange Doritos powder, trying to beat the big dungeon boss.

No matter how Gamergate started, or how it's grown, I fear this is what it wants: to build an impossibly high rampart that keeps women and girls out. But technology is not a unique bastion of workforce sexism. The boys' clubs have planted their ugly tree houses and hung their "no girls!" signs in any number of industries, albeit not as violently. Women are vastly underrepresented and underpaid in media (especially among opinion columnists and in sports journalism), Hollywood (on screen and behind the scenes), engineering, industrial design, manufacturing (where the gender gap has drastically widened since the 1990s), and too many more. That means, in case you've blessedly forgotten, that a very narrow segment of the population controls and makes just about everything we use and consume, including our gadgets, apps, gear, cars, buildings, movies, TV, books, newspapers, magazines—et cetera on into infinity.

Unsurprisingly, depressingly, it's been proven that men target

men in talent hunts and men talk to men when showcasing exper-
tise. In 2013, a US study revealed that, for the first two months of
the year, only 19 percent of newspaper stories quoted women. That
statistic is not uncommon. *New York Times* reporters are four times
more likely to interview a dude. Women consistently account for less
than 30 percent of speaking roles in Hollywood. No wonder: we also
comprise only 7 percent of directors. We could, all of us, in every
living-wage job or high-paying industry, have "ones we lost" folders.
Everywhere we turn, women are being silenced, shut out, emphatically and implicitly told to go away. Well, let me repeat: Fuck that.
If those of us who've been pushed out ever want to be more than
squatters in a man's world, we need to acknowledge our dismal sur-
roundings, do a feminist Miley Cyrus "Wrecking Ball," and then get
to building our own awesome shit.

Of all the many social trends that are emblematic of women's
inequality in the workplace, none is as longstanding or as starkly
evident as the wage gap, and, thus, none has been so consistently
attacked and dismissed. It's so battered that, in September 2016,
during the height of the presidential PR war in the US, the Institute
for Women's Policy Research (IWPR) released a tip sheet titled "Five
Ways to Win an Argument About the Gender Wage Gap." The 79.6
annual wage ratio figure in the US, the sheet acknowledged, is often
derided as "misleading, a myth, or, worst of all, a lie." (Canada's
wage gap ratio is actually slightly worse at 72 cents, down from
74.4 in 2009, giving it the seventh highest gap out of the thirty-
four countries in the Organization for Economic Co-operation and
Development.) The IWPR authors contended, however, that the naysayers were often disastrously simplifying a complex figure, usually
explaining it away as a woman's "choice" to work in lower-paying
jobs or her "choice" to leave the labor force once she had children
(sarcastic air quotes are totally mine and 100 percent intended).
In reality, a plethora of research has shown that underlying factors

are far more complicated, ranging from discrimination in pay, re-cruitment, job assignment, and promotion, and—yes, sure—lower earnings in traditionally women-centered occupations, as well as women's disproportionate share of the family-care pie. (Why can't we ever get a larger share of, say, the lemon meringue pie? Wouldn't that be nice and also delicious?) But that doesn't make it a lie, argued the authors, and what's more, the very reasons it can be ex-plained away—those listed above—are precisely the reason we can't fall into the mythical-thinking trap.

The myths IWPR countered in its tip sheet made regular appear-ances in my interviews with anti-feminists: that women choose to work in crappy jobs; that the most commonly used wage gap statistic doesn't take account of differences in job sectors or hours worked; or (as we tackled in the previous chapter) that women just don't want to work. It's true that some industries and occupations don't re-flect the annual earnings wage gap. Some are even worse. In the US, women physicians and surgeons earn 62 percent of what men earn; financial managers earn 67 percent, despite making up a larger per-cent of the job sector; chief executives earn 70 percent, and make up only one-quarter of that particular high-earning, high-power slice; and, even in jobs such as retail (sales) and housekeeping/ janitorial (supervisors), the number hovers at 70 percent. In oc-cupations where women's earnings are close to on par with men's, including maid/housekeeping positions, food preparation workers, office clerks, and even bus drivers, certain glum caveats remain. Those women a) also tend to comprise the majority of workers; or b) the jobs tend to be especially low-earning and precarious; and c) any higher earnings reflect successful collective bargaining among unions, making those jobs the exception, not the rule. Sometimes, there's even option d) a nasty combination of the above factors and other less easily identifiable ones.

What's more, studies are now showing that the gap is already evident one year after college or university graduation, and it only continues to grow over the course of a woman's lifetime. Call me morbid, but it makes me picture the wage gap as a big skull with a gaping maw. In 2012 the American Association of University Women (AAUW) released a study called "Graduating to a Pay Gap" that examined this grim trend. It discovered that one year after graduation, women were already earning just 82 percent of what their male peers earned. That number shrank after the study—perhaps anticipating ant-feminist outcry—controlled for hours worked, occupation, the former student's major, and their current employment sector. But it didn't disappear. Women teachers earned 89 percent of what men earned. In sales occupations, the gap sat at 77 percent. And among business majors, women earned just over $38,000 in their first year's salary, while men earned a tad more than $45,000. Women tended to also dedicate a higher share of their salary toward paying off student debt. "The pay gap has been part of the workplace for so long," wrote AAUW authors, "that it has become simply normal." But it doesn't have to be.

In the previous chapter, I challenged the opt-out myth, arguing that, in many cases, evidence shows that the phrase "push out" might be a more accurate one. But just how bad is the so-called motherhood penalty? In her research work on the wage gap, Claudia Goldin, the Henry Lee Professor of Economics at Harvard University, discovered that the opt-out penalty can differ greatly by occupation. Among those who took an eighteen-month hiatus in employment over the course of fifteen years, women with MBAs experienced a 41 percent earnings decrease, women PhDs experienced a 29 percent wage decrease, and those with MDs saw a 15 percent drop. Goldin's work also showed that MBAs tended to take more time off, largely because their jobs prohibited them from working more flexible schedules. As a result, they opted out entirely.

In subsequent research, Goldin also discovered that women with high-earning spouses tend to have lower labor force participation rates. And if you think women fare better once their children are no longer infants—a logical assumption given the time demands post stork drop-off—think again: the impact of birth on a woman's workforce participation only grows over time. High-earning jobs, particularly in our always-connected modern world, tend to reward long and continuous work hours. Such hours are not often tenable for women who are expected to take on the primary caretaker role. "A flexible schedule," noted Goldin, "often comes at a high price, particularly in the corporate, financial, and legal worlds." That price can be even higher, however, for employees in fields in which a missed work day or an inability to meet a rigid schedule won't just result in a lost promotion but very possibly a lost job. Many of these women don't have a higher-earning spouse to fall back on, either because they're single parents or because their partners tend to be in just as much of a jam as they are. To get an idea of just how much family can affect work and how reticent employers are to enact policies that might retain employees, we can examine the Athena-sized jump of Family Responsibilities Discrimination (FRD) cases in the US.

As the name suggests, FRD cases are those that are filed based on discrimination against employees because of their family obligations, whether that's pregnancy, motherhood, fatherhood, or even caring for a family member. Over the past decade, such cases have risen 269 percent; employees have won 67 percent of those cases, and employers have forked over half a billion dollars in settlement fees. Cases that involve pregnancy are the most common FRD claim. Some of these cases, as reported in WorkLife Law's 2016 report "Caregivers in the Workplace," can involve subtle discrimination: women, for example, who are denied professional development opportunities because supervisors see them as less committed or more unreliable after they have children, or supervisors who believe mothers *should* be home with their kids and give new mothers less challenging assignments, later telling them they can't advance because they aren't ready.

Discrimination can also be blatant. Here's a small sampling of the 4,400 cases the WorkLife Law report surveyed. In one case, after a front-desk worker took time off to care for her sick daughter, a supervisor allegedly asked her, "How can you guarantee me that two weeks from now your daughter is not going to be sick again? So what is it: your job or your daughter?" In another, a woman who was called into work on scant notice received a text from a supervisor that read, in part, "Look Melissa you have a child whom is medically disabled you do not belong in the workplace or in my clinic…! Go home [and] stay with your daughter—that's where you belong, not here." A pregnant part-time grocery store worker provided a doctor's note informing her supervisor she couldn't lift more than fifteen pounds and was terminated in response. A pregnant woman security guard, diagnosed with anemia, asked for permission to wear a second coat and was fired. In still another case, a woman was passed over for a promotion and was told it was because she already "had a full-time job at home with her children." And it just goes on and on.

It's important to remember, too, that any solutions must take into account women's various work experiences and their various lived experiences. Just as we must not default to white, middle-class, able-bodied, straight women when we're discussing the challenges, we can't default to them while we're discussing the solutions either. The near 80 percent gap that's often quoted is a better representation of white women's earnings relative to white men's. As discussed in previous chapters, that number shifts dramatically when we consider race and other factors that can influence employment and employment opportunity. "The solutions that you come up with will depend on what you diagnose as the problem," Chandra Childers, a senior research associate with IWPR, told me. "And if you don't understand the specific circumstances of each group of women, and even differences within those groups, that's really going to influence what you think the problems are and then what you think the solutions are." Still, some universal things could help.

Canada and the US have the most expensive child care in the world, sharing the top three spots with Ireland. (Hi, Ireland!

Welcome to our sad club!) In thirty-three states in the US, the annual in-state college tuition costs less than full-time child care for a four-year-old. In Massachusetts, for example, the annual cost of infant care is $17,062; annual tuition is $10,702. Infant care is also 15 percent more than average rent and takes up nearly 20 percent of an average family's income. A minimum-wage worker would need to work 43 full-time weeks to pay for one year of care. And that's just for one child. No wonder most can't afford it.

In Canada, Toronto is the most expensive city for daycare, at a median of $1,649 per month for infants and $1,150 per month for preschoolers. Vancouver and Calgary aren't far behind. Indeed, the only province where parents fare well is Quebec, where the government subsidizes care; in Montreal the median monthly cost is just $164. And though Quebec's system isn't perfect—wait lists are long and spots don't necessarily go to the families that need them most—it isn't hard to imagine how big a difference affordable child care could make. That's particularly true for women who are more likely to be the parent who leaves the labor force to care for children. Women's lower earnings are often used to justify moves like these, putting women in a vicious cycle.

Stronger maternity and paternity leave polices, particularly in the US, would also go a long way in guaranteeing that women on-ramp easily back into the workforce. Think of it as collectively helping them train for the sprint and the marathon. And the hurdles. Hell, everything. Raising the minimum wage would certainly help, especially the tipped minimum wage in the US, which sits at a terrifying $2.13. More laws allowing transparency when it comes to wages will also help. They would allow women to see just how persistent their wage gap is and to use the information to better bargain. Women and girls can be encouraged to enter traditionally male-dominated fields. Even negotiation training can be rethought so it doesn't implicitly reinforce the idea that women are simply the pits at bargaining, and if they could negotiate better the gap would disappear. Neither are true. "What I worry about is sending the message that if women just negotiated, that would make the gender gap go away," Hannah Riley Bowles, a senior lecturer in public policy at Harvard Kennedy School, told me. "And that's just not an okay message." Her pioneering research has shown that women aren't just imagining things when they perceive they'll be treated more negatively than a man for attempting to negotiate. Employers like their women to fall into stereotypes: to be team players, to be selfless, to not ask about money. Never mind that her research also shows at-home negotiations — the division of domestic labor and child care — also factors into a woman's ability to negotiate shrewdly and successfully at work.

This is where it gets really sticky: determining how much those gender expectations hamper a woman's success in the workplace. Even if we enacted more policies and actually followed them this time (ahem, pay equity legislation), even if we untangled the thicket of reasons for the wage gap and gender disparity in the workforce, how much would plain discrimination still stand in the way? A January 2016 National Bureau of Economic Research working paper found that "unexplained factors" accounted for 38 percent of the wage gap. That is, even once you establish control variables — differences in jobs, experience, and hours worked, for example — the gap remains. These "unexplained factors" are usually attributed, in large part, to discrimination, a shadowy thing that no control group can eliminate. Combine these challenges with the blatant discrimination women can experience in the STEM fields and you have a real-time case study of what happens when an industry has a thousand ways, both subtle and overt, to let women know the workforce is a difficult place for them to thrive.

Then again, if you're an anti-feminist, widespread workplace discrimination is feminist make-believe and none of this is true. As we saw in the last chapter, the anti-feminist movement largely tends to breeze past the complexity of women at work, capitalizing on the anxieties and impossibilities of work-life balance to present an answer that is seductively simpler: women don't want to work, or, at least, *most* women don't want to work, especially in male-dominated fields. Let's remember what Karen Straughan told me when I asked her why she thought feminism was restrictive and prescriptive when it came to the ways in which it told women they could behave: *How far are you willing to push people to do things that they otherwise would not do?* The anti-feminist world view dictates that feminism is making women feel guilty for not studying physics, or engineering, or other male-heavy post-secondary fields. Feminism is also designed to make men feel awful, said Straughan, for even being in an engineering class, because, according to feminism (apparently), they are actively and meanly pushing women out. While most feminists would likely agree that it's worth examining learning environments and diversity as well as the roadblocks women, people of color, and those who are LGBTQ-identified must hurdle over to reach those classrooms (or else land smack facedown on the pavement), I haven't yet heard any say men don't belong in them at all. Advocating to open the door wider surely disrupts the status quo and challenges "the way it's always been," but it doesn't close the door on men. Neither does the push to examine and dismantle existing workplace conditions, culture, structures, and supports (or rather, more accurately in most cases, the lack of support).

Yet Straughan didn't seem to put much stock into the idea of an old boys' club either, suggesting both that it doesn't really exist and that, if it does, it's the natural pecking order. "If *she's* happier studying to be a psychologist than she would be studying physics, then why are we making her feel guilty for not studying physics? Or making her feel like a failure to the [feminist] cause?" Straughan asked. "And why are we making *him* feel guilty for being in an engineering program? Why are we saying, 'There aren't enough women there. What are you horrible men doing to keep women out?'" This sort of argument provides a convenient loophole: it doesn't dictate what women must do, but preaches acceptance of what a woman is naturally inclined to do. It also removes systemic barriers and reduces everything to (unfettered) personal decisions. Straughan once told me she doesn't like feminists because she can't imagine them ever doing rough-and-tumble stuff, like climbing trees, so I doubt she adheres to the traditional idea that a woman must be dainty and sweet. But like other anti-feminists, she strongly believes if a woman wanted to do something, she'd do it, period.

Anti-feminists are fond of accusing any feminist who criticizes structural barriers of "damseling," a derisive term that is particularly popular when it comes to discussing labor equity challenges. While talking about workforce discrimination, for instance, Alison Tieman once told me that "presenting narratives of female victimhood inclines women to see the world not in terms of what they can do but in terms of what is done to them." If we really want women to fulfill their potential, she adds, society should encourage them to view the world in terms of not how they're acted upon but how they act upon it. This can-do message that anti-feminists consistently return to celebrates women who have *toughed it out* while simultaneously condemning to their sad fates those who haven't been able to do the same. Of course, they likely wouldn't put it that way. They'd call it choice, and a *natural* one at that. Then they'd not-so-kindly ask feminists to stop making shit up, to stop making such a fuss, to stop calling out sexist work culture, and to just let everybody do what they do best: namely, the same sorts of things they're always supposed to have done.

Because they're such a funny bunch, anti-feminists also like to claim that labor laws and the workplaces they govern have skewed too heavily *in favor* of women. A lot of really bad men's rights editorial-style cartoons, for instance, lament affirmative action and claim that women have lighter workloads, better work-life balance (ha!), and more flexible work days. Women are also apparently blessed with lower expectations and easier performance evaluations from superiors and are less likely to be injured on the job, which is true but (whoa!) *context matters*: women are underrepresented in industries, such as construction, that have high workplace injury rates.

This particular anti-feminist crowd likes to troll social media for prime "But, men!" opportunities. Toronto restaurateur, feminist, writer, and all around badass Jen Agg provides an example of this in her 2017 book *I Hear She's a Real Bitch* (a nod to the kind of sexist BS any women with strong opinions faces in male-dominated industries, like the restaurant biz). When the *Toronto Star* ran an exposé on the truly disgusting sexual harassment one woman pastry chef faced on the job at a Toronto restaurant, including having her breasts grabbed and her rear violently smacked with a metal flipper, Agg started tweeting about breaking the culture of silence and later spearheaded a one-day conference called "Kitchen Bitches: Smashing the Patriarchy One Plate at a Time." In response she received tweets that asked her whether she believed young men also had a hard time in kitchens. Agg agreed it was true that it was an "industry-wide" culture problem that needed to change "from the top down." So then she got tweets like: "[Jen Agg] thinks abuses women suffer in the kitchen is more important than the more common male abuse." Typical.

By capitalizing on women's anxieties about doing/having/being it all and simultaneously crafting these neat little pretzel knots of logic, anti-feminists have helped strengthen the silence. Many women wholeheartedly believe the narrative that they must not rock the boat or that they can rise up the corporate ladder if they just focus on their success. It's a palatable enough lie to swallow. Few of the women I approached to talk about their experiences in the technology field wanted to draw attention to themselves. Few agreed to speak right away. And when they did, many of them brushed off their sexist experiences or spoke of them in hushed, but-it-could-have-been-my-fault-actually voices. After one office tour, I stood incredulous as my guides, two women who'd co-founded an innovative environmental app for businesses, told me the tech industry had no problem with their gender. They munched on wasabi-covered crunchy peas from the communal kitchen in their shared office as I looked out onto the warehouse-style floor. Of all the dozens of tech companies in the space, theirs was the only one with female staff. In our fifteen-minute tour, I saw more foosball tables than women. But still, they told me emphatically, it's no big deal. I grew to expect the accusing look and admonition. Stories that highlight discrimination and harassment, these women told me, don't make it easier for them — as if I'd conjured up the sexism on my own. Over dinner, Janet Bloomfield did, of course, accuse me of that exact thing and asked me, quite pointedly, if I was a "stupid bitch."

It was like these women had all read the same self-help book. I imagined it was called something like *How to Move Past Violent Misogyny in the Technology Industry*, or even *Nine Habits of Highly Effective People in Denial.* As much as it frustrated me, I understood. Some women just want to work, not be Xena, Warrior Princess, defender of women who like computers (or math, or finance). But it's dangerous to push the sexist tech culture to the back of the closet, like an old Super Nintendo. Dismissing such a damaging culture is too much like buying into the post-feminist lie, like saying, "We are beyond all that. Women can make it if they want to, if they really try, but only if they stop whining." If only it were that simple. If we ignore the sausage party, we'll simply be served a different menu.

The tech industry is, in fact, unkind to many women. Claims of a sexist, fratty culture have followed Uber for years, finally coming under a particularly harsh spotlight when Susan Fowler, a high-profile engineer, detailed her year at the company on her blog. In addition to charting a drastic drop in the number of women at the company (from 25 percent down to 6 percent in under a year), Fowler wrote about some truly jaw-dropping treatment of women.

For example, she says the HR department ignored numerous complaints of sexual harassment and discrimination. In most cases, HR staff said the men in question were too important for the company to discipline and appeared to blame Fowler for making a fuss. When she pointed out how few women were site reliability engineers (SREs), like herself, she was again shrugged off—by a woman HR rep. "She [countered] with a story about how sometimes certain people of certain genders and ethnic backgrounds were better suited for some jobs than others," wrote Fowler on her blog, "so I shouldn't be surprised by the gender ratios in engineering." Sound familiar? Fowler quit shortly after. When she left, the number of women SREs had dropped to 3 percent. This was also around the same time that Uber's CEO, Travis Kalanic, joined Trump's economic advisory council. More than two hundred thousand people reportedly joined the #DeleteUber movement in protest, and Kalanic quickly resigned the advisory council position. Uber has denied it has a misogynistic culture and pledged to investigate.

"Technology is becoming less and less hospitable for women," Brenda Bailey Gershkovitch told me during our interview at the height of Gamergate. I'd spoken to her and other women for a *Flare* magazine article on the harassment and discrimination of women in technology. The piece was assigned before Gamergate, but I eventually switched focus to cover the newest "get out" campaign focused on women in the tech industry. Gershkovitch reminded me that discrimination was present in the industry long before GG boiled over, too. Looking at the harassment online, in her life, and in the industry itself, she added, "This is the version of us being in the house in the 1950s." She was right, of course, but women weren't being told just to get back inside the proverbial house. They were told to spend the twenty-first century's economic boom forcefully stuck in their homes, safely making Bundt cakes (or whatever) while men got to remake the world. Sure, some women, like Gershkovitch herself, aren't stuck in a millennium version of Pleasantville, but they are woefully few. If anything, the handful of women at the top, like

Yahoo CEO Marissa Meyer, Facebook COO Sheryl Sandberg, and YouTube's Susan Wojcicki, have fooled us into thinking this means women are everywhere.

Across Canadian universities, only 39 percent of technology, engineering, math, and computer science grads are women, and men overwhelmingly land jobs at the top tech firms. In 2014, only twenty-four of the Canadian companies included in Deloitte's list of the fifty fastest growing technology firms had women in their executive ranks. Only two of those included CEOs, and only six listed women as founders or co-founders, a coveted title in technology that can help lead to a chain of bigger and better start-ups. Even though the head of Twitter Canada, Kirstine Stewart, is a woman, women make up only 10 percent of Twitter's tech staff, 15 percent of Facebook's, and 18 percent of Google's. At the time I spoke to Stewart for the feature article in *Flare* magazine about women in technology, she was busy penning her answer to Sandberg's bestseller corporate feminist call-to-action, *Lean In: Women, Work, and the Will to Lead.* She acknowledged tech's culture was a problem of a chicken-and-egg nature. "But I think you can't change that culture unless there's more of you," Stewart said. "We need to make sure there's more of us." Stewart's book, released in 2015, is called *Our Turn.*

I liked her optimism, but is it our turn? I was first drawn to this question in June 2014, during what I thought would be the most controversial no-thanks-don't-want-any-women-in-tech scandal of the year (thanks, Gamergate; how wrong I was). At the end of that month, Whitney Wolfe, the twenty-four-year-old former Tinder vice president of marketing, filed a sexual harassment and discrimination suit against the popular dating app company. Her case was rife with allegations of sexual harassment on the part of Tinder chief marketing officer Justin Mateen, who was Wolfe's boss and also her ex-boyfriend (they dated for only a few months before Wolfe broke it off). She alleged the company stripped her of her co-founder title in November 2013, claiming having a "girl" co-founder devalued Tinder and "[made] the company look like it was an accident"—presumably meaning no tech start-up would dare have a female co-founder on purpose. (And, indeed, at that time women had founded only 3 percent of tech start-ups in Silicon Valley.)

Screen captures of dozens of disturbing text messages sent during work hours show Mateen's increasingly possessive and demeaning post-breakup behavior toward Wolfe. He sent especially vitriolic texts after he saw her talking to other men. Wolfe repeatedly asked Mateen to stop threatening and harassing her; he did not. Instead, his campaign against Wolfe allegedly culminated at an April 2014 company event in Malibu, at which, in front of CEO Sean Rad, he called her a "whore," a "gold digger," "a disease," and "disgusting." Humiliated, Wolfe headed toward the exit, where one of Rad's guests spat on her. Rad soon sent her a text reading, "Your employment continuing is not likely an option at this point." Wolfe felt bullied into resigning shortly after.

For many working women, and not just those in the tech industry, news of the Tinder scandal landed like a punch in the gut. A trio of Toronto women in the advertising and marketing field were especially livid and felt compelled to do something. Together, Shauna Roe, Rachel Kennedy, and Monica Remba, in the heat of a furious discussion on how a dating company could fail to recognize the value of women, landed on a brilliant idea: What if the women of Tinder just left? How would the company survive? Would Tinder realize it needed women? The three launched a Tinder boycott campaign, in which they called upon women to replace their Tinder profile pictures with a giant X. The campaign, dubbed "Swipe Strike," went live less than a week later but failed to connect with women of the Tinderverse (where active displays of feminism did not, often, equal successful hook-ups). "We were so rattled," Kennedy told me shortly after the launch. "Is it really that bad [out] there? In this day and age, is it really that bad?"

Stuff like this made me feel like it would never be our turn, but I was eager for someone to prove me wrong and to answer Kennedy's question. In search of that answer, I turned to Martha

Ladly, a professor at OCAD University in Ontario, whose PhD in the philosophy of technology focused on the ways women do — and don't—occupy spaces in technology. (Ladly was also one of the Marthas in the late 1970s Canadian New Wave band Martha and the Muffins, whose single "Echo Beach" won her a Juno.) We spoke in 2014, during the height of Gamergate. Ladly told me that, while hard data did not exist, she'd heard anecdotal evidence that the representation of women in tech was improving, but slowly. Without proof—indeed with most data showing the opposite—this struck me as wishful thinking. Either way, we both agreed one big caveat should keep women from feeling self-congratulatory: being a little bit better than our start of near nothing still wasn't anywhere close to something.

Ladly recounted one recent experience in which she'd volunteered to do an outreach program at the Lassonde School of Engineering at York University in Ontario. It was geared toward kids and teens interested in entering the engineering and technology fields. The workshop, said Ladly, was packed, and yet only two of those in the room were girls. After the workshop, as Ladly wandered through the university's halls, she noticed that the higher-level classes suffered from the same ratio: mostly men, with so few women they may as well have been playing hide-and-seek. Those that were in the room, she added, were usually at the back. She saw no women professors. Describing the experience to me seemed to make her baffled and angry all over again. "We have to make it more attractive for girls to go into these fields," she said. "Somehow we've got to figure out how to do that."

Two years later, it seemed we hadn't. In September 2016, Suzanne Stein, an associate professor and director of the Super Ordinary Lab at OCAD University, and Prateeksha Singh, a graduate research assistant at the lab, published an article in the *Globe and Mail*. They revealed that women's representation in the tech field was actually better in the 1980s. So much for progress. Stein, borrowing a phrase from mathematician and design theorist Horst Rittel, called it the "wicked problem." The particular wicked problem in the technology industry, she and Singh wrote, was that despite numerous insights and proposals for change, no significant change occurred. Or in other words, as Stein put it to me later, "It's this big hairy whole idea, and there is no solution." The problem with sexism and society, she said, is that it's so deeply ingrained it manifests itself in numerous ways, so how do you tackle an infinitely headed hydra?

Take, for instance, the surprise connection she found between her research into the tech industry and her other, separate project looking at domestic abuse. She discovered many shocking and undeniable parallels. Rules of engagement within both realms condone the disrespect toward, and bad treatment of, women. Compare the two, and the power and control wielded by abuser and co-worker or supervisor become mirrors. And that's just one disturbing observation among many. "Many of us have stopped talking about solutions and started talking about interventions," Stein added, "because there's no one answer."

Stein has a throaty laugh. It burst forth often during our conversation, when she seemed to find something funny or ridiculous, or even, it felt like to me, as a ward against some darker, dismal truths. She laughed now. "I think some of the reluctance to embrace feminism," she said, "is that once you open that door, everything comes out of it." This is not to say that feminism can't be fun as well. As part of their research project, Stein and her team developed several games to help with solution building to increase diversity in tech. One of those games, the *Feminist Theorist Card Game*, encourages women to embrace the pluralities of feminism and to problem solve though different theoretical lenses. Another game is *Ceiling and Ladders*. The idea with these games, Stein told me, is to encourage brainstorming, reduce finger-pointing, and take the high stakes out of crafting solutions. Stein called it the "magic circle of gameplay."

Through these actions and many others, feminists try to tackle the wicked problem, though, of course, it's tricky. Women in the field can't seem to agree on how to make it better. We step carefully because of the many minefields. Women are wary of rocking the boat, of not being team players, of others targeting us, of losing our "cool girl" status, of further pigeonholing ourselves. To that last point, Martha Ladly told me that women are often still viewed as assets because they're supposedly more emotionally intelligent than men, or are better communicators. Not enough hard science backs up these widely held assumptions, she added, and what science exists is mostly of the junk variety: poorly executed studies that, in the end, show no causality (woman + company = more feelings!). Besides, Ladly quipped, "I don't want to be the one that has to wear the emotional-intelligence hat."

As she spoke, I wondered what a feminist hat would look like. A 3D vagina? An abstract pink triangle? A 1990s ankh? Sparkles? I feared no matter what it looked like, nobody would wear it. The anti-women faction in the tech industry was winning because it had eroded feminism. We could see similar effects in other industries. The new message was that feminism would *hurt* women, not help them. If women wanted to participate peacefully in these male-dominated industries, particularly the tech world—if they didn't, in other words, want to face death threats, rape threats, or have a loogie hawked on them at a party—they had to abandon the f-word. They could be bro-ish, and they could be nice, and maybe they could even feel like they could belong, if only they weren't feminists. That was the deal.

Except it's a lie. After months talking to women in the technology field and beyond, I learned it doesn't matter what they call themselves, they are still on the other side of the castle wall, and sometimes those inside even catapult rocks at them. We have to acknowledge all the multitudes of challenges if we want to work toward solving them. I desperately want women to succeed, but it seems impossible if we continue to characterize Gamergate as anything but a full-scale, far-reaching, and coordinated attack on women; if we go on pretending the wage gap doesn't exist and workplace policy doesn't harm us; if we continue to accept and even celebrate the opt-out narrative; if women continue to remain silent about their experiences (both good and bad) and be satisfied with the few who speak out; if we inadvertently feed the false belief that sexism in the industry affects only an unfortunate minority; and if we continue to follow the post-feminist narrative that just because some have made it, all will make it.

We have so many reasons to fear speaking out, but if we don't I am more afraid our future daughters will have even fewer good career choices than their grandmothers and great-grandmothers. It will never be our turn; we will be left behind—again.

And this (un)merry-go-round cycle of history repeating doesn't apply only to women at work.

7 It's your fault: How anti-feminists narrowed the definition of rape and revived the deadly, viral culture of slut shaming and victim blaming

From age sixteen to now, the night I was raped has played on a loop inside my head. I must have thought about it a million times, and never when I wanted. It's an intrusion that doesn't end, sometimes lurid and Technicolor bright, other times like I'm watching a scene behind a thousand panes of stained glass. It all depends on how much I allow myself to remember, how much I can't forget.

I can tell you I said no. I can tell you I struggled. I can tell you the rough carpet rubbed a burn against my bare back. I can tell you that we were underneath his parents' pool table; it felt like a cave with only a few feet between the floor and the table's stained underside. I can tell you there was a condom, purple and grape flavored: a latex slime that made me gag. I can tell you that it didn't last very long, that my kicking feet and my screams freed me, made him afraid his parents would hear. I can tell you that I ran, but he grabbed me tight before I could reach the stairs. *Don't tell. You're overreacting. You wanted it. Just calm down. I love you. Just. Don't. Tell.*

The next day at school, he followed me through the halls, wherever I went: "I popped your cherry." At my locker he whispered in my ear, leaning close: "Slut." When I told him to stop he called me a bitch. Pushed me up against the locker, hands on my throat until his friend saw. *We're just goofing around.* This was my friend, a boy I trusted, but also, I see now, an obsessive, controlling seventeen-year-old with duck feet and spiked hair held up with Elmer's white glue.

With all the irony that high school can muster, that was also the year I took Dr. Porter's gender studies class, which included a unit on rape, assault, and violence against women. And so, just a few weeks after my own rape, I sat in class, suddenly panicking as Dr. Porter was trying hard to break through our teenage apathy. "These are serious issues," he boomed. Though he was an older man with a proclivity for turtlenecks, his lecturing method was vigorously cinematic. Often, when he wanted to make a point, he'd pace the rows between our desks like a drill sergeant, first wrenching off his oversized glasses and then using them to jab and gesture wildly.

He did so that day, on cue, as he shared the new-to-me statistic that one in six North American women past age fourteen have been raped or have had someone try to rape them. "Look to your left! Look to your right!" he shouted, glasses pointing. "Look around you! There is a chance that someone in this room—someone you know—could be that woman." As over-gelled and hair-sprayed heads turned left and right, my eyes dropped to my open binder. The rapist's campaign of shame had worked. I hadn't told anyone what happened, not even my best friend, Jen, sitting beside me.

I wanted to whisper to her, "It's true. That's me. It happened to me." But I couldn't. I may as well have been playing Chubby Bunny, that camp game we liked as kids, the one where you stuffed marshmallow after marshmallow into your mouth until you couldn't speak anymore and you lost. I was filled with shame, silent and sweaty, rooted to my seat, bargaining internally with any deity that might listen. *Don't cry,* I pleaded with my brain, as if it were a switchboard separate from my body, which, ever since my rape, was exactly how I felt. I could only think that if I cried now people would notice. I wasn't ready for my rape to stop being a secret.

As Porter droned on, saying who knows what, my mortification

ebbed. I could only identify the feeling years later, after surgery
for a badly broken leg. It felt like it did when an intravenous line
was hooked into the crook of my elbow, the first pump of saline
and morphine that turned from a pinpoint drip to a full-body flush
as it moved like a current through my veins. It felt like that, but
in reverse, drawn out instead of in—like what happens on those
survival shows, when musclemen suck poison out of snakebites.
Maybe it was like that. Out went shame and in came a slowly brewing
rage. One in six? One in six?! Over and over. I was just a kid; I had
no idea the number was so high. If you'd asked me before, I would
have estimated the statistic closer to one in six hundred, maybe
more. For those past weeks, I'd been convinced I was the only person
in the entire school whose crush had done what mine had done.
Certainly, I told myself, I didn't know anybody who'd been raped.
But one in six? I started tallying all the women I knew on a blank
page. I suddenly didn't feel so alone. It wasn't a relief.

After the rape my nighttime prayers and dreams turned to death.
I wanted to die. It took a long time not to feel that way.

Whenever I watch or read news stories of high school rape now,
I think I was lucky. Lucky to have been raped before the internet
or Twitter or Facebook or Instagram. Lucky that my story didn't go
viral. Lucky I didn't have to play out the "it's-your-fault-you-slut" or
the "she's-making-it-up-for-attention" or the "but-he-is-such-a-nice-
guy" narrative in front of the whole school, city, country. There's
never been a good time for a woman to be raped (what a stupidly
obvious sentence), but I didn't believe fifteen years ago that it could
get worse. That my own fears—Was it rape if it was my friend? Was
it my fault? Would anyone believe me?—would become mainstream
conversation, as if they were plucked from my chest and thrown up
on the world's largest jumbotron. I couldn't have guessed that a culture that told my sixteen-year-old self I was right to be afraid would
drown out decades of anti-rape activism.

So hush, now. Don't tell.

Society's attitudes toward rape haven't changed much in the past, oh, thousand years or so. Imagine a young unmarried woman of modest means in the 1200s. She lives with her parents and siblings on the outskirts of London, population eighteen thousand. Let's call her Alice. So here's Alice, minding her own business, strolling down the street, or milking cows, or thinking about that delightfully handsome assistant at the baker's shop — what have you. Alice is a wearing a fluted lapis-colored hat and a sack-like robe tied around her waist with rope. It isn't revealing by any standards, if that matters, which it does seem to for every lawmaker from Alice's time to ours. And then, in the darkest of dark moments, Alice is raped. Let's not dwell on the details; we know it was horrible.

Back then, Alice didn't have much recourse. If she were raped in the early 1200s and was a virgin, the rapist had to pay her father some cash and then marry her. If she were ten or younger, Alice would benefit from a small blessing: the concept of statutory rape existed and applied to very small children. Alice would not be helped any time after her eleventh birthday, however; any female over that age, the men in charge of making the law reasoned, should be able to fight off her attacker. Laws changed for the (slightly) better in the mid to late 1200s. A raped virgin like Alice could charge her rapist. She also had to tell everyone in her hometown, plus the surrounding towns, that she was raped and show them "the blood and her clothing stained with blood, and the torn garments" immediately after her rape; otherwise, it didn't count. If her rapist maintained his innocence, four women would examine Alice; they could, apparently, read her vagina like tea leaves to tell if she'd lied. Pity her if they decided she was: her rapist would be released, but Alice would be taken into custody.

If her rapist were found guilty, he would be dismembered. Alice could choose to save him, if she wished, by marrying him. If Alice was not a virgin, her rapist's punishment was far less severe. The law decreed rape was not equally detrimental to all women. Rape wasn't viewed as an assault on women and their bodies so much as an assault on their worth as sexual property. Raping a virgin was akin to ruining a Beverly Hills mansion. Raping a "known prostitute" was equated to breaking a window in an already dumpy cottage. If a woman didn't struggle adequately or became pregnant, it wasn't considered rape, an idea that has persisted through the centuries, surfacing again and again in rape trials.

Let's jump to today. These attitudes have only cemented over time, urged on by the internet, Hollywood, pop culture, sports, and, basically, every modern thing. Yet things aren't totally bleak, thanks largely to feminists who have fought back. In 1975, Susan Brownmiller's book *Against Our Will: Men, Women and Rape* became what the author later called an instant "rape classic." When it debuted, *Time* magazine decreed (kind of grossly) the feminist journalist "the first rape celebrity who is neither rapist nor rapee" and later named her one of its twelve "Women of the Year." *Against Our Will* is widely credited for bringing the feminist fight against both rape and regressive sexual assault legislation into the spotlight, helping to shape the passing of the first marital rape laws in the US. The book's central thesis also sparked a shift in the perception of rape as a crime of lust to one of power. Another essential shift: the push to believe survivors, not demonize and ridicule them. But as great as Brownmiller's book was for advancing the feminist anti-rape cause, some prominent feminists criticized it, rightly, for promoting racist views of both men and women of color, and we must pause here to acknowledge that these frankly shitty stereotypes still linger in many discussions of rape and rape culture today. Brownmiller also told *People* magazine that it was a "biological impossibility" for a woman to rape a man, which is blatantly untrue and does a disservice to male survivors of sexual assault and childhood molestation. Still, it's undeniable that *Against Our Will* was a game changer at the time and one the feminist movement sorely needed.

As *Against Our Will* hit bookstores (eventually in more than a dozen countries), other feminists were working to open the first sexual assault crisis centers and hotlines in Canada and the US. In 1972, the DC Rape Crisis Center in Washington opened, one of the first in the US, and issued a pamphlet, "How to Start a Rape Crisis Center," that helped other groups establish their own in other cities. In Canada, Johanna Den Hertog, Janet Torge, and Teresa Moore founded the Vancouver Rape Relief Society in 1973 and shortly after opened the country's first rape crisis center and 24-hour hotline, run out of one of their basements. Other provinces followed suit. After a Philadelphia woman was murdered in 1975 while walking home, feminists in both countries started to hold Take Back the Night marches to protest sexual assault and, more generally, widespread, randomized violence against women.

The work of forward-thinking feminists in the 1970s also ushered in the US's first rape shield laws; the 1994 Violence Against Women Act made the laws federal, ensuring (in theory) that no woman's sexual history could be used against her in trial. Canada passed its own rape shield laws in the early 1980s, to combat what the Supreme Court called the "twin myths" that a woman who's sexually experienced is less credible and is also more likely to have consented to the sexual act in question. These myths result in judges who declare things like: "Women who say no do not always mean no. It is not just a question of saying no, it is a question of how she says it, how she shows and makes it clear. If she doesn't want it, she only has to keep her legs shut and she would not get it," and "Unless you have no worldly experience at all, you'll agree that women occasionally resist at first but later give in to either persuasion or their own instincts." Though the laws were challenged in Canada, and struck down in 1991, the federal government cemented a reworded version of the legislation shortly after.

Combined, these early initiatives formed the foundation for survivor support and today's anti-slut-shaming and anti-victim-blaming movements, both of which are core tenets of modern feminist work.

That's not to say feminists have won. Would Alice, transplanted nearly a millennium, feel on firmer legal ground if she were raped today? Would she be able to tell the difference in setting and time? The answer is not as easy, or as optimistic, as women would hope. Both Canada and the US abound with modern-day medieval thinkers. The idea that you cannot "thread a moving needle"—a phrase uttered in the nineteenth century—persists. Rape crisis centers remain underfunded and under attack, mostly by conservatives and anti-feminists. Rape shield laws do not always protect survivors from invasive, traumatic questioning on the witness stand. Archaic attitudes persist.

In 2011, for instance, Toronto feminists launched the inaugural SlutWalk after reports that a police officer told York University students participating in a safety forum: "Women should avoid dressing like sluts in order not to be victimized." The march means to reclaim and redefine the word "slut" and also emphasize that rape is never the victim's fault, no matter what she is (or isn't) wearing. Though SlutWalk has also been criticized, in some cases fairly, for its whiteness, its cis-gender focus, and its sometimes loose political message, I think using fishnets and nipple tassels to reclaim your body, your space, and your right to exist freely and fearlessly is powerful and amazing. Feminism can be fun! The SlutWalk movement is now worldwide, speaking both to feminists' furious action and the global, ubiquitous potency of slut shaming and victim blaming.

Even the FBI preferred to rather euphemistically call rape "indecent assault" until 1929, when it finally decided rape was rape. Less happily, it still stuck with a medieval definition—"the carnal knowledge of a female, forcibly and against her will"—effectively removing statutory rape, drugged rape, and rape committed against men from the list. It didn't update its definition until 2012: post–Mickey Mouse, the Empire State Building, Woodstock, Spongebob, Y2K, roofies, and the introduction of the term "date rape." Before we let Alice breathe a sigh of relief, and think that men who make and enforce law have finally understood, let's consider the ways in which anti-rape attitudes, legislation, and protection are yet again under attack.

As University of Alberta professors Lise Gotell and Emily Dutton noted in their academic paper "Sexual Violence in the 'Manosphere,'" anti-feminists have recently intensified their counterclaims to anti-rape feminism. Much of this takes the form of declaring girls and women "sluts" and rape culture a feminist-invented myth. Anti-feminists seek to undermine women through assertions that false allegations of sexual assault against men run rampant, as Janice Fiamengo expressed in chapter three. Such ideas, argued Gotell and Dutton, "exploit" young men's anxieties around shifting sexual and gender norms and changing consent standards — like "yes means yes." In that exploitation, the anti-feminist movement provides simpler, more appealing answers to the complex discourse around consent and rape, namely that it's not usually men's fault, and women also bear some responsibility. "There is a real danger," wrote the authors, "that this highly visible MRA mobilization around sexual violence could foreshadow the erosion of feminist influence."

We're seeing the effects of some of this influence already. Back in 1913, a doctor explained, "The mere crossing of the knees absolutely prevents penetration . . . A man must struggle desperately to penetrate the vagina of a vigorous, virtue-protecting girl." (And if a woman was impregnated during her rape, it also wasn't rape because "without a woman's consent, she could not conceive.") A century later, Republican congress member Todd Akin, in attempting to counterarguments that the government should fund abortions in "forcible" rape cases, inadvertently coined the term "legitimate rape." If a rape really happened, he said, a woman wouldn't get pregnant because "the female body has ways to shut that whole thing down."

Consider also the letters of support Brock Turner's friends and family wrote pleading leniency for the convicted rapist, the ex-Stanford swimmer whose case dominated headlines in summer 2016 — especially after survivor Emily Doe's powerful letter to Turner went viral. One of his high school girlfriends spent a whole lot of time praising his BF qualities, adding the prosecutor unfairly tried to "demote" Turner and that she prays every day "for only the best for my dear friend," living in fear of the day he would go to jail. His mother wrote that he was telling the truth and lamented what had happened to him and their family: "My first thought upon wakening every morning is 'This isn't real, this can't be real. Why him? Why HIM? WHY? WHY?'" His father complained that prison would be a "steep price to pay for 20 minutes of action." Devastatingly, but perhaps also unsurprisingly, Judge Aaron Persky sentenced Turner not to the maximum of fourteen years, or even the minimum of two, but a mere six months, an act that jolted people into action, protesting the short sentence and the rape culture that underpins it. In the end, Turner served just three months. Despite a thunderous feminist outcry, cases like Turner's and comments like Akin's work to strengthen rape culture and chip away at women's rights progress.

Alice can be forgiven for thinking these actions, and others, are strikingly reminiscent of those made in earlier decades and centuries. Because here's the thing: if today's remnants of medieval law are a depressing reminder that we haven't made much progress when it comes to rape legislation and attitudes, the new rape culture, fueled by gleeful social media pile-ons and a vehement resurgence of tired, victim-blaming narratives, is a warning bell that we're actually sliding backward.

I'd like to pause here to note that I don't believe, not even for a second, that men can't also be raped. I agree that feminists must do more to acknowledge men can be victims. In fact, numerous studies show a man is more likely to be raped than he is to be falsely accused of rape. In 2013, the US National Crime Victimization Survey determined that, across forty thousand homes, in 38 percent of the reported incidents of rape and sexual violence, the victims were men. This surprised Lara Stemple, a feminist and also the director of UCLA's Health and Human Rights Law Project. She went as far as to call to ensure the statistic was right. Stemple was already an advocate for shining the spotlight on male victims. A few years prior, she'd written a paper called "Male Rape and Human Rights," arguing that "according to research, females are more likely to be victimized by rape than males," but that "despite popular perception . . . however, males comprise a sizable minority of rape victims. Perhaps unsurprisingly, given the lack of societal concern about male rape and the hesitancy of male victims to report, data about male rape is wanting." Discovering that the victimization survey statistics were, in fact, correct cinched her belief that we don't care enough about men who are raped, and we need to do better. She later released another study encouraging the challenge of old assumptions, telling journalist Hanna Rosin that awareness raising doesn't need to come at women's expense. "Compassion," Stemple said in the interview, "is not a finite resource." This opinion needs to be shouted from the rooftops.

What would my experience be like if I were raped today? The internet, still stuck on dial-up when I was a teen, is now a scary incubator of a culture in which rape is both ubiquitous and normalized, *cool* even. Take, for example, 2014's sick viral happening, #jadapose: teenage boys and girls tweeted photos of themselves lying in the mock pose in which an unconscious sixteen-year-old Texas girl named Jada was filmed post-rape. Like the video of her rape, these photos went viral. That same year, Jessi Smiles, a star on Vine, the super-short-form video-sharing service, accused her handsome internet-famous ex-boyfriend, Curtis Lepore, of rape and, in return, received death threats from his adoring female fans. Lepore later took a plea bargain in 2014 and tweeted, "FAV this if you would willingly have sex with me." It received thousands of "yesses" from women. A year earlier, people tweeted that the underage victims of New Zealand's Roast Busters — a rape club — "deserved it" because they were drunk, and besides, some girls and women argued, the "busters" were pretty hot anyway. Around the same time, this tweet went viral: "Why are girls so scared of rape? Y'all should feel pride that a man risked his life in jail just to fuck you."

More recently, in Canada, we've seen some gleeful anti-feminist pile-ons in response to headline-making cases. On March 24, 2016, CBC radio host Jian Ghomeshi was found not guilty of five charges against him, including four counts of sexual assault and one count of overcoming resistance by choking. These were just the cases involving three women that Crown prosecutors brought to trial; once the first allegations about Ghomeshi emerged (allegations that did not result in criminal charges), many more women, and a few men, came forward with their own stories of sexual violence at Ghomeshi's hands.

Justice William Horkins gave the anti-feminists plenty of fuel in a decision in which he slammed the three women accusers for inconsistencies in their recollections and for their supposedly too-friendly behavior to Ghomeshi after their alleged assaults. He seemed to find Lucy DeCoutere's media interviews particularly distasteful, noting more than once the number she had given: nineteen. She received, he said, "massive attention for her role in the case." *Oh, hello, attention-seeking trope — nice of you to stop by!* As one news outlet wrote, the resulting verdict sent Twitter into a "frenzy"; even before the verdict, newspapers in Toronto noted, "every detail and every opinion" played out over social media. Many of those tweets supported Ghomeshi's accusers, especially under the hashtag #IBelieveSurvivors. But many more did not.

Long before the acquittal, people were calling the women deceitful on Twitter. Anti-feminist Diana Davison became especially popular on social media during this time for calling the case against Ghomeshi a "hoax," making videos on her YouTube channel,

Feminism LOL, that argued in depth that the three women accusers made up everything. (Davison is equally adamant that Trump has never sexually assaulted anyone, despite his recorded boasts.) At the one-year mark of the verdicts, anti-feminists and their fans tweeted once more, promoting the narratives of lying, railroading women and the spotlight-loving victim mentality. Presumably they had forgotten about Kathryn Borel. Her charges against Ghomeshi — namely three documented incidents of unwanted physical touching, including one where he simulated intercourse against her backside — were settled with a peace bond. He did not admit guilt but he did apologize to her, stating only that he did not show the respect he should have to Borel, a former producer of his popular radio show, and that his conduct was "sexually inappropriate." But it's always her strong, chilling statement that's stuck with me; it read, in part: "Every day, over the course of a three-year period, Mr. Ghomeshi made it clear to me that he could do what he wanted to me and my body. He made it clear that he could humiliate me repeatedly and walk away with impunity."

Then there's Mandi Gray. A few months after Ghomeshi was found not guilty in a Toronto courthouse, anti-rape advocates still reeling from the decision were given something to celebrate. Ontario Court Justice Marvin Zuker found Gray's rapist, Mustafa Ururyar, who was like Gray a doctoral student at York University, guilty of sexual assault. "Gray was very credible and trustworthy. I accept her evidence," Zuker told the courtroom, which burst into applause at the decision. He went on to eviscerate many of our lingering rape myths, saying, "No one asks to be raped," and ordered Ururyar to pay Gray $8,000 toward her legal fees. Even though "these statements don't un-rape me," as Gray herself put it, the guilty verdict was seen as a righting of the criminal system ship — proof that survivors could win. But Ururyar appealed and, immediately, critics claimed those who were unhappy with the Ghomeshi verdict had used him as a scapegoat. Davison again called the accuser, Gray, a liar and she again rose to Twitter and YouTube fame. In the appeal hearing (from which, as of the press date of this book, a decision has yet to be released), Superior Court Justice Michael Dambrot called Zuker lazy, a show-off, and unmoored. The court system did not use outdated stereotypes, he insisted. "Of course it is important to dispel myths, but you do that by deciding cases correctly and appropriately, not by using your podium of reasons for judgment as a place for your own manifesto."

In response, *National Post* columnist Christie Blatchford echoed prevailing anti-feminist and MRA sentiment in a piece that chastised an exhausted Gray, who, facing the prospect of having to redo everything at a new trial, told reporters, "It's not worth it." Blatchford mused on Gray's hesitancy to retake the stand: "It would also feed into the emerging modern sexual violence complainant as a creature of curious delicacy who can talk to the media at length about her suffering, . . . campaign politically on social media, organize consciousness-raising events and behave as a social justice activist—and yet who can't face a normal cross-examination . . . without being grossly traumatized." Twitter was full of similar icky stuff directed at Gray, like, "I think I'll just make a false accusation like you did instead #liar," and "Every time I hear Mandi speak, I vomit a little. Is that normal?"

Often, especially when I see stuff like this, spending a mere hour on Twitter makes me want to write an open letter: *Dear Internet, thank you for reinforcing thousands of years of patriarchy and also the fears of women and girls everywhere. But could we call a truce? It will be a lot easier for everyone to thrive if you stop convincing them they are all liars and that their ultimate, personal validation as women is to be supremely fuckable. Sincerely, Lauren.*

This shut-up-and-take-it, victim-blaming, slut-shaming internet culture has bled the lines into vicious cyberbullying and is responsible for the deaths of several teens, most infamously Nova Scotian teen Rehtaeh Parsons. In November 2011, Parsons, then just fifteen, went to a house party where two teenage boys raped her (they maintain it was consensual and that everyone was in the "groove"). Very drunk, after about eight vodka shots, according to the boys themselves, Parsons didn't see one of the boys take a photo of the other, giving a thumb's up as he penetrated her from behind, as she was vomiting out the window. But soon she couldn't escape it. The boy in the photo texted it to two (female) friends. Soon, that photo was shared around town and in school and soon Parsons, like me, was called a slut, except it wasn't just her rapists taunting her. She faced an onslaught everywhere she turned from both classmates and strangers. Men demanded sex from her.

According to our modern culture, her assault didn't make her a victim or a survivor, but a slut. Together, the internet and her real-life peers obliterated her personhood, rendering her not only into a girl who could be callously objectified and used but one who supposedly both liked and wanted it. In April 2013, Parsons died after she was taken off life support following a suicide attempt. Later, the boy in the photo, who did not receive jail time, said he felt remorse but didn't believe he was responsible, even a little bit, for Parsons's suicide: "This has had a huge negative impact on me. Humans make mistakes. I will not live with the guilt of someone passing away, but I will live with the guilt of the photo." He added, "I have [pleaded] guilty to distributing child pornography, not a sexual assault," stressing (perhaps a bit delusionally), "I never played a part in the bullying [of Rehtaeh], nor would I."

Like, WTF. Rape, right now, is being remodeled into so many things it's difficult to keep up with the latest obscuration. It's a mistake wayward boys make in adolescence, like smoking or drinking one too many beers; it's something that ruins rapists' lives, so let's please feel sorry for them; it's a joke, something we can laugh at as we sing about it during frosh week, as many universities did in recent years to the acronym YOUNG ("Y-O-U-N-G! We like 'em young! Y is for your sister, O is for oh so tight, U is for underage, N is for no consent, G is grab that ass!"—or in some versions, more accurately, "go to jail!"). It's a fun thing frat boys write on banners in quippy jests like "Our couches pull out, but we don't." In other words, rape is anything but what it really is: a life-shattering violation of a woman's body—and both women and men are buying into the lie.

This devastating culture permeates university, college, and high school campuses, and efforts to combat rape culture are centered on these places. School campuses are a battleground of both feminist and anti-feminist action, making them collectively a useful lens for examining prevailing attitudes on sexual assault. The attitudes are the same from when I was sixteen—from when fictional Alice was sixteen—but today's technology has propelled the whispered jabs beyond school hallways and city streets and into poisonous ubiquity. In recognition of this, the US government and college administrations wrote an open letter titled "Dear Colleague" to boost awareness and focus on rape through Title IX, a piece of legislation originally crafted in 1972 to "prohibit discrimination on the basis of sex in any education program or activity that receives federal funding." With some success, it's tried to create new women-empowering sexual assault rules, rape crisis centers, and venues for recourse without necessarily calling the police, leaving the punishment decisions to faculty and student tribunals. Even so, the effort to boost women's safety on campus is, to date, controversial.

As an example, we can turn to *Slate*'s Emily Yoffe, who in 2013 and 2014 created an odd sort of victim-blaming brand for herself. Yoffe, kind of amazingly, almost single-handedly renewed the if-you're-stupid-drunk-it's-your-fault-stupid narrative with her October 2013 article "College Women: Stop Getting Drunk." She acknowledged that sober men prey on very drunk women. She also said, "Perpetrators are the ones responsible for committing their crimes." She said she wasn't victim blaming but trying to prevent more victims. *Okay, fine.* But she also admonished that matching men "drink for drink" is not a feminist issue. (And here I was thinking the feminist issue was combatting the perception that drunk women send out "rape me" invitations in fancy calligraphy.) "When you are dealing with intoxication and sex," she added, "there are the built-in complications of incomplete memories and differing interpretations of intent and consent." I wonder if Yoffe, despite her protestations, has looked up the dictionary definition of victim blaming. Probably not, considering that, in 2014, she also delved into the (apparent) epidemic of rampant false rape accusations in her article "The College Rape Overcorrection."

In this article, Yoffe took issue with what she saw as an overzealous approach to protecting women on campus, based on what she called shaky statistical research. "But the new rules—rules often put in place hastily and in response to the idea of a rape epidemic on campus—have left some young men saying *they* are the ones who have been victimized," she wrote. I agree with Yoffe that it is worth examining whether colleges and universities are equipped to investigate and render decisions on campus rape and sexual assault cases. Feminists and lawyers both have raised legitimate concerns about these schools' employment of due process and unfair treatment of the accused. But in Yoffe's hands—and in the hands of many anti-feminists—campus rape adopts an "us vs. them" construct. It seems we can protect either accusers or the accused, but not both. She takes particular umbrage with "affirmative consent" regulations, arguing they should be struck because they "dictate how young adults in college make love, and that's both ridiculous and quixotic." Huh. *Make love.* The danger in such thinking, and such articles, is that promoting the idea that society (but mostly feminists) has gone "too far" in protecting women in turn prioritizes the status quo: protecting men.

As a writer on the blog *Feminist Philosophers* put it: "It's sobering to think that Yoffe's article, which is focused on one-sided accounts from the perspective of the men involved in allegedly false accusations—accounts which are strongly contested by both the universities and the women involved—will probably not be subject to anything like the skepticism that is typically leveled at rape accusations." Certainly, this appears to be the case. I can't help but think we can find a better way. Surely, it shouldn't be so hard to mitigate false accusations without simultaneously elevating them as a more urgent, widespread problem than actual rape. Is it so difficult to acknowledge rape culture exists both on and off campus and that it can *destroy* young women?

Apparently it is. In recent years, dozens of groups have sprouted like weeds to combat the push for rape survivors' rights, and they're not losing. As one group, the superficially benign but sneakily named Families Advocating for Campus Equality (FACE) said, groups like it were urgently needed to "extricate their sons from this unimaginable nightmare" of false accusation. A lot of FACE's arguments are summed up as "sexism." As one father wrote in defense of his son: "Well, you can guess that it's always the boy's fault. Even though John reported to the student conduct office that the accuser had—after they'd decided to cool the sexual thing because it freaked her out—come into his room drunkenly and groped him in his sleep and demanded sex when John awoke, [they] waited two months to advise *him* that he might have a claim against *her*." Falsely accused men, FACE maintains, experience psychological trauma similar to or worse than that of those who've been raped. They argue that feminists use Title IX to enforce gender bias against men and create the perfect revenge vehicle for scorned women. In other words: Those lying, crazy feminists blow things out of proportion. Or even more simply: But, men!

Members of FACE and groups like it don't deny that rape exists or that those who commit it deserve to be prosecuted; they do believe, however, that most of what women say is rape isn't, that feminists are trying to "criminalize normal male sexual behavior." It's not enough for it to be unwanted: "If a man and a woman have any sexual contact whatsoever—a kiss, a hug, anything—and she subsequently claims this contact was 'unwanted,' 'unwelcome' or 'coerced,' then he is presumed guilty of sexual assault," the group Save Our Sons (SOS) ridicules, taking an eraser to decades of activism that states, as any three-year-old should know, "no means no." The rape, to constitute rape, these groups say, must be demonstrably violent and the victim must have fought back hard. Only then should the law "treat these cases with the seriousness they deserve, bringing those who commit this crime to justice." Sound familiar, Medieval Alice?

I want to dismiss these groups as hot, fetid air, but they're a terrifying new step in the campaign to shame and silence women. They're behind more than seventy lawsuits against women who have accused men of campus rape. I knew I had to talk to them, to see where their battle plan would take them. But even fifteen years after my rape, the thought of talking to someone who would validate all my victim-blaming fears gave me sweaty palms. I was afraid talking to these women would force my mind to whip back not to my rape, or my simmering rage in Dr. Porter's classroom, but to all the nights I spent huddled under my childhood stars-and-sun comforter, desperately hoping for my body to feel like mine again, and even more fiercely replaying the short, terrible minutes of that night, searching for a way to make it fit into my life, to make it make sense. I was afraid their voices and their arguments would reduce me. I wished I could get angry and wear it like armor.

It wasn't just these groups that scared me but the thought that their victory would inevitably mean more girls would feel like I had all those years ago. When a week went by and FACE still hadn't answered my interview request, I was happy. They didn't want to talk to me either! Hurrah! But then Sherry Warner-Seefeld, the group's president, said yes.

🌱

Warner-Seefeld Skyped me from her home in North Dakota. A blond high school teacher, she wore a slash of pink lipstick and a seafoam-colored long-sleeved T-shirt that matched her office walls. Family photos adorned the wooden ledge that wrapped around the room: a suburban altar of all that is good and godly in life. A cast iron single bed, a time-worn pastel quilt folded neatly overtop the black frame, was tucked in the corner. Warner-Seefeld's office, the place where she works tirelessly to redefine rape, was a bucolic guest room.

To my surprise, she opened our conversation with a declaration that she was an "ardent feminist"—or at least, she added, she used to be. She wouldn't go as far as to say she was anti-feminist; she just wasn't sure anymore. The sociology teacher reconsidered her feminist values as well as how she taught rape and rape culture to teens in her high school after her son, Caleb, was accused of rape in early 2010. She'll never forget that January call. Her second oldest of four sons, Caleb opened the phone call with, "Mom, you're going to be so mad."

Lots of things raced through her mind. At first, she thought he'd been arrested for drunk driving or, at worst, a minor misdemeanor. But she never thought rape. Not for an instant. Not her son. As he launched into his story, assuring her it would be fine, Warner-Seefeld remembers sinking into her couch. Caleb was insistent he didn't rape anybody and, as his mother, she believed him. He was also insistent the university wouldn't unfairly prosecute him; he was innocent. But Warner-Seefeld didn't trust the school. All the next day at work, her mind kept returning to the conversation, stuck like an awful jingle: *Dum-de-dum-dum, She's saying I raped her, Mom, dum-de-dum-dum.* Warner-Seefeld took emergency leave halfway through the day and started calling lawyers. They advised her to tell Caleb to zip his lips shut.

In the end, says Warner-Seefeld, a criminal investigation did not result in Caleb's arrest and no charges were laid. In fact, according to her, police issued a warrant for her son's accuser, who, she claims, made a false report. Apparently, the woman subsequently fled the state. The University of North Dakota, not bound by the justice system's decision, proceeded with its own investigation, and found Caleb guilty of assault and expelled him. According to Warner-Seefeld, the school's lawyer was "antagonistic and mean and cruel." The lawyer didn't believe that Caleb's alibi held up, since his main witnesses were fellow fraternity brothers—friends, the lawyer surmised, who could blur the truth for him. Warner-Seefeld saw this as deeply unfair; it seemed to me that if she believed women frequently lied about rape, she shouldn't have had such a hard time believing Caleb's friends would lie to protect him.

Upon hearing the guilty verdict, Caleb collapsed on the floor. He needed his lawyer to help him get out of the room. He was a puddle, said Warner-Seefeld, and once he saw her it got worse. "He alternated between rage," she told me, her voice wobbling, "where he was just unloading what happened in the hearing and then collapsing and sobbing on the floor. And then up again and raging about again, and then sobbing on the floor. It was horrific. I would never want to see it again." Even now, five years later, she blinked back tears as she recounted that day, throat bobbing and eyelids rapid-firing, and apologized for losing composure. It's hard, she told me, to get over remembering that part.

Today, she assured me, Caleb is thriving. Even though the university later reinstated him, he never went back. In the two years it took to overturn his expulsion, he got a job that paid more than his mom's salary as a teacher. While her son was making bank, Warner-Seefeld took her personal battle and made it national. Fueled by the perceived injustice, she joined forces with two other moms of accused sons and together they officially launched FACE in 2014, with the major goal of getting due process cemented into school tribunal hearings for sexual misconduct and rape cases, making them similar to proceedings within the justice system. If this happens, it will certainly make it harder for a university to come to a different conclusion than police about any alleged rape or assault.

Currently, accused men are allowed to have lawyers present during the hearings, but they may only advise or consult with their clients; they cannot speak on their behalf. In most cases, that's up to the accused men themselves. If FACE wins, the school tribunal will resemble a courtroom, with all the same rights to legal representation and also, likely, all the same pitfalls. (May the richest, whitest student win!) With this push comes FACE's less trumpeted, unofficial, but far scarier goal: the constant work to reshape the discourse on what is and isn't rape and sexual assault. It's hiding underneath every lobbying and outreach effort—a red sock in a basket of whites—ready to bloody the laundry.

"To me, you're being raped if you are being penetrated when you are very obviously not wanting it," Warner-Seefeld told me when I asked how she would define rape. Given her outrage that unwanted kissing currently equaled sexual assault, hers didn't seem to match my definition at all. "I mean very obviously not wanting it," she replied. "Not because you're too tired to say no, because that has happened. Not because you got bored in the middle of it. Not because of all these silly things. But you are like, 'No, I don't want to have sex.' You are like, 'Get away from me.' 'No.' You are very, very clear. And there's no ambiguity for this guy."

She's not the only woman I spoke to who feels that way. Hanna Stotland is a Harvard-educated lawyer who voted for Barack Obama. She runs her own business as an admissions consultant for students who are applying to university. About half of her clients are special cases—students who have, for instance, been expelled from their original university—and a growing percentage of those special cases are men who have been expelled under Title IX violations, i.e., those deemed by the university to have committed rape or sexual assault, even if the justice system has cleared them or declined to prosecute them. Stotland coaches these men through the reapplication process and helps them get back into school, though not necessarily the school that expelled them. A big part of her job involves co-crafting the best possible version of her client's rape story. She never encourages a client to lie and always gets them to own up to what they did wrong, whether it's cheating on their girlfriends or drinking too much the night of a hook-up. But it's always a hook-up, never a rape.

Like Warner-Seefeld, Stotland invoked feminism; she believes it's good but it's gone too far by arguing that rape is everywhere, that we should, as a matter of course, believe the accuser. Stotland, who admitted she has never been raped and, therefore, could not know how a woman reacts while being sexually assaulted, nevertheless told me, "I'm speaking for myself, but I don't find it an imposition to say no when I don't like what someone is doing." She feared the current brand of feminism encourages passivity and silence. The "yes means yes" trend, she reasoned, sets up both men and women for failure. Instead, she felt we need to teach women to own their desire—to know it's okay to want, or not want, sex, but above all, to know what, exactly, they wanted. Women, she assumed, didn't say no when they wanted to say no not because they were "idiots" but because they are taught it's their job to please men. "I don't think anybody is that stupid. I don't think that they behaved that way without instruction," she said, her voice strained tight—whether that instruction is from our hypersexual society, from history, from their own upbringing, or some other pervasive narrative.

I found myself thinking she wasn't entirely wrong. I'm sure many women have sexual interactions they don't want because they feel pressured to have them—that they ought to do it if they want approval, whether it's from specific men or the vaguely omnipresent capital-M men. I'd been under the sheets as a younger woman, doing things I wasn't jazzed about because I was desperate for a dude to like me. But to me that's not feminism gone wrong. The grin-and-bear-it bedroom games we should never have to play are a horrifying and precise symptom of rape culture.

I was, however, baffled that two self-proclaimed feminists (albeit one who was a conflicted and possibly former feminist) were still putting the blame for rape on the victim for not enacting the perfect protest. To me, their feminism didn't support women's rights; it actively undermined them. I asked both women what they'd want campus gender equality to look like today. "To me, it would look the same as it did in the 1970s and '80s," Warner-Seefeld responded. *Sigh.* Of course it would. That means no campaigns on consent, "yes means yes" messaging, or "believe survivors" advocacy; no "Dear Colleague" and no broadened scope for Title IX; but also, in many cases, no on-campus sexual assault centers, no safe-walk programs, no on-campus blue-light security phones. FACE and groups like it are at the head of a move to rewind rape legislation and public attitudes back several decades. Like Stotland, Warner-Seefeld sees today's push for affirmative, enthusiastic "yes means yes" consent as relieving women of their choices and robbing them of their independence.

Later, when I went back over my notes from these interviews, I saw that I'd carved angry circles into my notebook without realizing it, evidence of the effort it took to not lose it while talking to both women, to not unleash a tirade of emotion, a lifetime of what it meant to be a survivor. As I transcribed the audio from our conversations, though, I let loose, shouting angrily into the air, startling my cat out of his afternoon bask. Both women wanted to divorce their work from rape culture, but I couldn't escape the link. Not only were those links there, they felt like an iron-strength chain that could rope the world.

I'm not sure that, had I yelled at them, either woman would have done more than blink benignly at me, like my cat. They were so *convinced.* Even if the new standard of consent worked, stressed Stotland, universities needed to give men time to adapt. Why was expulsion the first step, she wondered. Couldn't schools just summon accused men to the dean's office and give them a good scare? Her voice took on a gravelly Dick Tracy I'm-gonna-whup-you drawl to illustrate: "If you break this rule again, you're out on your ass, buddy.

You got that?" Most men who found themselves in the "rape pickle," she added, weren't monsters. They were teenagers who *didn't even know the girl didn't want sex*, men who cried when told what they'd done, men who'd stop if the girl said a louder no.

Rape culture doesn't happen in a bubble. It happens because women like Stotland and Warner-Seefeld are telling other women their experiences, while unpleasant, could have been stopped if only they'd said no, emphatically. It happens because, as a larger society, we're telling women they could have stopped nice guys from making mistakes if only *they* were more responsible. It happens because we slut shame and invalidate and pressure survivors. It happens because it is terrifying to think our loved ones are capable of rape, that you don't have to be an evil, midnight bush-lurker to cross a line. It's so much easier to confirm a centuries-old status quo and blame women. But it's only ever men who benefit from this.

In a controversial September 2014 Canadian court decision, a federal judge acquitted a 240-pound man accused of raping a small, drunk, and homeless nineteen-year-old woman. Among many things, Justice Robin Camp, a man, told the alleged victim (he bizarrely kept referring to her as "the accused") that because she was drunk, the "onus [was] on her to be more careful" and "sex and pain sometimes go together, that's not necessarily a bad thing." He also asked her why she didn't keep her knees together and, when Crown prosecutors objected to his outdated and illegal views, he admonished the lawyer that the law doesn't prevent him from thinking. Get it? *HE'S A THINKING MAN, WOMAN!*

Camp did give the accused a stern talking-to, something Stotland and others suggest is a reasonable punishment in such cases. In court, Camp said: "You've got to be really sure that she's saying yes . . . So remind yourself every time that you get involved with a girl from now on and tell your friends, okay?" He added that men have to be very careful, because sometimes women make things up out of spite: "Is there not a possibility that a very unhappy thing happened here? Two young people made love, and somebody came afterwards and poisoned the girl's mind?"

An official complaint was launched in 2015. Camp strenuously resisted efforts to have him permanently removed from the bench (his only concession to wrongdoing was to take "gender sensitivity" courses, and he took the unprecedented step of asking the federal court to halt the Canadian Judicial Council's deliberation of his case), but he has recently accepted the decision of the council and resigned. The accused in the case was retried and acquitted; the prosecutor in the case has said the Crown may appeal.

Stotland, Warner-Seefeld, and their cohort acknowledge victim blaming is real but are adamant they're not doing it. They truly believe their toughen-up-buttercup approach will stem on-campus rape. Still, it's difficult to see how the "but he didn't even know he was raping you!" defense doesn't blame the victim. I mean, can we just stop for a moment and think about how ridiculous this is? Never mind that a dude's tears aren't magical unicorn drops that guarantee his innocence — he might be crying because he was caught, or because he's overwhelmed, remorseful, acting, about to shit his pants. A deeper problem is at work if a man can't tell if he's committing assault, and that's not a woman's fault. I doubt a stern lecture will stop this type of man, someone who so obliviously thinks he has a right to a woman's body. And, frankly, how dare we tell his victims they could have done more to stop or *educate* him?

Yet both Stotland and Warner-Seefeld adamantly believe the modern anti-rape movement encourages women to abandon responsibility for their choices. Bad sex, Warner-Seefeld said, does not equal rape. Regretting sex after a drunken hook-up, she said, does not equal rape. Not enjoying sex but still finishing it, she said, does not equal rape. She allowed that it was rape if a man had sex with an absolutely incapacitated woman incapable of giving consent or even knowing what was happening to her. It's also rape if it is forceful and violent. Prior trauma, added Stotland, can muddle a woman's view of what's actually happening to her, causing her to confuse her current lover with her prior rapist. Flashbacks do happen, but many studies (and my own experience) attest they don't happen like this; survivors can usually tell with whom they're having sex. "You can make a good faith mistake about whether you were raped," Stotland assured me, presumably benevolent, like a fairy godmother of victim blaming.

Warner-Seefeld, Stotland, and their ilk seem hell-bent on ignoring the numerous studies that have shown it is extremely rare for women to lie about rape — it happens in less than 10 percent of cases. In other words, flocks of women are not equating bad sex or regretful hook-ups with rape. That's an idea that's ludicrous at best and laden with slut shaming at worst. Warner-Seefeld laughed when I confronted her with this criticism, admonishing me for thinking women don't lie. "I don't know a young person in my school who actually doesn't laugh at that," she told me. "Because they literally know people who have done it." I'd rather we didn't blame and shame women based on the questionable authority of a high school rumor mill. Rape occurs in many different situations, but it all comes to down to simply this: a woman hasn't consented to sex. If she doesn't want it, or can't tell a man she does, it's rape. Full stop.

Emily Lindin, founder of the anti-slut-shaming project UnSlut, told me, "People don't believe there is such a thing as consensual sex for women." If that statement sounds bold, consider this: the ugly idea persists that if you were, as a woman, to have consensual sex and enjoy it, then you would deserve to be called a slut, which is just about the worst thing ever, so instead of being shamed, you lie about it and say it was rape. It's a giant shame vortex: we don't believe women who say they've been raped because we believe they should feel ashamed for having sex — so ashamed that they'd rather say it was forced. It's why police still ask women who make rape claims if they have boyfriends or husbands. But, as Lindin argues, a woman who has consensual sex is much more likely to just go on minding her sexy business than to call the police.

Warner-Seefeld was careful to say that FACE doesn't work with men's rights activists (MRAs). She has kept MRA groups at a distance because she believes they're radical and any alliance would keep her organization from getting a seat at the tables where legislative change happens. Stotland similarly scoffed at the groups, though she warned that the strange bedfellow syndrome—the partnership in ideology between MRAs and those who do work like hers and Warner-Seefeld's—means feminists are seriously getting the rape question wrong. FACE has received hundreds of calls from families who have sons and need help. She received three calls from families the day of our interview. She doesn't know what will happen to them—if they'll be expelled, stay expelled, or be acquitted. She's not willing to jeopardize that work with radicalism. It's worth mentioning, however, that much of FACE's literature references major MRA organizations and their work. For an organization that claims it wants to keep its distance, it both reinforces and applauds men's rights rhetoric.

One FACE document, titled "Title IX's Other Victims," quotes several blog posts from A Voice for Men, including one that says, in reference to the accused, "He sees very clearly that very few believe him while nearly everyone believes the woman. The system and our culture are failing him. His pain is invisible while hers is treated with reverence, even though she is lying." The article goes on to say that most women are believed, no matter what. We know that's blatantly false. Studies show only one out of about every one thousand rapes results in jail time, and conviction rates have decreased from 15 percent to 13 percent in the past three decades. That's not to mention the skeptical and downright hostile reaction that often greets accusers. And yet, as a society, we're primed to believe droves of women are unfairly sending men to jail. In a way, Lindin told me, she gets it, and I do, too. It's incredibly difficult to admit that our athletes, our brothers, our sons, our friends, our idols are capable of rape. It's so much easier to believe the girl's a slut. She's a liar. She made a mistake. She wanted it. But that doesn't make it right—in the sense of justice or accuracy. What it does make is a slippery slope, down which decades of the feminist reframing of rape is plummeting.

So what would the aftermath of my rape look like today? It's likely I'd have waited even longer to tell somebody what happened, knowing my own assault didn't fit into a perfect box. Back then, as a competitive kickboxer, I knew enough self-defense to make it stop immediately, but my brain turned off. I didn't fight hard enough to end it fast enough, which would have been instantly, clicked off like a TV. I struggled, but my body didn't catch up to my brain, because I couldn't process what was happening. My shock and my fear overtook me. And what if Warner-Seefeld had been my high school teacher? Would I have squashed the voice that said it wasn't my fault? Would I have been convinced I'd just made bad choices? That it wasn't rape at all? And even if—*if*—she hadn't convinced me it wasn't rape, would I have been too afraid to tell any authority figure, knowing my relationship to my rapist could have been used against me? After all, in many of the seventy FACE-backed lawsuits, prior text messages between the accused and accuser comprised a major piece of evidence, as if talking to a guy is blanket consent for sex and an exoneration of rape. When the victim-blaming voices are reaching rock concert decibels, how would I, or any other victim, be able to step forward, especially when the loudest of those voices belong to other women?

It would have been so tempting to stay silent.

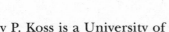

Mary P. Koss is a University of Arizona professor who is a leading voice in sexual violence research. In 1982 she worked with the Ms. Foundation, which runs *Ms. Magazine,* and feminist icon Gloria Steinem to conduct the first ever US national survey on campus rape. Koss has been studying rape on campus for longer than I've been alive, and yet she told me the researchers have made little progress.

On the whole, she said, studies that show rape on campus exists and is a proliferating problem, but not much funding or time has been put into figuring out a way to reduce campus rape numbers. In other words, she lamented, we keep proving and re-proving rape is a problem to satisfy naysayers, but we never do anything about it.

This failure to act on the studies, Koss argues, has left room for men's rights activists and rape truthers and apologists, as well as those with presumably good intentions, to skew the conversation. "Virtually nothing that is happening today is touching base with science," she said. "It's being propelled by assumptions, belief systems, and cherished icons." In her mind, men's rights groups and rape apologists are keeping the public outraged, no matter what side of the issue they're on. For example, said Koss, recent years have seen much rallying around the need for rape kits and even more anger over the backlog of already completed kits. The result has been a tornado of fundraising and awareness activity, but not much else. None of this, maintained Koss, will fundamentally change anything. Piles of research show the kits rarely get used and even more rarely help secure a conviction, especially when it comes to rapes committed by someone the survivor knows. These assaults tend to be less violent but also account for the majority of rapes on campus.

"It keeps us busy," Koss told me, referring to the intense focus on rape kits and the fundraising surrounding them, although she doesn't necessarily mean "busy" in a good way. It's projects like these (ones that put the focus on catching so-called real rapists) that can keep us from achieving real change. From the outside, it looks as if we're making progress and empowering women, but the effect is the same as if we'd dismissed them entirely. It's a curious, chilling game of PR strategy, and one that's working. We look like we're doing something, yet our surface actions keep us from tackling root causes, factors that are often more thorny to parse and difficult to confront. Koss was astounded that so much of today's policy is politically driven, which to her is like creating a public health strategy on cancer without consulting any actual cancer researchers. She's even more worried that said policies push us further and further away from nuanced definitions of rape and toward simplistic, limiting ones, ones that use the same parameters women like Stotland and Warner-Seefeld impose.

I'd spent years punishing myself for my own rape, and it depressed me that we were, more than ever, encouraging women en masse to do the same. I can tell you that rape breaks us, even when we want to be strong. We carry it with us always, tucked in an invisible pocket, even when that pocket's small and zipped shut. We don't need anybody to tell us what we could have done better, because we've told ourselves thousands of times. We don't need anybody to blame us, because we've done that, too. Everything the worst rape apologist has ever said, we've likely whispered to ourselves, alone in the dark of the night but also during a romantic candle-lit dinner, or driving to work in rush hour, or eating grilled cheese for lunch with a friend.

Here's what we do need: support, real prevention strategies, well-funded research, women's centers, and a society that values women and allows them, in turn, to value their sexuality. Rape is used as a weapon in war for a reason: it can make you never want to get up again. If we ever want to reach true gender equality, we need to engage in the mountainous task of eradicating rape, not in the far too easy, and dangerous, one of convincing women they're making up the whole damn thing. Of course, that would also mean ensuring women have bodily autonomy, something for which we've always had to fight. Instead, we're seeing a thicker and thicker veneer of "empowerment" painted on, a shiny gloss over all sorts of anti-feminist work, from the undoing of feminist work on sexual violence to the dismantling of reproductive rights and resources. My next steps would take me into the height of this rebranding: the mission to portray the anti-abortion activist as the ultimate feminist.

8 Teen spirit: Clinic closures, access attacks, and the pro-woman rebranding of today's anti-abortion activists

A week after his inauguration day, US president Donald Trump wrote a tweet in the sand: "The #MarchForLife is so important. To all of you marching — you have my full support!" That day, Vice President Mike Pence, who proudly describes himself as "a Christian, a conservative and a Republican," headlined the flagship March for Life rally in Washington, DC, becoming the first VP and the highest-ranking White House official to speak at the annual anti-abortion protest since its inception. Briefly, for those who may have missed this anti-abortion bulwark: the March for Life was founded in 1974, the year after Roe v. Wade, the landmark United States Supreme Court decision that asserted abortion rights, and has been held on its anniversary date ever since.

"President Trump actually asked me to be here with you today," Pence told the undulating crowd, the wind whipping their cheers into the air and across the Washington Monument park grounds. "He asked me to thank you for your support, for your stand for life, and for your compassion for the women and children of America." The giant flag behind him, emblazoned with a red rose, flapped shadows over his face, but the expression as his head bobbed a yes-yes-yes beat throughout his speech was unmistakable: victory.

With every sentence, a responding WOOOOOO! thundered out, spreading like contagion into the surrounding streets where thousands more waited. "Life is winning again in America," Pence trumpeted. The first rows of the gathered crowd were young and exuberant, all pumping fists and jumping bodies. Signs rose into the air. "I am the Pro-Life Generation." And "We Don't Need Planned Parenthood."

Pence wasn't the only speaker with political star power. At her turn on the podium, Kellyanne Conway, counselor to the president and Trump's former campaign manager, echoed Pence's promise for change. "This is a new day, a new dawn, for life," she told the crowd, pausing to flash a toothy smile, her blond hair lacing across her face and against her blood-bright suit. A few days earlier, Conway was widely ridiculed (and, in some cases, celebrated) for coining the term "alternative facts" in an interview with Chuck Todd on NBC's *Meet the Press*. But she didn't need smudged truths now to reinforce her boasts at the march. For those who cared about women's reproductive rights, the real truth was scary enough. Already, Trump had reinstated the Mexico City Policy—or as its critics called it, the Global Gag Rule—prohibiting foreign organizations that receive US family-planning funding from "providing counseling or referrals for abortion or advocating for access to abortion services in their country." Though administrations had repealed and reinstated the policy before, anti-abortion supporters saw it for how it was intended: as both a signal that Trump was on their side and a promise that more "good news" was to come.

At the close of the speeches, a triumphant rallying cry sprang up through the crowd, soaring through the city core like a bird in flight, ricocheting between the marble buildings like gunfire. "Hey! Hey! Ho! Ho!" the mass chanted. "Roe v. Wade has got to go!" For the first time in a very long time, it actually seemed possible.

In Canada, we have our own March for Life, held in May to coincide with the federal government's first step toward decriminalizing abortion in 1969. Back then, abortions were still only available in hospitals and only if a committee of doctors deemed pregnancy would threaten the woman's life or health, though the move was also part of the same legislation that, at least, made contraceptives legal. When Campaign Life Coalition (CLC), the political arm of the anti-abortion movement here, launched the march in 1998, only seven hundred people showed up to protest on Parliament Hill in Ottawa. In 2015, more than twenty-five thousand marched, with an estimated 80 percent under age twenty-five. And, the next year, when an equally large and young crowd gathered, it murmured its agreement as one MP called the Liberal government "the government of death." Behind the speakers, women, their mouths pressed into silent lines, as if paying penance, held white-on-black signs that stated: "I regret my abortion." Footage from that day shows legions of high school and university students dotting the hill, many of them wearing black T-shirts that read #EndTheKilling—that year's theme. Mothers pushed their children in strollers. Fathers piggybacked their toddlers on their shoulders. Dimple-kneed children held up protest signs, and others wove through the crowd. As in the US, Canada's March for Life is a (nuclear) family affair.

The happy vibe is a sharp departure from the more militant and murderous history of the anti-abortion movement. National Abortion Federation (NAF) statistics from 2015 show that since July 1977, the US has experienced eleven murders, twenty-six attempted murders, forty-two bombings, and 185 arsons, plus thousands of other acts of violence and intimidation against abortion providers, clinic workers, and women seeking health care. The violence crossed the border to Canada in 1992 when Henry Morgentaler's clinic in Toronto was firebombed in the middle of the night. In 1994, a sniper hid in the back lane of a residential neighborhood in Vancouver, BC, and shot doctor Garson Romalis while he was eating breakfast. Romalis survived the shooting. Six years later, a man stabbed Romalis as he left his clinic. Romalis survived again. Shootings in Hamilton, Ontario, and Winnipeg, Manitoba, followed. Nor is this old history: in 2015, Robert Dear Jr. fatally shot three people at a Planned Parenthood in Colorado.

While the shootings are clearly the work of extremists, in 2015, in the aftermath of the initial "baby parts" smearing of Planned Parenthood, harassments and threats against clinics rose exponentially, according to NAF numbers. Clinic blockades nearly doubled from 2014 to 2015. Meanwhile, picketing, which had been decreasing, jumped from about 5,400 incidents in 2014 to nearly 22,000 in 2015. Hate mail and email harassment has skyrocketed to nearly 28,000 incidents, up from less than one hundred — a huge difference that's largely the result of the NAF's decision to respond to the resurgence by hiring an outside security firm to track online threats.

These actions are all because feminists would like to see abortion treated, and thus protected, as a normal part of a woman's health care regime. Though those on the other side often deride this philosophy as an "abortion on demand" method, as the fictional politician Selina Meyer (played by Julia Louis-Dreyfus on the HBO show *Veep*) once quipped: "If men could get pregnant, you could get an abortion at an ATM." But the idea that women might *abuse* their right to control their own bodies (look out, that nasty woman has too much autonomy!) has stuck. In this alternate universe, women are wanton vixens who use abortions as easy birth control fixes. What a near laughable stigma, considering the dearth of abortion access in rural Canada and the US, not to mention that surveys have repeatedly shown that women most often seek abortion after contraception failure. Unfortunately, abortion is an uncomfortable topic, making it a prime target for public-opinion rebranding. The linguistic pairing of anti-abortion and pro-women messaging is like a conversational escape hatch for those who don't want to admit they're limiting women's rights, even though they are.

As Tomris Türmen, former senior policy adviser to the Director-General of the World Health Organization and current president of the International Children's Center, put it more than fifteen years ago in a *Health and Human Rights* paper:

> For families, the ability to choose family size offers increased choice as to the use of family resources, education, and employment. For communities, individual choices can result in increased options for economic and social development. An enabling environment is a necessary prerequisite for people to be able to promote and protect their own health and that of their partners, as well as for them to be able to act on the decisions they make.

Türmen was writing in support of entrenched, worldwide views on reproductive rights and also asking her readers to consider how to move those rights forward. In doing so, she made it clear that any effort to ensure women reached their full potential must move in lockstep with reproductive rights, lest it eventually fail. Reproductive health access enables women to decide when, and if, they want to have children, a choice that can extend to more freedom in the labor force, in relationships, at home, and beyond throughout life. Or, if you're an anti-abortion activist, it can mean the opposite of all those things: a way for society to *control* women.

Though the anti-abortion movement is often seen — and sometimes dismissed — as predominately made up of the Christian religious right, many of its members are working hard to make their message connect with those outside their core. In Canada, this means broadening the movement to include everyone from Muslims to atheists. At the January 2017 march in the US, Democrats had a visible presence. (Few, however, would describe the march as either racially or religiously diverse.) For both countries, however, this bridge building means a shifting rhetoric, one structurally predicated on both a civil rights and a pro-woman mandate. This new narrative is as deliberate as calling fetuses "the unborn," for whose civil rights anti-abortion activists mobilize. When these messages combine, we get popular slogans and hot pink signs that claim the anti-abortion movement is where one can find "real" and "true" feminists. Forget those counterfeit feminists over there demanding reproductive rights, they suggest; bona fide feminists protect women "from womb to tomb." Outlawing abortion is seen as gifting women with the inalienable rights of life, pregnancy, and motherhood. Oh, gee, thanks. Does that come with "baby parts" gift wrap?

Changing the approach to the conversation targets both the hard and easy gets: those who aren't fully swayed by religious arguments and those who haven't yet fully reconciled what it means to have reproductive control. But is it working? In Canada, the last significant piece of anti-abortion legislation, Motion 312, was put forward in 2012 and called for a re-opening of the debate on when human life begins. Conservative MP Stephen Woodworth wanted to form a committee to review the Criminal Code's definition that "a child becomes a human being only at the moment of complete birth," and we can easily guess to what end. Although the motion was defeated, and the Conservative-heavy government ousted a few years later, a surprising number of MPs (ninety-one), ten of them cabinet members, voted in favor of the motion. More recently, MP Cathay Wagantall introduced Bill C-225, the "Protection of Pregnant Women and Their Preborn Children Act," a slippery-slope piece of legislation which would have made it "an offence to cause injury or death to a preborn child while committing or attempting to commit an offence against a pregnant woman." It was defeated in its second reading (209 nays to 76 yeas), but note the lurking terminology shift: *preborn.*

We can attribute these defeats, in part, to public opinion. A 2016 Ipsos poll showed that 57 percent of Canadians believe a woman should be able to have an abortion whenever she wants one, up from

36 percent in 1998. Men and women also agreed at about the same rates. Only about a quarter of Canadians believe that abortion is morally unacceptable. However, it's interesting to note that when surveyed about what their fellow Canadians think, respondents overestimated the rigid thinking of their neighbors, guessing that 40 percent of the country deemed it unacceptable. This, perhaps, nods to the growing visibility of the anti-abortion movement here, particularly among youth.

As promising as this Ipsos poll is, we shouldn't confuse it with real, on-the-ground access to abortion services. Even if women wanted to treat getting an abortion as casually and easily as an ATM pit stop, we couldn't. The overall picture is grim, despite recent access victories, most notably in the province of Prince Edward Island, which until January 2017 provided no access at all to services, not even in hospitals. For an idea of just how grim, consider what one PEI woman who tried to access abortion services in the no-go zone told authors of a 2014 report on the effects of the province's restricted policies: "Oh, god, it takes something away from you that I don't think men ever get taken away. A certain sense of I am my own person, I can do as I choose, as who I am, express myself fully, and everything."

As of fall 2016, there are only a few dozen abortion clinics across Canada, and in several provinces, including Saskatchewan and New Brunswick, an in-hospital abortion may be a woman's only viable option, although New Brunswick women have the option of paying for their abortion at a private clinic. Yet fewer than 20 percent of hospitals in Canada offer abortion services, and the vast majority of them require at least one doctor's referral. It's not unheard of for women to face an additional hurdle: doctors who refuse to give a referral because of their personal anti-abortion beliefs. What's more, if you look at a map of where those hospitals are located, the visual truth is startling: services are largely clustered around city centers, close to the US border. The number of doctors who

learn how to perform abortion is trending down: in the US, that
number has plummeted more than 40 percent since the 1980s, and
a similar trend is suspected in Canada, perhaps because doctors
conscientiously object or because they believe, wrongly, that abortion
rights are a done deal here. Already, the number of abortions in
Canada has decreased to 81,897 in 2014 from 98,762 in 2007.
More than 10,000 of that drop can be attributed to the number of
abortions performed in hospitals.

If we want a crystal ball view into what Canada might look like
if the anti-abortion movement continues to gain ground, we need
only look south, from where many activists are now taking cues. A
2016 Pew Research Center poll reveals that, similar to Canada, the
majority of Americans believe in abortion rights. A full 57 percent
of Americans believe that in all or most cases abortion should be
legal, though only 23 percent believe in unfettered access. A May
2016 Gallup poll showed the two sides as nearly evenly split, with
47 percent of Americans calling themselves "pro-choice" and 46 percent declaring themselves "pro-life" (their words). But, thanks in
large part to anti-abortion elected officials, this split is not necessarily
reflected in policy. As of 2011, 89 percent of US counties had no
known abortion provider, including 97 percent of non-metropolitan
counties.

More disturbingly, in the political quest to undo Roe v. Wade,
seventeen states have enacted state-mandated pre-abortion
counseling and twenty-seven have enacted wait periods. In the first
case, before an abortion, women are required to receive counseling
on at least one of the following: the supposed link between abortion
and breast cancer (five states), the ability of a fetus to feel pain
(twelve states), and/or mental health effects (nine states). The
waiting periods are generally twenty-four hours and the timer usually
starts after the woman has received said counseling, whether it's
mandated to occur on the internet, over the phone, or in person.
In addition, twenty-three states require an ultrasound before an

abortion is performed, though only three of them force the woman to view the image or hear it described.

Proponents deny the tactics are meant to bully vulnerable women into guiltily or shamefully choosing not to have an abortion. Rather, all of this is done under the guise of *helping* women. Proponents claim they bestow true informed choice upon women. "Whoomp, there it is!" (again): the benevolent gift of empowerment. Apologies to Tag Team (one of my favorite early '90s groups), but, no, I don't dig it. Though it's difficult to determine the effects of these policies (in part because US states report abortion statistics according to where the procedure took place, not where the woman resides), a 2009 Guttmacher Institute study looked closely at Mississippi, which requires in-person counseling and waiting periods and where researchers have delved more deeply into the data. Abortion rates did indeed fall, though it doesn't seem that a woman's desire to control her own body dropped correspondingly. Instead, both out-of-state and second-trimester abortions rose, not exactly what those on either side of the debate would consider a success. Yet as unrestricted access stands on increasingly shaky ground, those clamoring to give it the final push into oblivion are not who we might think—nor is the message what we might expect.

The day before the 2017 March for Life, anti-abortion activists took over the hulking Renaissance Washington, DC Downtown Hotel. After lunch, I joined about fifty activists, lawyers, law students, and others for the adjacent Law of Life Summit, designed to advance the anti-abortion movement through putting forward more anti-abortion legislation, attacking Planned Parenthood as a (supposedly) criminal organization, and encouraging more lawyers, prosecutors, and judges to embrace the mission. Besides a handful of nuns in habits and one or two priests, the staid crowd looked like what it was: a room full of affluent lawyers. Before Royce Hood, founder of the summit and a not-so-long-ago graduate of the Catholic-run Ave Maria School of Law, stepped onto the podium, the crowd milled around the coffee stations hemming the room, treading across the chocolate- and mocha-colored geometrical carpet to pump hands and clap backs. The men favored well-cut suits and Archie-style hair, while the women wore smart blazers, tasteful jewelry, and sleeveless work dresses. From what I could see, the only exceptions to this seemed to be two young women: one in a green shirt carrying a magenta sign that read "Conceived from rape/I love my life" and another in a leather motorcycle-style jacket who wore her electric violet hair in a deep side part.

The latter woman, Destiny Herndon-De La Rosa, founder of New Wave Feminists (slogan: "Badass. Prolife. Feminists."), was on stage. As part of a panel featuring "young leaders," she sat with two other women. One was Alexandra Swoyer, another Ave Maria graduate and a *Washington Times* journalist who covered the presidential campaign for *Breitbart*. The other was Alison Howard, the director of alliance relations at Alliance Defending Freedom. Each had their cell phone out, fingers swiping and connecting. Moments earlier, by way of introduction, the moderator, Jill Stanek, the national campaign chair of the Susan B. Anthony List, crowed, "I have surmised that you all know that we won, right?" She went on to say that the anti-abortion movement must prepare for "the most evil tricks that we can't even possibly imagine" and called feminists "perennial losers." She cheered what she deemed feminism's "generational in-fighting" and its "reluctance to pass the torch"—stoking the divisiveness within the movement. "My observation of the pro-life movement is exactly the opposite. We first demonstrate the love of our young people before they were even born," she said, emphatically if not grammatically. She was so proud of the women on stage, she beamed. "These women are so precious."

Herndon-De La Rosa had recently catapulted onto the national stage after New Wave Feminists applied to become a partner at the Women's March on Washington and was, to her great initial surprise, accepted, and then, swiftly and much less to her surprise, rejected. The march pointed to its pro–abortion rights stance as the reason for its rescinded partnership, but Herndon-De La Rosa "invaded" the totally public march anyway (the audience applauded wildly at this, as if she'd infiltrated the Gestapo) and welcomed the publicity boost the controversy created. She went on to say there were no hard feelings and joked that she "needed to send them a fruit basket, because this is the best thing that's ever happened." I'm not sure what she said after that because the room erupted in laughter and clapping, drowning her out. A few minutes later, she won the room again when Stanek asked the panelists how they saw the movement's future. "The future is pro-life female," answered Herndon-De La Rosa, riffing off a popular feminist T-shirt with a similar slogan. She added that it was important for anti-abortion advocates to promote the pro-women narrative. "We're not trying to control women or take over their bodies — that's not it at all," she told the crowd. "We believe that you should have control over your body from the moment it first exists."

Yikes.

Moments later, after the panel ended, the audience voted to skip their bathroom break — they were too engaged to stop. Hood, who emceed the conference, his face permanently pink with excitement, encouraged attendees to step out if they needed to, directing them to the men's room. "There are restrooms," he added, hesitating, before jovially breaking off to responding laughter and shouts of "Good for you!" as he confessed, "I don't know where the women's room is." A few minutes after that, the audience broke into another round of rowdy, gleeful laughter when John-Henry Westen, editor-in-chief of the website LifeSite: Life, Family & Culture News, jumped up on stage, holding his laptop, voice hiccupping in excitement as he interrupted Hood.

"Breaking news! President Trump just did it again," he cried, emphasizing "again" with Shakespearian drama. "He once *AGAIN* called out the mainstream media for not coming to cover the March for Life." Giddy noises rippled through the crowd. "He's like our best advertisement tool right now." Westen broke off into giggles that were answered with more laughter and riotous clapping. "President Trump is also confirming—officially, sort of—that Mike Pence is going to show up tomorrow." At this, the audience lost composure, filling the room with shouts of "Wow!" He continued quoting Trump, and the audience continued mirroring his excitement, hollering victory.

What a fun crowd!

The blending of traditional conservatism and new feminism made for a strange but effective mix. In one breath, we got speakers who asserted things like "mom's the real issue"—referring to the presumed superiority of the traditional family structure and the sanctity of motherhood—and, in the next, other speakers who praised feminism and lamented what they saw as a you-can't-sit-with-us mentality in the movement. Both, however, preached a brand of pro-women activism rooted in restriction, no matter how often it employed "dank memes," risqué language, or Urban Outfitters–style (ahem, sorry, Pro-Life Outfitters) "All Lives Matter" shirts shilled on tattooed bodies. While it's beyond my purview to define someone's feminism for them, the more I became exposed to the Anti-Abortion Movement Dictionary's meaning of feminism, the more I became convinced it wasn't as advertised: a sort of modern feminism-for-everybody with a "pro-life" twist. Take one of New Wave Feminism's memes, for example, a funky pink text on a black, distressed background: "We reject the failed feminism of victimhood and violence, for ourselves and for our unborn children." In the corresponding Instagram caption, Herndon-De La Rosa added, "The fauxminists can have #victimhood if they want it. Real #feminism is beyond that."

Well, now, doesn't that sound familiar?

Outside the conference room, teenage girls clumped together. The youth rally had ended at the same time. I was surprised to see how many of them carried signs that read "True feminists protect human life." (The signs were hot pink, of course, a shade so ubiquitous that day it might as well have been the event's official color.) At the bottom of the sign, a pink banner highlighted the Guiding Star Project, accompanied by #NEWfeminism.

Curious about what, exactly, new feminism was, I hunted down the organization's booth at the nearby trade show, where teenage girls carrying the signs were even more abundant. I scanned through a pamphlet at the booth, which was bordered by still more young girls, trying to master my poker face. "'Old feminism,'" read the pamphlet, "is based on the idea that men and women are interchangeable and that women have been unfairly held back from achieving their potential in society because of their role as mothers in the home." (Oh, geez.) "New Feminism," the pamphlet explained, "views femininity through a lens of hope and joy. We honor the unique feminine genius — the way women think, perceive, and love *as women* — and celebrate that these strengths are compatible with the strengths of others. We know that true feminine success is measured by a woman's love of others" [italics theirs]. Sure, fine, but I had just one question: By what bar is true masculine success measured? The pamphlet didn't say, but I'd seen enough that day to guess.

I wandered through the trade show, checking out the other feminist-branded booths. For all their dismissal of "old" feminism, these groups tended to promote a feminism that was — well — musty, like first-wave, nearly-a-century-gone, make-sure-you-have-mothballs-handy-because-it's-so-old kind of old feminism. Non-profit *Life Matters Journal*, a publication of Rehumanize International, an organization that describes itself as "a non-partisan, non-sectarian/secular group dedicated to the cause of life," displayed a giant mint-and-pink standing banner that asked, in lettering reminiscent of both tattoos and Pinterest, "Can you be Pro-Life and Feminist?" On it, they'd given Rosie the Riveter a makeover, rendering her face blank except for a piece of tape over her mouth that read "life," a nod to the Silent Siege project, which calls its tactics a "divine strategy from the Lord"—a strange choice for a supposedly secular group. As the banner pointed out, early feminists, including Alice Paul, who spearheaded the battle for women's right to vote in the US, and Dr. Elizabeth Blackwell, the first woman to receive a medical degree in the US, largely protested abortion, at least in public. Still, as much as we owe a debt to these women, I'm not about to grab a petticoat and try to be them. I might picture myself standing on their shoulders, but it's not in a straight and unwavering line. Rather, it's an inverted pyramid that allows for pluralities and expansion, a rejection of this idea that it's good to go backward.

"I think the feminist movement has gotten off track," Lisa Stover, the national programs coordinator for Students for Life of America, told me. "But we do have this new wave of feminists now who recognize to be pro-woman also means being pro-life." Borrowing from the same logic lines pro–abortion rights activists use, and infusing it with the bitterly steeped tea of traditionalism, she continued: "We're not just advocating for the child, we're advocating for the mother as well. But I do think that women shouldn't have to deny their fertility in order to be just like men. And no woman should be forced to choose between her child and her education, her child and her career, her child and her goals."

Like many of the "new pro-life generation," Stover believed only the anti-abortion movement could, in its full support of pregnant women, allow women to "have it all"—well, at least until they ran into all the stumbling blocks (or Great Wall of China–like barriers) the rest of the feminist movement is trying to break down. "By our nature women are nurturers, we are protectors of those who we love," she added. (If you're wondering if these women all take the same class to learn how to robotically recall, or unify, their message, the answer is yes, and it's called apologetics.) "As a pro-life feminist, I'm all for women's rights," she concluded, "but not the type of rights that don't belong to us."

Even anti-abortion activists who don't embrace the f-word are quick these days to say that they're pro-woman. "I like to say I'm feminine. And by that I mean I embrace my femininity, and I don't believe that being female is a hindrance to equality with men," Stephanie Gray, the former executive director and co-founder of the Canadian Centre for Bio-Ethical Reform, explained from her home in British Columbia. "I think the feminist movement has done something right when it fights for, for example, equal pay for equal work or the right to vote, so women have a voice just like men do. But I think the feminist women — some women of the feminist move-ment — have done harm by saying that women should have a right to kill their children, because no human ought to have that right. I would say that goes against the nature to be feminine, which is to celebrate the fact that we biologically get to nurture offspring in a way men never will. That's something to be embraced and turned into and celebrated, not rejected." Whooo boy. Gray has now struck out on her own. Her new ministry, called Love Unleashes Life, also the name of her book, aims to change the minds of the influential: current and future doctors, lawyers, and legislators.

A few months before the 2017 US March for Life, I met with Alissa Golob, a woman in her late twenties and the former executive director of CLC (Campaign for Life) Youth. Golob attended her first anti-abortion protest at age thirteen, when her pen pal invited her to attend the Show the Truth tour, in which activists hold up posters on busy streets, intersections, and high school campuses. The images on the posters, purportedly of fetuses aborted during the first or second trimester of pregnancy, are intentionally gory and shocking. A suburban Ontario woman named Rosemary Connell started the campaign in 1997 after a trip to the US where she participated in a similar protest using the same gruesome tactics. (It's worth mentioning here that in both Canada and the US more than 90 percent of abortions take place in the first trimester, during which, at its twelve-week maximum, the fetus is no more than two and a half inches long. Studies have shown that most women would have their abortions even earlier into gestation, when the fetus is about the size of a pencil eraser, if access—and, in the US, funding—were better.) After her first Show the Truth protest, Golob was hooked. "I think children have this innate black-and-white [view]," she had told me when I interviewed her for the first time in 2014. "Everything is black and white to them: 'Oh, dead baby, bad.' And that's what you want. You wish it could be that easy for everyone." For the next decade after that, she went every summer. When she was with CLC, she organized her own youth-led protests, decorating busy Toronto intersections with similarly horrific photos. She's emceed the Ottawa march, driven across the country in a "No to Trudeau" van, and grown the movement's youth contingent, marking herself as an important leader in the Canadian fight to end abortion.

Golob's place in the movement shifted again in early 2016, when she left CLC to co-found a youth-centric, politically savvy organization called Right Now—its mission to "nominate and elect pro-life politicians." It does so by pushing people to vote at local nomination meetings and training volunteers to create campaign teams in ridings across the country. It took a month for us to set an interview date because she'd been traveling across the country. On the day we finally met over coffee in downtown Toronto, she hadn't been home for most of the month; despite the fact that Canadians generally treat abortion as a hot potato, Golob had been busy.

Dressed in a trendy black velvet dress, she often tugged thoughtfully on her choker as we talked. Golob didn't like Justin Trudeau, but she was not particularly a fan of Trump, either, her expressive eyes rolling in exasperation when I mentioned he was moving her cause forward in the US. She later wrote on her website that she couldn't "fully support" him because of his "outrageous and derogatory comments toward women." She would, however, readily take a note or two from the American movement's tactics, and she would be thrilled if Canada's conservative political leaders spoke with such openness and enthusiasm about their own anti-abortion convictions.

Her frustration at the anti-abortion movement's reticence to evolve leaked through. "The world that we live in and the society we live in right now is completely different than the society we lived in in the 1980s, when abortion was completely decriminalized, or even in the early 1970s, late '60s when it was initially decriminalized, so we can't keep doing the same tactics," she said. She respected the founders of the anti-abortion movement, but felt that what may have worked in the 1970s or '80s wouldn't work now—not, at least, as the movement's sole focus. "There's social media," she said. "There's different shifting world views; there's science that has changed; but most of all there's technology. And I just don't see that the pro-life movement is utilizing that. They're just sticking to continuing to be loud, but not effective." She paused before adding, "To a certain extent." She described her position as emphatically "pro-woman" and identified two elements to the issue: "There's the element of the humanity of the unborn, and then there's the element of the woman and what she's going through." She noted that she'd spent a lot of time working in pregnancy crisis centers, which are often located near abortion clinics and actively seek to counsel women against abortion under the guise of offering "pregnancy resources." The stories she heard convinced her that many women were coerced or felt forced into having abortions and that, because of this, the pro–abortion rights movement treated women "like they're disposable trash, basically." She added that "it was so completely disrespectful and sad and not doing anything to women except making us revert back to not having a say."

If we want further evidence of how essential this pro-women messaging has become to the new generation of anti-abortion activists, consider Lia Mills. Sixteen years old when I first interviewed her in 2012 (for the piece that caused my mother and grandmother so much anguish), Mills rose to fame after posting an anti-abortion call to action on YouTube when she was twelve. Over one million views later, Mills had traveled across North America, growing her army of "life warriors" wherever she went. I've met seven-year-olds in sparkly pink pants who wanted to be just like her and bubbly, blond-haired teens who, after meeting Mills, started anti-abortion clubs in their own high schools. By 2014, thanks in large part to her influence, the majority of the tens of thousands who descended upon Canada's Parliament Hill for the anti-abortion movement's annual March protest were enthusiastic youth.

Now twenty and identifying as a pro-life feminist, Mills published her first book, *An Inconvenient Life*, in fall 2016. I heard from her shortly after I started interviewing pro-life feminists after she, in turn, had heard from someone — not me — that I was delving into the front lines of post-feminism, anti-feminism, and new feminism. She sent me a friendly note and an encouragement to check out her new video. Compelling as always, Mills addressed her audience in a spoken-word beat, condemning both the knee-jerk dismissal of anti-abortion activists as misogynists and what she perceived as a forced societal silence against their advocacy. "Is it at all humanly possible to be pro-women, pro-choice, and pro-life?" she asked. "Third-wave feminists will scream no. As a women and gender studies student, I would know." In the video, Mills asserted that she supports a woman's right to choose — her bodily autonomy — but added, in a plea for her audience to understand, "It is choice without restriction that we oppose and condemn." She used rapists, pedophiles, and other criminals as examples of those who have pushed choice too far, into the realm of harm.

These emerging conversations about women, feminism, and abortion rights often get mired in variations of the question: Who owns feminism? Can the feminist majority really pull a *Mean Girls* and tell the women who call themselves pro-life feminists, "You can't sit with us"? While the abortion debate undoubtedly exposes broad divisions between North American women, to me it feels like a lot of this is a distraction ploy. It's the same one anti-feminists use to undermine all sorts of issues and is meant to force feminists into the exact kind of exclusionary infighting for which we're too often ridiculed. I doubt pro-life feminism is about to completely usurp the other, more popular feminisms, not because reproductive rights are such a solidly built pillar of today's feminism—though either side would likely lament or applaud the truth in that—but because pro-life feminism is so dang narrow. Some of it pays lip service to diversity and also condemns the objectification and hypersexualiz-ation of women and girls (morals, ladies!), but pro-life feminism is, for the most part, solely concerned with pro-life feminism. Those who espouse the pro-life model rarely discuss or address the other structural and systemic barriers women face; I'd hazard a guess that's because they're wound wire-tight with reproductive rights. Instead, it often feels that, like post- and anti-feminists, they assume most women's rights are a done deal.

But that hardly matters: their end goal isn't really to broaden the feminist movement, it's to broaden the anti-abortion one. As Mills said in her video, the movement is often viewed as misogynistic and limiting, with a modus operandi rooted in controlling women's bodies. Anti-abortion feminism, in other words, may not engage in contemporary feminist issues, but rubber-stamping a newly branded "girl power" decal on its anti-abortion politics helps ease its own stigma—you know, so long as it doesn't have to engage in the actual, challenging work of feminism. I don't believe that, deep down, most people, anti-abortion activists included, would like to see themselves as working to send women back through time, like Marty McFly in some weirder, all-girl version of *Back to the Future*. If one thing unites all the many types of "Nah, I'll pass on you, feminism" women I've met it's that they sincerely believe they're helping women. They're *convinced* of it.

Whether other feminists accept their pro-life sisters or not, whether women who fight reproductive rights call themselves feminists or empowered pro-women, the anti-abortion message is the same: only we can answer womankind's SOS call! And that message is alluring to those who ultimately want to diminish and restrict women's rights but sure as hell don't want to admit that's what they're doing (even to themselves). In their minds, not only are pro-lifers rescuing women from feminism, they're also rescuing feminism from women. How *utterly* benevolent. As a result, we're told the same old BS: we can embrace feminism so long as we keep it palatable; so long as it's more about easy empowerment and less about the complex, exhausting, and difficult fight for real rights; so long as it, at its rotten core, promotes anti-feminism. So, no, I can't see pro-life feminism one day dominating the feminist movement; that would imply a coexistence or even a partnership, albeit an imbalanced one. But can I see it working alongside the anti-feminist and post-feminist movements to crush modern, intersectional feminisms and the reproductive and sexual rights around which they mobilize? Well, yeah, sure, I can see *that*.

Next to the trade show in the hotel's ballroom, men in plaid shirts dismantled the sound system from that afternoon's youth-only rally. Neon lights still illuminated the stage when I peeked my head in. About an hour earlier, music from Transform DJs — "high energy, Christ-centered Electronic Dance Music" — had pounded through the floor of the room where the Law of Life Summit was held, traveling up from the anti-abortion rave. The next day, the all-male group, whose "hits" include "I See You Moving" ("Hands up! For justice! For life!"), and whose members wear shirts like "I survived Roe vs Wade/Roe vs Wade will not survive me," opened the March for Life rally with the promise: "You are the generation that's going to end abortion."

I snuck in and grabbed some of the pamphlets and postcards left on a few seats. One advertised an event for that night: a mega–prayer session called One Voice DC. Another encouraged students to get behind the #StandForLife social media movement. A postcard for Stover's organization, Students for Life, detailed how to equip the "pro-life generation," with tips on how to get a starter activist kit and how to request one of the group's traveling displays. I also found, among other things, a photocopied *Cosmopolitan* feature on Brandi Swindell, founder of Stanton Healthcare and a speaker at the youth rally.

Swindell's Stanton Healthcare in Boise, Idaho, is a good example of how the mawkish "pro-life, pro-woman" doublespeak works. Named after suffragette and women's rights activist Elizabeth Cady Stanton, the center fills a huge gap in women's health services, providing everything from ultrasounds to pregnancy testing to baby supplies, and offering no- or low-cost options. I'm not about to slam any center for offering women's health services, particularly those that help low-income women, and I can see how Stanton's traveling ultrasound clinic, which services rural communities and refugee populations, fulfills its purported pro-women mandate. I might have been swayed to see it like the *Cosmo* writer presents it: an alternative center for women who need help with their pregnancies. *Might have*, if not for one teensy tiny—okay, colossal—problem: that's not its central mission. The clinic dubs itself a "life-affirming medical clinic," which is another way of saying "pregnancy crisis center," which is another way of saying that it's located next to a Planned Parenthood and also includes "options counseling" and "sexual integrity consultations" on its list of services. It does not offer any form of contraception, and, of course, does not provide abortions. Stanton Healthcare's motto is "Replace Planned Parenthood." Its marketing material reads "We will not just COMPETE. We will not simply EXPOSE. We will not only DEFUND. It's time to REPLACE Planned Parenthood."

It's this end goal of "pro-life, pro-women" and "pro-life feminism" that undermines any posturing the movement makes toward what it claims are its new, sparkly women's rights objectives. The more deeply I dug beyond the seriously cool hair, Instagram posts, and trendy T-shirts, the more at odds the anti-abortion movement's women's rights makeover and the wider feminist movement seemed. Feminism, after all, generally works to broaden what we can do and achieve, not restrict it. If anything, these women wanted to narrow women's roles, honing who they were and all they could be into a strict faith-based prototype. They may have advocated individualism and independence, but they also prescribed how to do it: be yourself, but only if you color within the traditional lines of family and femininity. Of course, that's not how they put it to the new legions of anti-abortion activists at the youth rally, or the hundreds that milled about the trade show next door. The aisle housing the Student for Life booth, its affiliate Rock for Life, and their Pro-Life Outfitters clothing arm was especially congested, looking less like a trade show and more like a rock concert merchandise table. I had to hand it to them: they knew how to market to millennials.

On the table, a Rock for Life postcard urged "Be Active. Save Babies. Get Free Stuff." Another asked "Know someone who has had an abortion?" A friendly twentysomething handed out bright pink (of course) stickers that read "Don't fund Planned Parenthood." She peeled them off by the dozen and smoothed them over teens' backpacks and shirts. The throngs of young women ogled selfie-perfect shirts. In addition to the ones I'd seen earlier, I spotted a baby blue T-shirt with the silhouette of a pregnant woman that read "#ImWithBoth." Another, on hunter green, said "Former Embryo." A third, the most popular according to the website, featured a little arrow, just 'cuz, and cool graphic print that read "Human Rights for All." Teens handed over cash and clutched their purchases. Some had already thrown them over their old clothes, modeling them around the show. A lot of them carried hot pink signs with feminist slogans. "I think that this generation craves authenticity," said Student for Life's Stover. "We want real solutions to real problems.

We don't like abortion because it poses a quick fix to a deeper issue. It's like putting a Band-Aid on a bullet wound. We want a real authentic solution."

In many cases, this authentic solution is abstinence. The front of one Students for Life hand-out card showed a smiling white couple, college-aged, next to a heart that read, in cursive writing, "Dispelling the myths about 'safe sex.'" On the back, one of the truths offered was "Condoms simply act as a barrier for preventing pregnancy. They are not designed to protect from STDs." Umm. Another: "The claim that hormonal birth control will 'prevent' sexually transmitted diseases is scientifically false." Well, yes. That's something students commonly learn in (non-abstinence-based) sexual education classes. Earlier that day, I'd also picked up abstinence-based curriculum books, one of which included a real-life story from a woman named Stephanie who attributed her success and admission to Oxford University to her sobriety and virginity: "I will wear this ring on my wedding ring finger as a symbol of my promise to not have sex until I am married. One day, on my wedding night, I will give this ring to my husband as a symbol of the love I have for him...a love that is so strong it made me wait for him." I guess pro-life feminism missed the memo on anti–slut shaming, as well as the one about working to ensure women have healthy, confident, and *informed* sex lives.

Another missed memo: the one about not criminalizing women who make their own choices about their own bodies. Although the new wave of anti-abortion organizations are largely against punishing women who have abortions, less is said about what would happen if—or when—they succeed in obliterating Roe v. Wade. Many laws that do punish women who have abortions are still on the books, kept in check only by Roe. Once it goes: *poof!* States will be able to start prosecuting under them once more, an even scarier thought considering many of them are designed to punish women who perform their own abortions, a practice that is likely to increase if anti-abortion groups also succeed in diminishing Planned

Parenthood. Already, as of 2017's March for Life, four American women had been charged for self-inducing their own abortions, three of them with drugs purchased online and one with a coat hanger. These desperate women had not visited a clinic because of cost and distance, and also, in at least one case, shame. Ultimately, Roe saved the women from serious jail time, but their cases provide a chilling glimpse into our possible future.

Drifting through the conference, I couldn't help but wonder the same thing many leaders in the anti-abortion movement had been asking themselves, both in Canada and the US: What happens when the new faces of the anti-abortion movement can vote? What will those 80 percent of marchers in Canada, those cheering pro-life feminists, decide? I doubt we can count on them to uphold the progressive spirit of feminism — to fight against the creeping Islamophobia and rising anti-immigration sentiment in our countries, to protect LGBTQ rights, to expand Indigenous rights, or to recognize the vital importance of movements like Black Lives Matter. I'm not sure how they'll interpret even the most basic rights for those who are not like them. The next day, at the march and outdoor rally, I drained the battery on my phone taking photos and videos of the new "pro-life generation," still marveling at their pink signs, their ardent use of the word "feminist." There! And there! And there! One group of young high schoolers burst from the crowd, blond and bright, their cheeks rosy from the howling wind or maybe excitement, their voices clear and loud, triumphant laughter marking the end.

"Build the wall!"
"Build the wall!"
"Build the wall!"
"Pro-life!"

THREE

The future is feminist

9 Reason for hope: The young women and girls who are giving misogyny the middle finger

When I was in Washington for the March for Life, I visited the Belmont-Paul Women's Equality National Monument. The brick house was built in 1800 on a Capitol Hill street corner and burned in the War of 1812, only to rise again, phoenix-like, in 1929 as the headquarters for the National Women's Party and hub of the American suffrage movement. I made this side trip because I wanted to see where the first wave of feminism had flourished into being. For all its flaws (hello, white feminism, meet your deeply rooted origins), the suffrage movement eked out women's first rights and rose defiant against its contemporary anti-feminist culture, and the irony of its status among today's anti-feminists was not lost on me as I padded through the house, its stained-glass windows making a kaleidoscope of light. Suffragist women were jailed, beaten, and force-fed if they went on hunger strikes to protest, and still they fought for the right to vote, a right that some anti-feminist women today, nearly a century later, want to repeal. For feminists, this was the moment things started looking up; for anti-feminists, it was the moment the world went to hell.

Inside, I planted myself in front of a door-sized ornate mirror decorated with a gold decal sticker of another frame. A small plaque beneath the mirror encouraged museum goers to take a selfie: "See yourself here." I turned that phrase over in my mind as I stood there, staring at myself, face puffy with exhaustion, hips full with a too-steady diet of chocolate, and really thought about it. What would it take for us to make a shift as seismic as women's first emancipation? The white marble busts of Alice Paul, Alva Belmont (who, if you don't know, was not just the pocketbook of the movement but a woman with a wicked taste in feathered hats), Susan B. Anthony, and Elizabeth Cady Stanton surrounded me. I may not have wanted their feminism, but I knew all of us today owe them a debt. If they were alive, I thought, we'd likely have much to teach each other.

Turning to go upstairs, my guide, dressed in full park-ranger attire, pointed out the seven gold-tipped, spiked poles mounted to the stairwell. They, the actual poles the women used to fly their protest flags, were taller than I, their surfaces slightly knotted and dinged. "You can touch them," the guide, Lauren, said as we walked up the steps. "Rub off a little courage." As I walked through the house, I admired the suffragist women's knack for flair and pageantry. They knew how to make a dope sign. Often in the gold, white, or purple of the movement—or sometimes all three—the huge cloth signs balanced hope and demand, shame and surety. One sign, gold on gold, read in all capitals: "Forward. Out of the darkness. Leave behind the night. Forward out of error. Forward into light." Another, purple on white, with a scalloped and fringed edge: "Mr. President what will you do for woman suffrage?" And perhaps the most famous, some of the last words Inez Milholland Boissevain, the woman on the white horse, uttered: "Mr. President, how long must women wait for liberty?" It was the last sign I saw, though, that sent chills skittering up my spine—the good kind of chills that told me even these early feminists knew the movement needed to keep building, building, building to thrive. Framed behind glass, a watermark cracking down its middle, it read, "The young are at the gates."

They say you can't go home again. But if you pester the principal enough, you can go back to high school, which is almost the same thing. Since starting this project, I'd wanted to return to my old high school gender studies class, a place that had played a formative role in my own feminism. It's likely that, in the early 2000s, my high school was one of a handful in the entire province offering gender studies classes. That's since changed, thanks to a group of young women called the Miss G—— Project for Equity in Education. (Julie Lalonde, whom we met in chapter two, was one of its members.) The project is named after a case study in Dr. Edward H. Clarke's 1873 book *Sex in Education; or, A Fair Chance for Girls*. Miss G——, a young woman of remarkable intellect, died, doctors declared, because she tried to compete with young men in the academic field. "Believing that woman can do what man can, for she held that faith, she strove with noble but ignorant bravery to compass man's intellectual attainment in a man's way, and died in the effort," at least according to Clarke. The goal of the Miss G—— Project was to implement gender studies electives in high schools across Ontario (and, ideally, spark similar curriculum changes across the country). After an eight-year advocacy and public awareness campaign, the project succeeded. In fall 2013 the first gender studies classes debuted across Ontario high schools.

I'd badly wanted to sit in on those first classes, and in January 2017 I finally got a chance. What kind of young women and men would sign up, I wondered? Would this new generation of budding feminists sense the fault lines across generations? How did students engage with these new feminisms, and how had the class changed in the fifteen years since I'd been a high school student?

On the day I arrived, freezing rain had slicked the sidewalks and popped my umbrella open like a muffin top. Pathetic fallacy: something I'd learned in high school. I walked up the front steps, paused. Reoriented to the office. Nausea swam through my déjà vu, a physical feeling that started at my toes and made my hands lurch a lopsided signature when I signed my name on the visitors' log. Then Erin Crawford, teacher of the grade eleven gender studies class, appeared, carrying a clock (seriously—pathetic fallacy!), and her presence saved me from folding time in on itself like an accordion.

We walked down the same sticky linoleum hallways I'd walked down every day for five years (I went to school when there was still a grade thirteen). I was chatting away about how long it had been since I'd been back, when suddenly my insides dipped. We were passing it: the locker, my old one, the one that my teenage rapist had pushed me up against, his hand to my throat, warning me not to tell. In that instant, I thought: And still we question whether these young women and men really need gender studies—if they're ready, if they're interested, whether they'll relate.

In the classroom, Crawford hoisted herself onto a desk, hanging the clock, while I looked around the room. The desks were old, with the same seafoam green and faded blue hard plastic chairs that I remembered, arranged in a fan. At the back wall, fluorescent paper letters demanded "Be the change!" They hung over a long, rainbow-colored grid of pictures of famous people captioned with phrases like "She happens to be a lesbian" and "He happens to be gay." Another wall was decorated with posters the students had made. One said "Feminism is not a bad word"; another "Be happy, be comfortable, be yourself!" A few simply prescribed "love." One stated "Love is love." Posters celebrating transgender rights and trans love decorated every wall. On these walls, body shaming was condemned, feminism was intersectional, and both J. K. Rowling and Ani DiFranco held places of inspiration.

A poster asking "What is wrong with this picture?" featured a collage of magazine cut-outs showing hypersexualized men and women (Axe ads had their own special column). Another, tucked beside Crawford's desk and taped to the blackboard, read "Feeling uncomfortable is a necessary part of unlearning oppressive behaviors." On the way into the class, I passed a small alcove covered in yellow Post-its. A sign reading "Positive Posts" invited the students to leave some nice words. There were more than fifty, with short bursts of solidarity. "Smile." "You matter." "I love you." "Shine." "You are worthy." The class credo had even spilled out into the surrounding hallway. Giant sheets of paper advised fellow students on consent, gender fluidity, and preferred pronouns; slut shaming, anti-feminism, and not staying true to yourself were all told to take a hike. It was Instagram feminism meets intersectionality, and damn, was it effective. Combined with a truly barrier-breaking, highly inclusive brand of feminism, the self-love side of this new feminism ceased to irk me. It seemed more about protecting mental health and real self-worth—valuable goals for high school students—and less about superficiality. It's something I could have desperately used as a teenager. This was nothing like my gender studies class fifteen years ago; this was so much better.

The students shuffled in at 10:20 AM, a bundle of sweatpants and leggings, mostly young women, but also a few men, chattering giddily. Racially, they were a diverse group. Crawford opened the class by asking the students for updates on their independent study unit, a research project for which each student must investigate women's rights in a particular country. Students talked about femicide, access to education, domestic violence, women's legal rights, sanctioned rape, cultures of obedience, and more. One young woman summarized the problems facing women in her assigned country as such: "But it's, like, so whack." The comments made her classmates laugh and also bob their heads in agreement. Crawford stood up. Tall and lithe, she wore an eggplant hoodie, gray skinny jeans, and oxblood Blundstones, which she called "Blunnies." Her hair was short and asymmetrical, and when she lifted her arm to gesture I noticed a small tattoo on her wrist. In a word, Crawford was cool. "I think in this class we've taken away our rose-colored glasses and thrown them out a long time ago," she said, miming a toss toward the door. "But sometimes, it's still like, 'Holy smokes!'"

Next she handed out an infographic showing statistics on women worldwide. Example: "Women preform two-thirds of the world's work, yet receive only 10 percent of global income." When Crawford asked the class what struck them about the numbers, more than half a dozen hands flew up. They were particularly bothered by the wage gap and the implications of earning less, not to mention the idea of possibly picking up the domestic slack. One teen, her eyes rimmed with black kohl and a Monster Energy drink perched on the corner of her desk, remarked that if the wage gap didn't budge, "like, change won't happen." The students were engaged, thoughtful, and daring. They were so much more daring than I had been in class at that age. While watching Sheryl WuDunn's TED Talk on the Half the Sky movement to help women and girls, a conversation erupted over periods and the high costs of menstrual products. Crawford had just commented that many women in India drop out of school once they begin menstruating because they can't afford pads and are ashamed.

"What do they do then?"

"Shove a towel up there?"

"Oh god."

"Pads and tampons should be free!"

"Nobody wants to bleed everywhere."

The conversation evolved, touching on the stigma associated with periods and how more light needs to be shed on homeless women's access to menstrual products. It's not something I ever would have mentioned in high school, especially not in class and *especially* not in a class with boys. But these students dug in with aplomb. When the class bell clanged, they dragged their feet, still chatting. WuDunn's talk on women who'd overcome oppression inspired them. One student with long blond hair remarked, "How they're rising above—it gives me the chills." She sat for a moment, thinking. A quick current shuddered through her. The chills. She grabbed her backpack and slung it over her shoulder. As I started to pack up my own stuff, Crawford told me about how she was the first person to teach the official gender studies course, HSG3M, in the school board district. Every year, about twenty students enrolled—not a big class, but an invested one. I was scheduled to come back tomorrow to interview the students about their thoughts on the class and feminism. We mused about what they would tell me, and I remarked that her class was so different from the one I'd taken. We agreed that was an incredibly good thing; feminism has to evolve.

I navigated the hallways out, dodging the teeming students. To complete my high school redux, I'd planned lunch with one of my oldest and best friends, whose family home sat across from the high school. She happened to be there and to have the day off. We used to head to her house almost every day at lunch, dodging across four lanes of traffic (this time, I crossed at the light), cutting through the apartment cluster we called the Red Bricks, then through the alley and into the shelter of her house. Once, we laughed so hard, mushroom soup shot out of my nose. It was that kind of friendship: the kind that fades out the bad parts of your day, and we both had many of those bad parts in high school.

I burst through her front door, rain clinging to my hair. "They're so young," I said, by way of greeting, peeling off my coat. I thought about it. *"We were so young."*

She didn't miss a beat. "I know."

In March 2015, when *This Magazine* boldly declared, "Canada needs more feminism," we were, quite literally, saying "fuck that" to the previous year's heap-ton of messed-up stuff: the charges of violent sexual assault against Jian Ghomeshi, the Dalhousie University dentistry students whose private "Gentleman's Club" Facebook group talked about using chloroform on women and polled which female classmate they'd like to "hate fuck" the most, the multiple rape allegations against Bill Cosby, and, yes, the rise of anti-feminism. *This* advocated for intersectional feminism, strong alliances with men, and universal child care. We challenged the idea that feminism needs one woman to be its brand ambassador, celebrated pluralities and grassroots movements, and cheered the power of social media. As editor, I was nervous about how it would be received—I, of all people, knew what a charged issue feminism had become—but it became one of the best-selling issues we ever did during my five years at the magazine (though I did receive a couple of middle fingers and one very angry monologue from a woman anti-feminist at that year's Word on the Street festival in Toronto). The launch party, which featured talks from two women of color and a transgender woman, was packed.

The perception that young women don't care about feminism stubbornly persists, but that's an unfairly broad characterization. The *Washington Post*/Kaiser Family Foundation poll reveals that young women, on the whole, are actually more likely to say they are either a feminist or a strong feminist. A full 63 percent of women aged eighteen to thirty-four embraced the f-word, the second highest out of all age groups; women aged fifty to sixty-four nudged them out of the top spot at 68 percent. The younger group was, however, far more apt to say it felt the current movement focused on issues that mattered to them. Nearly 60 percent of them agreed feminism had zeroed in on the right issues, and more than 80 percent agreed the movement was empowering—a marked difference from older generations. They were also the least likely to call it outdated, at only 16 percent. If anything, a closer examination of all the "Are you a feminist?" surveys shows that young women care deeply about feminism; it's just that their feminism may often not resemble that of those who came before them. As discussed in previous chapters, that difference, when expressed in individualistic or even commodified attitudes, can be problematic. But, frankly, it can also be incredibly inspiring.

I created my own informal survey in January 2015 and largely promoted it, on purpose, through social media. I knew it wouldn't be the most scientific study, but I didn't just want to know the numbers; I wanted to know what women today *thought* about feminism. I wanted millennials, those who grew up with, and were now possibly even entrenched in, our digital culture, to answer me. To my surprise, the survey received over one hundred responses in the first few hours it went live. In the end, more than three hundred people answered, and most of them weren't even trolls! On average, those who filled out the survey were close to my age: in their late twenties and early thirties. All genders responded (close to 15 percent of those who completed the survey were men, actually), but I was most interested in the answers of those who identified as women, transgender women, or gender fluid. The idea was to hear how women themselves, and particularly the age segment we seem to puzzle over the most, interacted with the f-word and what it meant to them.

Of the women who answered, 88 percent said they identified as feminists. Though I didn't give them the option of choosing the degree to which they were a feminist, these variations emerged anyway. The word "feminist," I acknowledged, can be loaded. Tell me more, I asked. Why do you identify with it? Some of the answers were so short and to the point, they made me laugh. "I believe in equality for women, duh," said one twenty-four-year-old. A twenty-eight-year-old responded, "Equality yo," and a thirty-four-year-old offered possibly my favorite answer: "Next." It really should be that simple! I also appreciated the bit of snark I received: "I believe in equality and I know what the term 'feminist' actually means," said a thirty-year-old. Some were emphatic and fed up, for example: "Because gender equality is not a reality. I'm sick of accepting the status quo," said a thirty-seven-year-old, and, "The idea of not standing up for my own rights to equality, not to mention the rights of women and girls around the world, is reprehensible," said a twenty-nine-year-old. Women talked about reclaiming the word and taking it back "from people who have twisted it or turned it into something negative." They talked about the importance of intersectionality and elevating long suppressed and oppressed voices within the movement. And they talked about the importance of doing more than just using the word: "Feminism is an everyday life practice, not an identity to slip on and off whenever it suits you," observed a twenty-nine-year-old.

By far, though, the most common answer I received relied on the dictionary definition of feminism, with many young women born in the 1980s, '90s, and '00s asserting they believed in feminism because they believed in equality and equal rights—no elaboration necessary. At the same time, some of the more interesting answers came from those who were grappling with the term and what it meant to them. In some cases, these women actively positioned their use of "feminist" or "feminism" against perceptions of the wider movement, both external and internal. There were a lot more of these answers than I anticipated, such as those included below, all from women under forty, across the LGBTQ spectrum:

"I consider myself a feminist in the original meaning of the term: absolute equality in work, life, and relationships as well as complete control over one's own body. I do not advocate aggressive blaming or finger-pointing at the opposite gender, and I do not believe in women perceiving themselves as perpetual victims of the patriarchy. Sisters need to do it for themselves."

"Yes to equal rights, pay, treatment. Not picket signs."

"I haven't completely unpacked that yet. Injustice and inequality infuriates me. What infuriates me more is how passively we all accept it. Rape culture and sex shaming are so deeply ingrained in all of us and I want it to stop."

"I do, but I didn't always. I find many people who identify as feminists go to the extreme to identify women as victims or do not acknowledge the intersectionality of gender. After all, white women only have so much to complain about; we need to be listening to our sisters of color."

"I believe in equality, although the term 'feminist' is starting to annoy me."

The uncertainty revealed many things: a fear of doing it "right," a retreat from the traditional political expressions of feminism, a frustration with the trappings of the word, a need for a fuller commitment to intersectionality, and worry over whether they could take ownership of a term they felt was historically rooted in fights outside their everyday experiences. But nowhere did I sense a complete ignorance of what feminism meant, nor any sign that post–*Mad Men*–era women had collectively hit themselves on the head and suffered mass amnesia. They knew the political actions from which they benefitted. Though today's feminists may have shifted their focus to different issues, many of which reflect our modern, messy anxieties over gender, and some of which can be considered trivial, they had not, as is sometimes suggested, forgotten that it mattered. Young women have spearheaded some of today's most energizing campaigns, utilizing social media and technology to connect, share, and discuss on an immense scale. Some of us like to dismissively call this "slacktivism," that catchy portmanteau of "slacker" and "activism." Pop science writer Malcolm Gladwell disparaged it in his 2010 *New Yorker* article "Small Change," in which he argued, "We seem to have forgotten what activism is." I think we're underestimating how powerful and courageous a loud, expansive, public conversation on feminism can be, particularly at a time when we're so averse to dropping the f-bomb.

In spring 2012, a group of Duke University students who enrolled in a class called "Women in the Public Sphere: History, Theory, and Practice" underwent a feminist awakening. While they learned the history of women's activism in the US inside the class, outside there was a renewed focus on sexual assault on the Duke campus and much discussion about the university's party culture. The move to defund Planned Parenthood was just getting started. Rush Limbaugh had called Georgetown University law student and birth control advocate Sandra Fluke a "slut" and a "prostitute." As a result, classroom discussions were lively, in-depth, and intersectional. "But," wrote course instructor Rachel Seidman in a later analysis, "when my students tried to talk about these ideas outside of class, they were often shut down by their peers' refusal to engage or by accusations that they were 'man-hating feminists.' Deeply frustrated, they asked, 'How can we make any progress on any of these issues if we can't even talk about them?'" As a solution, the students decided to open dialogue on campus through a social media "PR campaign" for feminism.

Together, the class recruited a diverse cross-section of their family, friends, and acquaintances, giving each a black marker, a small whiteboard, and instructions to finish the sentence "I need feminism because . . ." Each posed with their answer for a photo, which the students used to launch the campaign "Who Needs Feminism?" On the morning of April 12, 2012, they plastered the Duke campus with campaign printouts and wrote an op-ed for the school newspaper. "But as these posters remind us," students wrote, "the goal of equality is not yet achieved . . . It takes a lot of people to change a stereotype." Online, students created Facebook and Tumblr pages to share the photos. They were not prepared for the reaction. Even now, wrote Seidman in her analysis, "Who Needs Feminism? Lessons From a Digital World," they have no idea how the campaign became so popular so quickly.

But soon, women and men from around the world were sending in their own photos. Buzzfeed, Mashable, and Huffington Post called. *Good* magazine named the campaign its Good Gone Viral national winner. High schools and colleges around the world have now participated in their own versions of the campaign. In 2013 Oxford University organized a photo shoot and more than five hundred people showed up. Today, years after the class graduated, the Facebook page is still active. The conversation has moved past "the already converted," as Seidman put it, and connected many people who'd never otherwise meet to discuss feminism.

And that isn't the only example of social media getting loud. In Canada, the hashtag #BeenRapedNeverReported became a global phenomenon within twenty-four hours, with nearly eight million people taking part in the conversation, many of them young women. (I wonder if Antonia Zerbisias, one of the women who first sent this hashtag into the world, and also the former *Toronto Star* journalist who'd ridiculed fourth-wave, intersectional feminists, realized that many of them were the ones carrying on her hashtag.) The hashtag #MMIW was created to draw attention to Canada's many missing and murdered Indigenous women and to pressure the federal government into launching an inquiry. Toronto teens Tessa Hill and Lia Valente started the online We Give Consent campaign in 2015 to get consent into Ontario's provincial curriculum. They won. The hashtag #YouKnowHerName trended after Canadian courts enacted a publication ban on Rehtaeh Parsons' name, the Nova Scotian teen who died following a suicide attempt after she was mercilessly bullied when a photo of her rape was shared around her school. Saying her name was a way of honoring her and keeping the conversation about cyberbullying, rape, and consent going. And then there's #YesAllWomen, the global movement that arose after the Elliot Rodger killings and also in response to the reactive #NotAllMen chorus. It continues to underscore women's daily experiences with misogyny. These online conversations aren't the only way young women are engaging with feminism, but it's time we stop discounting them. Perhaps what's truly outdated is thinking that these conversations don't make it offline into real, live action. Thousands of young women are practicing their feminism every day in their communities and in their lives. I know that because, despite all the women I've met who say feminism is passé, I've also met a whole helluva lot of young women who say it's not.

I returned to my old high school to meet with a few of Crawford's students and hear more about their lives as teenage feminists. I met them in the library, a huddle of feisty, thoughtful sixteen-year-olds in plush red chairs, positioned at the back of the two-tier room, next to the manga. The group who volunteered to chat with me was diverse, including two young women of color (Victoria and Areeja), two young white women (Kaitlyn and Josie), and one teen named Sam who identified as genderless and prefers the pronoun they/their. ("There's male and there's female," Sam told me, placing one hand to the far left and one to the far right. Then Sam stretched one arm far to the back. "Then there's me. I'm, like, outside getting McDonald's.") When the term started, Sam told me, Crawford had asked the class to raise their hands if they were a feminist. The only person who did so was Sam, whose mother is the president of the board of directors of their local chapter of Girls, Inc. Even so, Sam once recoiled from the word, too, particularly when Sam's mom tried to send Sam to a Girls, Inc. summer camp. "I told her, 'I don't want to go to a quote-unquote feminazi camp—especially since I'm genderless.' I didn't want to be surrounded by girls because I knew I'd get called 'she.'" But that wasn't what Sam experienced at all. "One, everybody called me 'they,' and that was great. Two, I learned more about what feminism is. It's not what some people might think it is. It's not all about 'women are better than men.' It really is about equality and raising girls to believe they are equal—they are strong enough."

"I didn't raise my hand," said Victoria. "I don't really think I thought about it ever. You pick up on little things that people do to put down girls. You don't really think you need to do anything about it. It just happens all the time so you just go with it. Being in this class and being aware of what happens to women everywhere—I am a feminist." Kaitlyn added that the stereotypes about feminism had also stopped her from raising her hand that first class, but the more she realized the word is not "what people have made it," the more she changed her mind: "I would say that I identify as a feminist now." Areeja agreed. She had always questioned the "girls are supposed to" thinking she heard, but until she got to class, she said, "I never questioned it *too* much." Now, she's more confident in her opinions. Josie, who played on the boys' hockey team for six years growing up, and was the only girl on the ice, said that she always identified as a feminist but never understood why it was important to voice it out loud. Plus, there was a stigma. Still, if asked that question today, she and the rest of the group would all raise their hands — at least, if they were in class.

"Although has anyone noticed that when you tell somebody you're in the gender studies class they give you the look?" asked Sam, demonstrating a facial expression that conveyed disgust for all things losery, a look I perfected during my high school years but have never been able to effectively pull off since. Sam called it the look of "Oh, really?" The others murmured assent, and stories emerged in rapid fire.

"A friend was like, 'Ugh, really?' Are they teaching you that there are two genders?" said Sam, referring to an internet meme that pokes fun at the assertion there are more than two genders.

"That's the number one question that I got," added Josie.

"Or that it's a girls' class," said Victoria.

"Or it's like, 'You actually like that class?'" added Kaitlyn. "Stuff like that."

When I asked them what issues are most pressing for them and their peers, and how increased awareness of feminism might help tackle those issues, the group didn't hesitate. Slut shaming. Sexual harassment. Consent. Josie, who told me it was the first week she'd come to school without makeup on since grade six, felt that girls in the school were taught not to complain if they were assaulted. "A guy can come up to me and grab me by any part of my body, and that's okay because he *wants* me," she said. Victoria smirked, "It's flirting." If sixteen-year-olds were encouraged to dismiss this kind of stuff, Josie wondered, how would they react when they were older? She added that she was thankful she'd never been harassed or assaulted at school. She let the words hang in the air for a moment and then reconsidered. Actually, she added, that kind of behavior was so normal at school, she *had* experienced it; she'd just never known to call it that before. Someone once grabbed Sam's crotch to "see if I had a dick." A teacher once said it was okay for students to ask Sam about genitalia because the students might be curious. Sam had been called a "special snowflake" a lot.

Then there was that Instagram thing. The year before my visit, they told me, a group of male students from the schools in their region started posting nude photos of girls online. *Everyone* was talking about it. Girls were named and rated and called fat sluts. Victoria spent a lot of time blocking on social media people who were following the account. Eventually the ringleaders were caught, and it fizzled out. But boys at the school are still constantly asking girls for nudes and then sharing them as soon as they get them. The group was disappointed by the administration's response, which, they felt, was often to simply delete the photos. Girls were told not to send them. Fair enough, they said, but what about the culture of pressure, of learning consent and respect? What about that?

Victoria added that she'd been the target of slut shaming. "It happened to me. I had a bad reputation in grade nine," she told me. "People would yell 'slut' to me in the hallway. No one ever stood up for me. Because I had a bad reputation, they had no respect for my body. A guy would talk to me and be like, 'OK are you going to send me nudes?' Or people would come up to me and just grab my waist. Even though I did do dumb things it didn't mean that *anyone* could touch me. I was just supposed to take it. If I didn't, guys would get mad at me: 'Oh, you're ugly anyways—you're gross.'" Then she said something that made my skin prickle: "And like it was my fault." On some level, it seemed, she still hadn't been able to shake the feeling that she'd deserved it. My mind flashed back to the "positive posts" that decorated the entrance to the gender studies classroom. Suddenly, the little affirmations of "You're worthy" and "Love" scrawled on the pale yellow squares didn't seem the least bit hokey. They seemed vital. This, I realized, was a feminism of healing.

The most important thing many of them had learned in gender studies, they agreed, was that things can change, even if it starts out on the tiniest of scales. I've learned this, too: once young women start engaging in feminism, amazing things can happen, whether they're aiming big or small. Victoria, like others in the gender studies course, has started to live by a creed she'd learned in that unique classroom: Little things do matter. "When you speak up, just in little groups," she told me, "or in response to things that you hear in the halls, it does make a difference. Even though they may not change the way they think or believe, you may get them to start thinking about it." In these small ways, the group agreed, you can make progress. Just then, the bell rang out through the library. We'd lost track of time. I was supposed to have met with a second group, but there had been too much to say. They could have talked for hours more.

As they packed their bags and headed to lunch, Sam lobbed out one more thought, an endnote to the conversation: "Consent and respect, my friends!" They all nodded. *Consent and respect.* And then they walked away, each back to their own friend groups, soon swallowed up in the crowded hallways.

Minnah Stein held up a colorful drawing of a woman with a very big head. "This is Marie Antoinette," the sixteen-year-old told me. Her smile stretched wide as her hand dipped to grab the next drawing. "And this is Catherine the Great." When Stein was little, she loved the book *Lives of Extraordinary Women,* written by Kathleen Krull and illustrated by Kathryn Hewitt and first published in 2000. "I drew all the women in it," she explained. Around that same time, her parents would bring her with them to the voting booth, explaining why it was so important to vote and what the suffragists had done so she could have that right. They told her how hard it had been for those early feminists: the violence, the beatings, the jail time. "Feminism isn't just a label that I put on myself," she told me. "It's part of my core beliefs. It affects who I am, the decisions that I make, and how I interact with other people. Feminism is something that I was taught, but now growing up it's a choice I make to practice every day through my thoughts and actions."

Stein founded the organization EMPOWER U to help other students in Sarasota County, Florida, take a stand on the issues that mattered to them. For Stein, that issue is sexual assault, which she calls one of the biggest civil rights issues facing youth today. She easily rattled off the statistics for me: one in five girls and one in sixteen boys will be sexually assaulted in college; it happens in our elementary, middle, and high schools at the same rates. Two years earlier, she said, she held a pledge drive at all the high schools in her county, encouraging students to stop sexual assault in their schools. Last year, she screened the documentary *It Happened Here*, which tells the stories of five young women who were assaulted on their college campuses, throughout high schools in her county—a total of more than 1,500 students. That's not to mention all the volunteering she does.

When I asked her how she keeps motivated, Stein responded that she has ambassadors at schools across the county who help her spread the word and get things done. Even so, it wasn't like they were talking about the f-word 24/7; it was simply an ethic by which they lived. Besides the occasional remark at a debate event (the very classic "Girls can't do X because they're girls"), she stressed that she hadn't even experienced much sexism in her own life. But that wasn't the point. She wasn't trying to improve only her own life. "My friends and I don't sit around and talk about how we're feminist and all the feminist things are going on," she said. "We support each other in our feminist views, and I think that's something that's really important. I think some of that is because we're still young and as we start to get older, we'll start to see sexual discrimination more and more, especially in the workforce and the colleges. Maybe that is what leads to being more vocal about identifying as a feminist. When you see things like this happening, you want to get involved and make sure that you can help stop it."

And she's far from the only young woman who's getting involved. In Toronto, Kasha Slavner took six months off school to travel around the world with her mother, Marla. They documented the adversities people faced worldwide as well as how they triumphed over them. Her idea was to tell these stories through a feminist lens but also through a teenager's viewpoint. Kasha raised funding for her documentary journey, called the Global Sunrise Project, through crowdsourcing and in-kind sponsorships. When I spoke to her after the film's completion, she told me that the response had been so great that she had decided to delay university, so she could ride the momentum and keep working on the project. The idea for the project first sparked when, at fourteen, the organization Canadian Voice of Women for Peace selected her as a youth delegate to attend the United Nations for the fifty-seventh annual session on the Commission on the Status of Women. Surrounded by eight thousand men and women who were passionate about women's rights, she realized that almost every issue could be tackled through a feminist or gender-equality lens. "I was seeing people from almost every kind of community in the world, every continent, both rural and urban settings," she told me. "And the fact they were so knowledgeable and passionate about the issues was really inspiring—to learn from them and hear their stories and what drove them. I felt really empowered coming back from that." She's never missed a UN Status of Women session since.

Although young women like Slavner and Stein are extraordinary and raising awareness on a large scale, I also spoke with many other girls and young women who were all practicing feminism in their own ways—working, through routine actions, big and small, to shift the conversation. When I put a call out for interviews in 2016, I was inundated with responses. For days, my phone buzzed frequently with new email notifications from girls who were eager to talk about their views on feminism and the issues affecting them. In the grocery store. While I was in kickboxing class. Out for drinks at a Harry Potter–themed bar (yup). I got the sense that these teenagers were thankful for the opportunity to parse their feelings on feminism and to have someone listen enthusiastically to the concerns they had about issues facing them and their peers. I heard from women all over the world. I spoke for nearly two hours with a young blind woman in Brunei who wanted to start a feminist club, even though, she said, such a thing was unheard of. An Indian teenager going to school in Dubai told me about heading and co-founding a forum called Fem that holds talks and competitions related to gender equality, as well as campaigns that focus on different themes. She had faced a lot of flak recently, she shared, because she'd decided to make a career in biological research. People had been telling her it would harm her marriage chances. "My success," she told me, "will be my rebuttal."

I heard from a young woman who was in the process of starting a girl-only model UN club. She was tired of the boys always talking over and interrupting the girls in her school's current club. Another young girl living with a physical disability talked about the need for intersectionality and why it must expand to focus more on those with disabilities. Many of the girls I spoke with named slut shaming and rape culture as the issues they're most urgently fighting. Body image came up frequently. Reproductive rights were high on the list of issues they wanted feminism to meet head-on. They talked about transgender rights and defying the very construct of gender. One seventeen-year-old in New York told me she was going to be the first woman president, but then, laughing, said she hoped it wouldn't take that long. "The future of this is bright," she said, speaking of her generation. "I think it's an unstoppable thing." They were hungry for change.

These young women inspired me. They made me think. And they challenged my own biases around our new generation of feminist activists. These girls and young women are all giving misogyny the middle finger. They're doing it on their own terms. And in all the many reports I read, historical accounts I unearthed, and conversations I had with women of all ages, perhaps my favorite definition of feminism came from a fourteen-year-old girl in central Indiana who was too nervous to tell her mother she was a feminist. "I was thinking about this before," she paused and let out a long *mmmmmm*. "What is feminism?" She went quiet, thinking. Suddenly, she smiled broadly as she landed on it. "It's about uplifting those around you."

Bingo.

Thank goodness my own answer to the question "What does feminism mean to you?" has evolved in the fifteen years since I first discovered it. And yet I think back tenderly to that young girl. I smile at her spiked hair and her wide-leg pants, purchased from the boys' department, of course, with money from her summer job as a camp counselor for kids with special needs. I laugh at the way she thought to defy beauty standards with safety pins in her ears and various found objects, including little plastic Barrel of Monkeys toys—I joke not—in her hair. But it's not a cruel laugh. I want to hug her when I think of the way she stayed up late writing poetry, chatting with friends on instant messaging, and burning mixed CDs filled with riot grrrl music, searching the depths of her young soul for the answer to the question "What does feminism mean to me?" These might be big questions for a young girl to ask, but then again, she's not precisely a girl anymore, is she? Certain things have a way of making you grow up, of making you realize feminism isn't a word or a theory but a way of living, of seeing the world as the place it could be. Idealistic? Sure. But ask her and she'd say: only if you stop working to make it happen. So, as much as her feminism — *my* feminism — was clumsy and narrow, as much as she needed to learn and be challenged and grow, I cherish her. I respect her.

That is, ultimately, what I want for the feminist movement, in all its pluralities, to do for the young girls and women who are discovering it: cherish and respect them. It's imperative for the feminisms of our future to draw a hard line against racism, ableism, classism, Islamophobia, homophobia, and transphobia — all the ways in which we promote hate and preach division. But we cannot smooth over our intersections; we must acknowledge those differences, make those shushed voices loud, and seek to remedy our mistakes. We must act. But what if we acted compassionately as well as courageously? What if we leaned into our discord with love and respect and trusted — *trusted* — that feminism is a constantly evolving politic but we can get to the right place together. Yeah, sure, this sounds like a Hallmark card for feminism, something you'd find tucked into the "Get well soon!" rack with little doodles of blooming flowers, halved fruit, and other euphemisms for vaginas drawn all over it. But there must be a way, I figure, to talk amongst our differences, to make the movement accessible and welcoming for newbies, to connect and disagree, and through this political force, to uplift all of those around us. So, yes, maybe it sounds cheesy. But is it unattainable?

Back at the Belmont-Paul museum, another old protest banner provided a potential answer. It simply read "Failure is impossible." It was a reminder not to underestimate women. The early suffragists faced a violent anti-feminism not so different from today's attacks. Back then anti-feminists distributed postcards that depicted suffragist women as ugly, overweight, and generally prone to having gigantic schnozzes. In these cartoons, they beat policemen with their umbrellas. Women were painted as actual fluffy cats in hats, complete with draped suffragist capes (a suggestion that granting women the vote was about as useless as giving it to Mrs. Tabbykins). Yet another, in a series by the same artist, Walter Wellman, showed a wavy woman who said of her demand for the vote: "I believe in a reduction on the tariff of Paris gowns." The artist helpfully added a bit of creep to the blood boil: "I'm just sixteen. Yours for votes." Silly, vapid young women! Oh, how these naysayers must have been surprised when women won, toppling voting restrictions like dominoes across the country. And today, the young are at the gates still—promising that, this time when feminism rises, it will listen and make change for everybody.

Or, at the very least, it will try.

10 Defining the new feminism: How we can harness the discord and create a better feminism for the future

The light bounced off the mist-dampened sidewalks surrounding Toronto's Union Station. It was a quarter past seven on the evening of January 20, 2017, and the gathered women were nearly an hour early. Mercifully, for once, so was I. Hoisting my backpack, I joined dozens of my soon-to-be bus buddies as they collected outside the city's transit hub, where raucous excitement immunized us against the chill. Earlier that day, far away in Washington, DC, Donald Trump had celebrated his inauguration, marking his first day on the job with a populist and eerily dystopian speech. He pledged to the world that America would be first again: selfish and mighty. He preached his own brand of unity: "It's time to remember that old wisdom our soldiers will never forget, that whether we are Black or brown or white, we all bleed the same red blood of patriots." To be fair, if you were a supporter, I suppose you might have considered his speech inspiring, truly patriotic, even. And, indeed, Trump retroactively declared it the National Day of Patriotic Devotion, an occasion with an Orwellian twist.

The women gathering at Union Station were not Trump supporters. They were part of the Canadian delegation of the Women's March on Washington, roughly half of the six hundred who would travel through the night, across borders and through the soupy fog, so they could add their bodies and their chants to the massive crowd. The women on the bus were not radicals. They were not experienced activists. Many of them had never done anything like what they were about to do. They brought with them brownies and granola bars, fanny packs, and sensible shoes. They also brought rage and conviction. Trump and the turning tide of their southern neighbors had unleashed something in them: resilience and anger and fear and hope and love—a cauldron of emotions that could be summarized in one word: *enough.* Even though it wasn't their country, they had decided, like thousands of others, that it was their fight. Stitched through with worry and shaken safety, they wondered—some for the first time—if their daughters' lives and their granddaughters' lives would be worse than their own. Would their own lives be more constricted than their mothers'? Were some things once thought entrenched already tumbling loose?

Later, I chatted with a group of women about why they'd decided to come. One, a young prosecutor named Sylvia, went silent as our footsteps pounded the pavement. "It's just..." she started, stopped, thought. "Well, how could I not be here?" How could all of them not be there?

On the way to the border our bus captain, Penelope Chester Starr, warned us not to utter the word "protest." She confiscated and tore up two signs that a couple of teenage girls had made. While hiding the signs in a plastic bag under some garbage, she explained that if American border guards asked us, we were to respond that we were going to a peaceful march—not a lie, exactly. The head march team in Washington also shunned protest language, deliberately shifting the focus to positivity, engineering the movement as more than a clap back against Donald J. "Grab 'Em by the Pussy" Trump.

We were clapping back against the whole damn system. Nobody on the bus risked defying the edict at the border, but it was easy to bristle at the watered-down semantics, to wonder if we'd yet again given the feminist movement a pastel makeover the political equivalent of a doctor's office painting: palatable and inoffensive. Hell, I'd prickled at it, too. Now, on the bus, surrounded by ceaseless voices, I rethought my initial reaction. Maybe we needed this openness before we got down to the difficult work of rebuilding the feminist movement. Maybe it was late, but it wasn't too late for us to see that the fight wasn't over yet, not by a long shot, not for everybody. The Women's March on Washington had built the biggest ramshackle tent it could and invited everyone inside, and just look at everyone who'd shown up.

We showed up because on November 8, 2016, as the US election results rolled in, Teresa Shook, a retired attorney and grandmother in Hawaii, realized that Donald Trump was going to win. What happened next has already passed into feminist lore. That night, Shook created a Facebook event page proposing women protest in DC on Inauguration Day weekend. She asked her friends to spread the word, and when she went to bed that night more than forty women had said yes. When she woke up, that number had hit ten thousand. It swelled even more after she merged events with Bob Bland, CEO and founder of the fashion incubator Manufacture New York, who had started her own Facebook event page.

The beginning was energetic but shaky. The march's initial name, Million Women March, was taken — absent of historical recognition — from 1997's march of the same name, which had rallied thousands of Black women in Philadelphia for social, political, and economic progress. This appropriation received widespread criticism, so the original organizers changed the name, issuing a press release with an apology and a promise to do better. They did. The organizing committee soon reflected the diversity of those they hoped would attend the march, as well as for those whose central rights the feminist movement must advocate.

The American mainstream press, however, pounced on the discord. One magazine ran an article, "Why the Women's March on

Washington Has Already Failed," in which the journalist highlighted
discussions around race and privilege (she called it bickering)
and contended that women weren't actually feeling threatened by
Trump. In a feature on the march, the *Washington Post*'s magazine,
Express, infamously (and hilariously) featured the male gender sign,
not the female one, on its cover. Inside, the headline reduced the
mass political movement to "When Venting Goes Viral," focusing
on the "rocky start" and the assertion that "minorities, particularly
African Americans . . . have felt excluded from many mainstream
feminist movements." (I don't disagree with this sentiment, but it's
a strange one to find in a basic news report.) In a dedicated online
section, the *New York Times* ran a series of opinion pieces on the
march, including several authored by women of color, who provided
valuable insight. It also ran a bizarre piece on the march's Facebook
discussion in which a white woman said she'd canceled her plane
tickets to the march after bristling over a Black woman's post that
encouraged marchers to use the renewed focus on women's issues
to consider their privilege. "This is a women's march," the offended
woman told the *Times*' reporter. "We're supposed to be allies in
equal pay, marriage, adoption. Why is it now about 'White women
don't understand Black women'?"

Such pieces fueled the discord, painting those who planned on
attending the march, and feminists in general, as petty, incompetent,
and shrill. Though the movement ballooned overnight, newspaper
articles rushed to point out that the organizers hadn't secured permits,
nor had they considered the march route, and so on and so on.
Women, the message went, cannot organize. Women cannot get along.

Some of that tone changed after march organizers released their
"Guiding Vision and Definition of Principles" document on January
12, 2017, displaying an unapologetic commitment to intersection-
ality. It paid homage to the abolitionists, the suffragists, Black Lives
Matter, Occupy Wall Street, and more. "We believe that Women's
Rights are Human Rights and Human Rights are Women's Rights,"

read the document's opening principle. "This is the basic and original tenet from which all our values stem." The document called for racial justice, economic justice, environmental justice, full reproductive rights, an end to racially motivated policing and police brutality, more accountability, a reformed criminal justice system, comprehensive health care for "our gay, lesbian, bi, queer, trans or gender non-conforming brothers, sisters and siblings," gender-affirming identity documents, equal pay, family leave, and more. It rejected mass deportation and family detention. It rejected hate.

I had booked my bus ticket because, like many others, I needed the reminder that I wasn't alone. After more than two years of wading through the sludgy waters of anti-feminism, I craved a reason for optimism. For a supposedly dying movement, feminism had undoubtedly roared awake, seemingly overnight. The first one hundred bus tickets from Toronto to Washington sold out in twenty-four hours. More than thirty sister marches were organized throughout Canada. More than 670 sister marches took place worldwide. But Washington was the epicenter, and like the rest of those on the bus, I wanted a front-row seat to the feminist revival.

Penelope Chester Starr, one of the four Canadian national co-organizers, told me that the overwhelming response was worth the exhaustion of organizing the event. Even though we sat together on the bus so I could interview her on the way down, we didn't get a chance to talk until after midnight. It was only then that everyone else on the bus had gone to sleep, and Chester Starr could, at last, take a break from organizing, answering questions, fielding media, documenting the trip, and ensuring the sister marches were on track. She leaned back on the plush seat, put her phone down for a moment, and exhaled.

She told me that her mother was French and her father was American. Though she was raised in France, she'd also spent some time in the US before moving to Canada in 2008. As an American citizen, she had been able to vote in the election, and she had:

for Hillary Clinton. She was devastated when Clinton lost. But the march galvanized her, stopped her from becoming immobile, helpless, stuck in grief. What many people didn't understand about the march, she said, was that it was not the end goal; it was only the beginning. Though she didn't know what would come next, she assured me that *something* would. She'd help organize it, and it would be intersectional and diverse, whatever it was. The point, she said, is that we, especially those of us who are more privileged, need to learn to listen to each other. "I hope we're starting something new here," she said, picking up her phone. "Look at what a group of strangers has already accomplished in eight weeks." Her phone blinked with missed messages. Her eyes darted over the stacks of texts and emails that needed her attention, her thumbs moving dextrously as she apologized for the disruption.

It was one AM. None of the women on the bus knew what to expect the next day, but they'd shown up anyway. *Wings of hope,* I thought blearily. As I burrowed into my makeshift pillow, a bunched-up scarf, Chester Starr was still on her phone. I don't know when she went to sleep.

Was the Women's March on Washington a crucial time for women to join together, or was it an opportunity for feminism to confront its historically privileged and narrowly rigid roots? Yes. And yes. For feminism to regain and maintain relevance it has to be both. The lesson to those of us who care about women and their rights is to remember both the march's messy, wrong-headed beginnings and its effort to do better, to be inclusive, to consider whose voices we are putting forward, and whose voices we are not. This is how we, as privileged women, settle into the discomfort: we listen, and then we throw open the doors that have been open to us, and then we listen some more. All of us must acknowledge our mistakes and then do better. This never stops. What I've learned from the front line of the new post-feminism is that feminism itself must never, ever reach a concrete definition. To thrive, it must always be a new feminism; it must always keep evolving without losing sight of its core principles of inclusion and equality.

Acknowledging our privilege is not the same thing as discounting our struggles. Intersectionality is the ongoing and fully committed practice of recognizing all those complex intersections of struggle and privilege and barriers. It's not about silencing voices, not about attacks, not about exclusion; it's about raising the voices of everyone around us. Does that not make us louder, together? Having examined all the ways in which we haven't achieved the goals of feminism at all—the ways in which we may, in fact, be in danger of stalling or even teetering backward—can't we take action to band together and move forward? Isn't the whole point of confronting the backlash that we have to look at where we're heading, change course toward a renewed commitment to a more equal society, not just in opportunity, but in policy and practice?

Certainly, we humans can be selfish and apathetic; we can also be courageous and selfless. Even in a culture of mounting division, violent discourse, and insidious sexism, we've shown time and time again that we do care about the rights and lives of women and girls. We've shown that we can respect our different opinions and experiences and fears and worries and democratically move forward. And we did. In the aftermath of Donald Trump's election, three hundred thousand people donated to Planned Parenthood, hitting more than forty times the organization's normal rate. Around 70 percent of those who dipped into their wallets had never donated to the organization before. The American Civil Liberties Union raised $7 million through online donations in just five days; its website crashed post-election thanks to a 7,000 percent increase in website traffic. Projects like Donated Bigly, launched by two women lawyers to help match donors to in-need organizations, sprouted up almost overnight. That's to say nothing of the many women and men who acted outside the US election to build a movement for hope and change.

In Canada, Indigenous activists and their allies have pushed the federal government to start a $40 million, two-year inquiry into more than one thousand cases of murdered and missing Indigenous women. Women-led grassroots initiatives such as Ladies Learning to Code, Dames Making Games, and the Pixelles are all dismantling the barriers women face when entering STEM fields in encouraging, creative, and fun ways. The National Film Board of Canada pledged to achieve gender parity in its funding and its films.

In the US, Hollywood stars became vocal about the gender pay gap. Activists rose up against the culture of victim blaming in sexual assault trials. Gymnast Simone Biles shot back against mega-sexist Olympics coverage with, "I'm not the next Usain Bolt or Michael Phelps. I'm the first Simone Biles." Two-time Olympic weightlifter Sarah Robles shared uplifting, badass messages about body positivity.

Throughout my own time talking to and working with women and girls, I've met a hugely diverse cross-section of activists, advocates, and community volunteers—all working to push back against cynicism and hate. They've organized conferences and meet-ups, talks and clubs, celebrations and solidarity, for women of color, Indigenous women, women with disabilities, LGBTQ women, women in business, women in poverty, women of size, those who've experienced violence and discrimination, those who cheer sex positivity, and all the intersections in between. It goes on and on, this resilience against the darkness.

Would it not be better, practically and possibly morally, to focus on what those women are doing rather than to shine a spotlight on those who are actively working against them? After all, have we not overcome impossible odds before? I'd argue the answer sits somewhere in between, along the scale of doing both. Let feminists engage with their critics, both inside and outside the feminist movement. In doing so, let us not be didactic, but open to many answers.

Though I can't define anyone's feminism for them, or provide a fix-all pill to do better, I can say this: Let us raise this conversation to rock-concert decibels. Let it be both a reminder to communicate with each other and a refusal to be silent. And, as we lean into the feminist movement's growing pains, let us also celebrate our victories and our heroes. We must remember that we can triumph. We've done it already, so many times before. Look around. We're doing it right now.

The buses barreled down the highway toward RFK Stadium, the current home of major league soccer team D.C. United and also where we were permitted to park. It was just a few minutes after eight AM, and my belly sloshed with the Tex-Mex breakfast I'd shoveled down earlier when hundreds of us swarmed a suburban Chevys. Nervous and excited, we leaned forward, our bodies at acute angles, anticipating the first glimpse. The stadium's parking lots were a sprawling doughnut ring that could fit eight thousand cars, or up to twelve hundred buses. We had all wondered how many would show up.

Our driver, Frank, was the first to see them. "Wow, look at all those buses," he breathed. *Holy Moses.* "I've never seen so many buses in one place." Then we saw it. From our vantage point, high above the bowl of the parking lots, the bus tops glistened, blocking out the asphalt and filling the lots to capacity. (Nearly one thousand other buses, it was later reported, had permits to park elsewhere in the city.)

"Look at all the people!"

"We could hold the march right here!"

"I'm going to have goosebumps all friggin' day," someone behind me said.

Chester Starr led the bus in a chant as it inched behind the line-up to the lots.

"What do we want?"

"Equality!"

"When do we want it?"

"Are you fucking kidding me?"

Dressed in matching red hats and unfurling contraband "Sisters of the North" signs, the Canadian delegations poured out. On everyone's arm, scrawled in black Sharpie, were the digits 613-996-8885 — the emergency consulate number for Canadians traveling abroad. "I don't believe you will need this number," Chester Starr said as she passed around the Sharpies, their chemical tang punching the air. "But just in case." She warned us against possible violence, uncontrollable anger. Organizers expected counterprotestors, whether they were cheering for Trump or holding up anti-abortion signs. Nobody could guess at the size of the crowds we'd soon encounter, or the expected mood. The night before, more than 217 people had been arrested, and someone had set fire to a black limousine. As we grouped outside, Chester Starr flicked her lighter against a cigarette. Tension crackled off her; she wanted to make sure we all stayed together, that she got us there okay. She grabbed a cardboard tube from the depths of the bus, her own smuggled banner announcing our delegation. I followed her outside the parking lot as we snaked behind hundreds of other marchers. She apologized for being "cranky," but I understood. Her phone was still buzzing with questions. Her fingers flew over the glass front, tweeting updates. Spark. Another cigarette.

It was a half-hour walk to our meeting spot with the other Canadians, including Marissa McTasney, an entrepreneur who'd taken the initial lead on organizing the Canadian delegation and who'd never engaged in activism before. Today was her birthday. In the weeks leading up to the march, McTasney had faced a deluge of online threats and horrific name-calling in response to media interviews. Men's rights activists and anti-feminists had hurled what was now, to me, a vile, familiar roster: she was called fat, ugly, and stupid. And she was threatened with rape. Some men reached out via email, spewing right into her inbox. But here she was. Here we all were. As we headed down Independence Avenue SE, cars honked their support and people emerged from their houses and shops to thank us, to ask us where we were from. One family passed out Starbucks coffee, another Hershey's chocolate kisses. By the time we met with the others, it seemed impossible that the day could turn to violence. Chester Starr charted our first steps on Facebook Live, wiping her brow before smiling wide: "Make some noise! All right, yes, this is exciting! We are going! We are on our way! We're going to march! Woohoo!"

At the National Mall, the downtown park, the crowd enveloped us. Before that day, estimates had pegged the expected crowd at two hundred thousand; after crowd scientists analyzed the pictures, that number soared to at least— *at least*—470,000, roughly three times the number of people who attended Trump's inauguration. (The Trump administration, of course, had "alternate facts" about the respective crowd sizes.) The crowd was so thick, I never made it to the speakers stage. I missed all the stars: Janelle Monáe ("Whenever you feel in doubt, whenever you want to give up, you must always remember to choose freedom over fear."); America Ferrera ("A platform of hate and division assumed power yesterday. But the president is not America. We are America."); Alicia Keys ("We will continue to rise until our voices are heard…until our dollar is the same dollar as a man's."); Scarlett Johansson (speaking to Trump: "I want to be able to support you, but first I ask that you support me . . . Support my daughter, who may actually, as a result of the appointments you have made, grow up in a country that is moving backwards, not forwards."); and, of course, Gloria Steinem ("You look great. I wish you could see yourselves. It's like an ocean.").

One reporter tweeted that, from where he was standing near the back of the packed park, it would take him nineteen minutes to walk to the stage, if the route were clear. After he tweeted, he realized he was no longer at the back; hundreds more people had closed around him. There were so many people that they filled the entire march route. I didn't move for an hour as we waited for the staggering crowd ahead of us to start. And even then, we moved not along the route, but beside it, uncontainable. I was so surrounded that I couldn't quite fathom how big the crowds were until a friend sent me an aerial shot. And pink was everywhere — *everywhere*. Anti-feminists and Trump supporters had mocked marchers for knitting pink "pussy hats," a cheeky play on Trump's own derogatory talk and a way to reclaim a word that was never meant to be ours. (Also, the cat-eared hats were cute.) A blogger with Chicks on the Right wrote the hats were "what happens when militant feminists from across the country put their 'deranged cat lady' knitting skills to use." And they call *us* killjoys.

The crowd itself reflected the deliberately, unapologetically diverse mandate of the march, a mishmash of messages and chants, people and goals. This was discord acknowledged and celebrated, a promise for the feminist movement to do better, written on the faces of everyone, and shouted in every hoarse voice, separate and together. Black Lives Matter signs punctuated the throngs of people moving slowly, the chants rolling through like a tidal wave. We shouted: "Show me what democracy looks like! This is what democracy looks like!" We shouted: "We want a leader, not a creepy tweeter!" We shouted: "No hate! No fear! Immigrants are welcome here!" We chanted for Muslim rights, transgender rights, queer rights, Indigenous rights, disability rights. We chanted for inclusivity and diversity, and a free media. Signs asserted: "Love trumps hate," "Let it rain glass," "Climate change is real," and "Women's rights are human rights and human rights are women's rights." We invoked humor: "We shall 'overcomb,'" "There shall be hell toupée," and "This pussy grabs back." Maya Angelou was a hero. Martin Luther King was a hero. Nasty women were heroes, too, and the motto "Love is love is love" thrummed through the crowd. So many women carried signs that simply read "Equality." Through it all I heard drummers, playing out a steady rhythm, like a beating heart.

I embarked on this project because I wanted to examine the growing influence of anti-feminist narratives, the paralyzing effects of the
"Ciao, feminism!" culture, and how both are polluting feminism's
necessary growing pains and intense self-analysis. This book joins a
number of recent titles that analyze how feminism is connecting today, how it's being attacked and celebrated and practiced, and what
it means to put feminism in the bright and glaring spotlight once
more. I've interviewed some of the authors of these other books and
discussed the work of others. I see all of us working together, even
those of us who are strangers, to ignite a sorely needed conversation
on equality and human rights, and how we, as a society, choose to
value, protect, and guarantee both. I've heard from so many feminists who, upon hearing that I actually spent a fair amount of my
research time with anti-feminists, remark on my bravery or ask me
what "they" were like, their curiosity akin to a five-year-old studying
an especially nasty bug. I hope these pages answer the latter question, and call for us all to have that same bravery, to learn from those
who disagree with us, if only to make ourselves stronger.

At its core, though, my subject has been how women today navigate their lives. My goal was to trace the trajectory of how women
define their choices and the contexts in which they make them, particularly in a world that historically and currently has prescribed who
we can and cannot be. That trajectory is not one line, but many; not
straight, but messy. It reveals both true steps toward equality and
also the fierce need to not let that be enough. We need a relent-
less, energetic force that doesn't stop until it has dismantled our
structural imbalances and barriers and built something better. Some
women *have* made great strides, sure, but that is not the same thing
as equality. And isn't that what's at stake here: the very definition of
what we mean when we talk about equality?

We all don't fucking have enough bread. If we continue to deny
that, we're heading for a dismal future. We'll never reach parity

in the workforce; structural support to keep women from opting out will remain stunted; we'll continue to make less while we do the same work; we won't have control over our own bodies; we'll continue to be raped at astounding rates; we'll continue to be told and to believe that we deserve it; we'll keep acting like this is the best we can do; we'll see bigger roadblocks placed in front of women of color, women with disabilities, and women who identify on the LGBTQ spectrum; Indigenous women will keep going missing; and we'll continue to categorize women, deciding who is worthy of attention and who is not, how a woman can be and how she cannot. We will tell ourselves we chose it. Some of our lives will get better, because that is the undeniable promise of anti-feminism and post-feminism (even, to some extent, mainstream white feminism).

These backlash movements are appealing precisely because they pin both success and failure on the individual. It's a heady mix of choice and can-doism that allows women to claim their own empowerment while not acknowledging what keeps others from claiming theirs. I don't believe anti-feminists and post-feminists truly want the worst of the Dark Ages for women, or that pop feminism only cares about white, middle-class women. But I do believe they work in their own way to protect a system that has given them power and protected their values while maintaining very clear roles — it promises them certainty in a time when uncertainty blooms like weeds. And I do believe we can do better. It's more important than ever for us to keep making more bread, until all our baskets runneth over.

If we ever hope to achieve this, feminism also has to do better. It must keep peering into itself and keep practicing inclusivity and intersectionality. Not to get too sappy, but *it must keep practicing love*. Whenever I think about this, I think back to what Colleen MacQuarrie, a PEI-based activist, told me about the successful campaign for abortion access in her province. She credited a lot of the success to hope and the celebration of different tactics and coalitions within the movement. Activists welcomed new ideas and responded with a simple, "Yes, and how can I support you?" For her, hope did not come from envisioning one single mass movement but rather a diverse upsurge of movements in constant dialogue about the principles of equity and respect for different peoples and the world we live in. "If we can have more voices and more actions, I don't worry that we won't be creative enough," she told me. "I don't worry that we won't be able to find the evidence. I know we will. What I worry more about is the silence. I worry when we're not hearing about the uprisings." She added that action is about hope responding to its antithesis: despair. "Despair is the gift to oppressive forces. To the extent that you can inspire despair and degradation, you're winning the status quo." Anytime we see a rise in despair, she argued, you hear a Mad Libs–style, fill-in-the-blank-here question: "What can we ever do about...?"

Hope is an antidote to that despair. It tells us that we can do something and then it propels us into action.

Later, I'd hear about the counterprotestors. A makeshift float, which its driver dubbed "Trump Unity Bridge," tried to truck Trump supporters through the march. Later, anti-feminists would troll the social media accounts of marchers, posting anti-abortion gifs and spreading misogyny. Later, at a bar with the Canadian marchers, I'd hear men jeer at feminists, drunkenly telling them to "go back to the kitchen." Later, as we prepared to walk back to the parking lot, locals would tell us which streets to avoid, warning us that it wasn't safe for women at night. We'd discover our bus had broken down, and our grassroots organizing would falter, stranding some of us in the parking lot, lost. American Red Cross disaster relief would swoop in and save us, doling out fleece blankets, Ritz crackers, and hot chocolate. We'd joke that it wasn't symbolic.

In the coming weeks, all the old tropes would dance by like

cardboard cowboys at a carnival shooting gallery. Anti-feminists and conservatives would point to Madonna's comment to the crowd — that she'd "thought an awful lot about blowing up the White House" — as proof of feminism's inherent violence, its terrorist intent. And, later, the women who marched would have tough conversations about how to keep the momentum going. They'd debate and discuss how to be intersectional, stumbling forward and back, striving to build a new feminist movement. Later, we'd remember that it was all so, so uncertain, this success. But right now, all of that was far away. Surrounded and embraced by a thunderous crowd with no edges, we were a reminder that, together, nothing could touch us. In that briefest of moments, we were unstoppable.

Epilogue

Months after my trek to Washington, the Women's March movement remains defiant. Post-march, Washington HQ, determined to capitalize on the march's infectious momentum, immediately launched its follow-up campaign, 10 Actions/100 Days, kicking off a new project every ten days. These mini-movements included everything from postcard writing to the hashtag-worthy A Day Without Women, which encouraged women to take the day off from both paid and unpaid work. The 100 Days campaign stood in solidarity with Syrian women. It supported immigration and preached unity. Quite frankly, it did some awesome stuff, and in April 2017, *Time* magazine put the co-organizers of the Women's March on Washington on its 100 Most Influential People list. "This is the rebirth of the women's movement," *Time* declared. "These women are the suffragists of our time. And our movement isn't going away—it's just the beginning."

The need for the women's movement isn't going away, either. April was a strange month. President Donald Trump signed legislation that allows states to deny federal family-planning funds to Planned Parenthood (as well as to other abortion providers), but in the semi-good news department that month, Bill O'Reilly was booted from Fox News following a storm cloud of sexual harassment allegations. Why only a tentative thumbs-up to O'Reilly's ouster? While it's encouraging to see conservative bulwarks condemn shitty treatment of women, I'm less thrilled that it took so damn long. I can hear the echoes of anti-feminist critics now: *But can't women just be happy they ruined him, Shrill Feminist Lauren?* Sure, we can be happy he finally, finally, *finally* (times infinity) faced some consequences for his alleged actions. Y'know, after a successful career of fame and fortune and all that—none of which he's really losing. The problem with such increased attention to feminist issues is that it can make it difficult to parse real political change from PR-motivated blips.

O'Reilly has been in the spotlight before for his gross behavior. The allegations against him date back decades and include settlements with five women. It seems likely that the withdrawal of fifty advertisers from the show had more to do with his departure than a newfound allegiance to feminist values. In response to all of this, O'Reilly trumpeted the ol' it's-not-me-it's-them line. "[It's] tremendously disheartening that we part ways due to completely unfounded claims," he said. "But that is the unfortunate reality many of us in the public eye must live with today."

Skip forward a few months, and we can see the same attitude on display with Harvey Weinstein. When media first broke the story of allegations of sexual harassment and assault in October 2017, the Hollywood bigwig released a statement, quoting Jay-Z, that said he was trying to do better and that he was also building a women's scholarship foundation to be named after his mom. Lisa Bloom, his original (and now former) lawyer, who famously built her career on *helping* women, called him simply "an old dinosaur learning new ways." And yet the story could not be stopped; this time women would not be quiet. On October 15, Alyssa Milano tweeted a suggestion from a friend: "If all the women who have been sexually harassed or assaulted wrote 'Me too' as a status, we might give people a sense of the magnitude of the problem." In twenty-four hours, the hashtag was tweeted over half a million times. In the following week, more than fifty women in the industry came forward to share their Weinstein stories. Then another thirty-eight women came forward, this time against director James Toback. As Amber Tamblyn said in the *New York Times* of the women bringing their stories forward: "Now that we have collectively spoken, we can never go back."

Yet, post-Weinstein both media and anti-rape activists had to rush to counter the rising victim-blaming narrative—the same one we always hear whenever survivors come forward, particularly in our new anti-feminist climate. That narrative, we know, is the one that attempts to draw a correlation between time and truth. Questions of why it took so long for women to speak up often seek to undermine the power of survivors sharing their stories and rising up together; it's a narrative that dismisses the consequences of speaking up even as it tries to enforce them. Myriad outlets, from *Bustle* and *Entertainment Weekly* to the *Guardian* and *NPR*, ran stories with headlines like "Why it took so long for accusations against Harvey Weinstein to come out" and "Why did no one speak out about Harvey Weinstein?" Despite the headlines' tone, the articles often sought to explain to their readers that such questions didn't have easy answers. But the fact that these articles are still appearing so early in such news cycles exposes a deeply anti-feminist symptom of a larger problem. We still rush to judge survivors; we still want to believe this isn't part of our culture. What a reminder that public outrage does not mean instant eradication of firmly held cultural, patriarchal footholds. In the months following the march, I ping-ponged between wanting two contradictory things: for us to be buoyed by little wins and for us, and others, not to mistake these wins as finishing-line markers. Feminists can, and did, protest O'Reilly and Weinstein, but what we can't do is stop. We cannot afford to be lulled into complacency again, to ever again let such abuse ever slip by unremarked.

Just writing that makes me want to take a nap.

It's an uncomfortable truth that the work of the Women's March movement, and all the feminist actions that rose with it, are nowhere near absolute victory. Our newest iteration will undoubtedly face further intense backlash, vicious mockery, and significant setbacks from without and within. For veterans of the feminist movement—those doing the hard work long before the headline-grabbing march—this will all likely feel like déjà vu, old wisdom. Still, it's hard to deny this new feminist movement feels like a necessary revitalization, a fresh beginning. It's not simply an opportunity to bring more girls and women into the movement or to get media (and, let's face it, marketing) attention, but also a chance to define what we want our feminism of the future to be. I still can't decide whether it's a wonderful or weird thing that I saw the same book highlighting the march in indie bookstores, drugstores, and ultra-trendy Urban Outfitters, but it's probably both. In this increased mainstreaming of feminism, though, we have to remember it isn't just a numbers game. Let's make more women invested in feminism, but let's also make it a feminism that's intersectional, diverse, anti-oppressive, and open to self-reflection.

When I first started researching this book, I heard "You go for it!" a lot. But I also heard two common criticisms—or, more accurately, expressions of disbelief. One, many people told me that feminism no longer mattered. And two, they told me that anti-feminism wasn't a thing, and if it was, it was an impotent movement. Sometimes, often, these were the same people talking, but not always. Either way, the underlying message is the same: Women have made it. We don't need feminism because we already have equality. Anti-feminism won't rise for the same reason. Men's rights activists and other anti-feminists, they reassured me, will never make it out of their online dens, their mothers' basements. Well, there's liberal pomposity and denialism for you (more on that in a minute). Perhaps what seemed inconceivable to them then still seems inconceivable now. But that doesn't change reality, as surreal and nightmarish as it now is. Women's rights—human rights—are under siege, and the anti-feminists have war cannons. The most powerful of them wears a splendid toupee and lives in a white house (well, sometimes).

As I finished writing *F-Bomb*, Donald Trump was in the early days of his presidency. Yet even I didn't think those impending-apocalypse jokes would bear out quite so quickly. Between Syria, North Korea, and building a wall (OMG, I hope we're not all living in *Mad Max* when this book comes out), it can be hard to keep the fight for women's rights going. Cue another criticism I heard as I was working on this: Why should anyone care about [insert X feminist issue] when we have [insert Y world issue]? It's a valid point. Manspreading on the subway is not anywhere on par with Syrian refugee policies. But it's also an argument that overlooks the unbreakable links between X and Y. Eradicating physical and sexual violence, guaranteeing sexual freedom and rights, and improving access to girls' and women's education, health (including reproductive health), and the workforce are irrevocably tied to ending discrimination and racial and religious violence, building pro-immigration policies, boosting the economy, raising populations out of poverty and—not to put too fine a point on it—ending tyranny. That is, if we can give rise to a truly intersectional feminism.

As we do this, let's also be wary of putting too much blame on Trump. He didn't magically poof anti-feminism into existence; he's powerful and popular because the anti-feminist movement is powerful and popular. For reasons I've explored in *F-Bomb*, he's found fans because his policies resonate—even, and in some cases especially, with women. Let's not pretend, also, that it's some side effect of America, contained like a contagion within its red states. It always surprised me when I interviewed people, particularly those in America, who gushed over Canada and our prime minister, Justin Trudeau, as if he'd inoculated us against anti-feminism, racism, xenophobia, and other generally crappy things. It's like everyone forgot we were the nation that put Stephen Harper and his super

Conservative friends in charge for *nearly a decade*. Harper, a lifelong politician, has the verve of a cardboard box, but just because he didn't say ridiculous, scary shit on Twitter, it doesn't mean his political stance was, at its root, wildly different from Trump's. Under him, Canada was just quieter (and more pragmatic) about its intentions. And even that might be about to change.

The Conservative Party picked a new leader in May 2017 and, in doing so, a new idea of what *conservative* means in Canada. Emboldened by Trump's win in the south, our own reality TV star, Kevin O'Leary, of *Dragon's Den* and, later, *Shark Tank* fame, threw his hat in the ring. Known on *Shark Tank* as the "shark with the sharpest teeth," O'Leary is famous in both the US and Canada, and reminds me of a smoother, smarter, balder Trump. He's a populist, and for similar anti-government reasons. "Now, with the election of Donald Trump to our south, Canada's largest trading partner is headed by a businessman with an aggressive strategy that could hurt the Canadian economy," O'Leary wrote on his campaign's "Why I'm Running" page, which boasts about his business acumen and, also, the fact that he's not a "career politician": "Since the start of this leadership race I have looked for a candidate with these qualities, but it has become clear that I am the only one that can defeat Trudeau." He eventually dropped out, but I'm not sure that matters; he resonated, and that's sobering enough.

Besides, other candidates offered scarier, more socially conservative platforms (and voting records), including opposition to immigration, LGBTQ rights, and access to abortion. Kellie Leitch built her campaign on a platform of "Canadian values" (whatever that means) and has met with a Canadian group that wants to ban Muslims; one of her Conservative Party opponents has likened her to a "karaoke Donald Trump." Maxime Bernier is A-OK with guns. Andrew Scheer is "pro-life" but also promised not to reopen the abortion debate (hmm). Of course, none of them was running on an explicit, thoroughly anti-feminist platform. But neither did Donald

Trump, really. Our bar shouldn't be whether or not someone is actively, openly trying to restrict women's rights.

In the end, Scheer won the leadership. In the months since, he's given interviews to Rebel Media, denounced Rebel Media (after the far-right organization faced criticism for its coverage of the August 2017 race riots in Charlottesville, Virginia), and then, a few months later, hired a campaign manager named Hamish Marshall, who is a corporate director at the Rebel and, indeed, helped build the media company into what it is today: the bulwark of the alt-right and a hotbed of anti-feminist feminist views. Scheer has asserted the hiring didn't portend a hard right shift for his party, and nor did he truly have connections to the Rebel, but it's unsurprising that his critics are skeptical. Such promises can seem hollow these days, and it's likely Canada will soon learn it isn't immune to America's current political upheaval. As the alt-right continues to rise, we'll all have to confront that just as women's rights are linked to human rights, so are human rights to women's rights. Obvious, right? Ushering in a new conservatism — one that focuses on not fiscal conservatism but a Trump-esque mishmash of social conservatism, blustery nationalism, and a certain economic isolationism — comes with a matching voter mindset. Sort of like his-and-hers ideological tracksuits for the right wing.

As we wade further into the opposing but jointly skyrocketing feminist and anti-feminist movements, I hope we can learn to listen more to the other side. I don't exactly mean that we should have a tea party with Hitler, Mussolini, and, oh heck, even Trump. Crumpets, tea, and facism! But I do believe we have to let go of our liberal superiority — this belief that clearly reprehensible views aren't powerful enough to gain mass traction. We've seen they obviously are. It means acknowledging that people we don't think have any right to be unhappy — the white middle class, mainly — are miserable, hurting. What's worse, they believe the left's policies will drown them. Unless we understand why, it will be impossible counteract and confront the ripple effect of damage that pain has caused. We can't fight what we so arrogantly ignore. I'm *so not* arguing that we stop trying to tear down the status quo or that we render feminism polite and palatable, like a ladyfinger cookie. But let's revaluate why, and how, we're distancing people (and women especially) from feminism, not just call them insufferable airheads.

I believe it is possible, still, to fight with compassion and humility. Not just possible, actually, but essential. At its heart, feminism is not about making *your* life better and more equitable; it's about making *everyone's* lives better. Those of us with platforms must continue to make room on them for those without, and then we must help them build their own, higher platforms. We must embrace criticism and change. We must live our politic. We must *make some fucking room.* I don't think any of this will be easy. With everything going on around us, it will be incredibly difficult to live with love and courage as guiding principles. It will be hard to remember that we can be angry without being hateful. Even as I write this, even as I believe it with my own angry and compassionate feminist heart, I feel like I'm auditioning for a staff gig at Hallmark—or maybe shopping around a new Lifetime special. Look, the feminist movement is messy right now, but maybe that's the point. Maybe it has to be a hot mess first so it can figure shit out.

In the months since the Women's March on Washington, I've seen feminist-branded, well, everything, flood the market. Pins. T-Shirts. Hoodies. Pencils. Pencil cases. Notebooks. Tote bags. Planters. Jewellery. Temporary tattoos. Wine glasses. Hats. Perfume. Lipstick. Blankets. Phone cases. Mugs. And so much more. I'm not sure it's a bad thing, though I can't bring myself to buy any of it. It isn't that I don't want to, literally, wear my feminism on my sleeve, but I do worry about turning feminism into a product. I'm all for women entrepreneurs making a buck, and even more for those who are donating sales proceeds to organizations in need (though I also recognize corporations are on this particularly saucy gravy train as well). Yet, if the legacy of the Women's March is T-shirts, then we've missed a huge opportunity and made it all the worse by boosting the impression we're doing something when we aren't at all, not really. It is incredibly easy to buy something, but it so much more important (and difficult and frustrating and exhausting) to live the feminist politic.

But there is one recent trend with which I can get on board. It will not surprise anti-feminists who make memes on the internet to learn that I have a lot of tattoos (but it might surprise my grandmother — sorry, Granny!). In March 2017, women began inking "Nevertheless, she persisted," in reference to US senator Mitch McConnell's smack down of Massachusetts Democrat Elizabeth Warren. He ordered her to, essentially, shut up as she tried to read a letter from Martin Luther King's widow during the confirmation hearing for Trump's attorney general pick. In explaining his decision, McConnell said, "She was warned. She was given an explanation. Nevertheless, she persisted." It's since become another rallying cry for feminists. She persisted. *We will persist.* My friends and I have given serious thought to joining the hundreds of other women who've inked it on their skin. As I pondered it, one of my guy pals (yes, a feminist who likes men! We're not mythical unicorns!) remarked that it was strange so many feminists were etching a conservative man's dismissal of a woman on their bodies. Sure, yes. But there's also something powerful about reclaiming statements like these — in reclaiming feminism and, in doing so, reclaiming ourselves, our lives, and all that we can be. It makes us mighty in a world that still wants us to be small.

Well, fuck that.

Acknowledgments

This book would be just a jumble of words without the brilliance of my editor, Jill Ainsley. Thank you for your thoughtfulness, your patience, and your keen suggestions. I also owe endless thanks to the entire team at Goose Lane, who took a chance on me and this book: Susanne Alexander, Julie Scriver, Martin Ainsley, Kathleen Peacock, and Karen Pinchin, as well as to my copy editor, Melva McLean, and my proof-reader, Jess Shulman. Without the hard work and faith of all of you, this book would not be what it is. Thank you, as well, to the wonderful team at BenBella Books, especially Glenn Yeffeth and Leah Wilson. Sarah Dombrowsky, thank you for a beautiful cover. You all deserve way more exclamation marks than is grammatically correct.

Thank you to my agent, Hilary McMahon at Westwood Creative Artists. Your boundless enthusiasm for this book and for my writing is like sunshine.

To my mentors at the University of King's College, Tim Falconer, Jane Hamilton Silcott, and Kim Pittaway: you are invaluable. Thank you for everything you did to make the manuscript stronger, and for all the stuff that doesn't show on the page: keeping my spirits up as I wrote the book, hit walls, and fully waded into the publishing world. Together, you cheered me on, kicked my butt when I needed it, asked tough questions, and encouraged me to think in new ways and consider new perspectives. You made me better.

A huge thanks to the team at *This Magazine*, and in particular my longtime work wife, Lisa Whittington-Hill. *This* will always feel like home, and the wonderful, hard-working team there is such a big part of that. Thank you for giving me the time and space to work on this book, and all the ideas connected to it. Thank you for helping me grow and for teaching me about all things pop culture. I'll always treasure my time at *This*, and your support.

The biggest thank you goes out to my parents, family, friends, and all the amazing women in my life. Thank you to all the editors who've helped make my words sing. Thank you to everyone who I've surely forgotten. Thank you to Link, who cannot read but can warm my feet expertly.

Mom, thank you for your countless pep talks and for delivering all that homemade food so that I wouldn't forget to eat during the intense writing periods. To my best sister, Kiddo, you always make me laugh and remind me what matters most.

Jen, thank you for always saying yes whenever I ask if you want to be my plus-one—no matter how weird it is—and for your unwavering support in all things life. Candice, you will always be the best part of King's. Thank you for always challenging me and for being your brilliant, sparkly self. Dana: No matter how you toss the dice, you've always been there. Thank you. And to my oldest, dearest friend, Andrea, it's been such a privilege to grow up with you—you're amazing.

I owe a big thanks to all the women and girls who spoke to me for this book and let me into their lives. Whether we agreed or not, I appreciate you taking the time to explain your perspectives and to answer all my questions. Let this discussion continue with respect and compassion. And, finally, to the feminists now and throughout history: your tireless work has brought us to where we are today. My thanks could span the universe.

photo: Yuli Scheidt

Lauren McKeon is an award-winning editor and
writer. She is the former editor of *This Magazine* and
a contributing editor at *Toronto Life*. Her essays have
appeared in *Hazlitt*, *Flare*, the *Walrus*, and *Reader's Digest*,
and she has spoken on gender issues at conferences and
seminars and on radio and television broadcasts.